THEY FACE EAST

A Memoir of Confederates in My Tree

by

Trae Zipperer

Dedicated to the two men whose deaths gave me life.

Pvt. John T. McElhaney
Co. A, 50th Georgia Infantry Regiment
Killed in Action, Battle of South Mountain, 14 Sep 1862
1st Husband of my GGG Grandmother Mary Ann Allen
On my maternal side

Pvt. Coleman Groover
Co. B, 5th Florida Infantry Regiment
Killed in Action, Battle of the Wilderness, 6 May 1864
1st Husband of my GGG Grandmother Lydia Ann Douglass
On my paternal side

Contents

Chapter 1

U-HAUL, YOO-HOO, AND ICE-COLD BEER

My first road trip to honor my DNA was in early June 1984 as a fifteen-year-old teenager accompanying my dad from central Florida to a fresh new life in Texas, a re-boot so to speak. It was my doings, the son of an alcoholic trying to save him, encouraging him to sell everything we owned and move to Houston where I thought maybe his parents would wield influence over his addiction. Certainly he wouldn't behave as a drunkard in front of his mom and dad, I figured, as best an over-achiever could plot at that age. Unbeknownst to me at that time, Jesus was the only one who could have saved him, saved me, saved all of us from the horrors of alcohol, because want-to and will power just aren't powerful enough to cast out demons.

The wheels had fallen off his life one at a time, the lug nuts of each loosened by his best friend, alcohol, but he remained in the driver's seat, determined to do it his way, no matter the cost to himself or those around him. My mom left. My sister left. His employer left, along with the company car, our only source of transportation. The beer, the cigarettes, the cockamamie pickled brain, get-rich-quick schemes—such as the worm farm, the feed lot for swine, and the rabbit barn, among others consumed our meager financial resources. All he had to do was submit to God, give it to God, humble himself to God's authority over him, but he chose to stay the course. As we loaded the U-Haul truck, he said, "Bub, go get Daddy a beer."

There wasn't much to load into the back of that rented moving truck. With no money in savings and no liquid assets, his friends showed up to buy anything of value, a form of charity, to pool the gas money required to purchase 1,000 one-way miles worth of fuel. The last belonging pushed up the loading ramp was the irreplaceable Sears Kenmore chest freezer containing our food stores. Fresh frozen inside was steer meat, deer meat, crappie fish, blue fish, homemade sausage in natural casings, Flavor-ice popsicles, and black-eyed peas. Anytime we stopped along the route, we'd park near an electrical outlet, close enough for the extension cord attached to the freezer to reach. As if life wasn't already embarrassing enough, the two of us were the only travelers plugging in our U-Haul truck, a frozen sustenance umbilical cord.

My uncle, hearing about our plight, had offered to give my dad a used blue Toyota Corolla station wagon. With no car and no money, we were grateful, and beggars can't be choosers. He probably slipped my dad some cash and called it a loan, knowing not to count on that money coming back anytime soon, if ever. My uncle's house, and the Toyota, were somewhere in Georgia, I guess, but wherever they were, the route to there from central Florida would follow northward up I-75, passing Valdosta, GA along the way.

My dad was fourteen years old when his great-grandfather, Charles Robert Lovett Zipperer, "Grandpa Tony" passed away, so my dad would have been old enough to have spoken with him about family history. Or, maybe my dad learned it from his grandfather, Frank, Grandpa Tony's son. Or, maybe my dad learned it from his dad, Jack, who had lived with Grandpa Tony. However he had heard about it, my dad knew Grandpa Tony had moved to Manatee County, FL from a town named Lake Park, GA, near Valdosta. My dad's name was Charles Robert Zipperer, his dad's name was Charles Robert Zipperer, and Grandpa Tony's dad was Charles Robert Zipperer, so it wasn't difficult to remember the name my dad wanted to find etched on a headstone in Lake Park.

Dad being a junior and considering III to be a stretch for our pedigree, my parents named me Trae. Not my first name, my middle name, because that's how it's done in the South. I think they came up with the idea while playing cards: ace, deuce, trey. They dropped the Charles, repositioned Robert up front, moved III to the middle, and spelled it T-r-a-e. Robert Trae Zipperer was typed on the birth certificate. From then on, they called me Bubba.

Crossing the Florida Georgia line, we knew we were getting close because billboards were advertising all things Valdosta. We exited the interstate at the first off-ramp designated Lake Park and pulled into the quick stop convenience store, backed in, actually, so my dad could roll up the U-Haul's overhead door enough to reach the freezer extension cord. Roadside cold spots like these were familiar to me. I'd visited similar places my entire life, along every back road within the central Florida geographic boundary of Orlando to Melbourne to Yeehaw Junction to Lake Wales to Lakeland to Groveland to Orlando. All had two gas pumps out front and no cover over the refueling islands, like you see today. Inexpensively constructed standalone buildings with flat roofs, the exterior walls were comprised of unfinished concrete block painted white, the kind where you can see the mortar outlines of each and every block. The entire front elevation was large panes of glass advertising "Ice-Cold Beer."

The only bathroom for miles was found on the outside back corners of these establishments. Reaching for the thin metal handle attached with screws just above the hole where the doorknob once resided, a pull provided a distinct creaking sound produced by the stretch of a long, thin metal spring. It was a low-tech door-closing assistance device. Greeting all upon entry was the distinct, pungent smell of old urine emanating from crystalized remnants deposited in error. The sole source of light and ventilation, a screen-covered rectangle high on the exterior wall exactly the size of a missing cinder block. Sometimes there was an old cake of soap, with deep soiled cracks, stuck to the porcelain sink. A rust-colored stain shined all the way from the drip spot to the drain.

Dad would pull open a condensation-dripping walk-in cooler glass door, reach inside, and clutch an ice-cold can of Miller Genuine Draft. My treat was always a chocolate flavored Yoo-hoo drink contained within a yellow label-wrapped clear glass bottle with a yellow twist-off cap. The chocolate flavored powder was always a half-inch thick layer of sediment at the bottom requiring a fair amount of agitation to give it the appearance of chocolate milk. I recall somewhere on the bottle the words, "Shake, It's Great!" The person behind the counter always had a small brown paper bag, just the right size to slide in a can of beer, concealing it from quick identification just in case the law pulled alongside. There must have been something special about the feel of that paper, the top of the bag rolled down just so.

Walking over to the pay phone booth at the corner of the building, a worn swollen phone book hung suspended by a metal cable. The white pages residential directory was at the front of the book, and the yellow pages business directory was at the back. Flipping to the last of the white pages, the entire text was nothing but Zipperers. I couldn't believe it. I'd never seen so many Zipperers in one place in my entire young life. I can't recall exactly how we ended up there from the quick stop, but I remember a building with a sign reading "Zip's Tire Service" at the top. My dad said Zip probably did a good business with the interstate highway nearby.

Sure enough, the owner of Zip's was a Zipperer, too. He'd never heard of any Charles Robert Zipperer, or a Zipperer graveyard. Stopping to think, he did recall his son, Johnny Boy, telling him something about some graves way back in the woods. Zip hollered for Johnny Boy inside the house. I guess Zip must have run the tire service out of his house. The young man, I think he was maybe eighteen years old, came to the front door, and Zip asked him about the old graves he had found. Johnny Boy told the story of how he and some friends had been exploring and stumbled upon some old graves with the name Zipperer on the headstones. Zip asked Johnny Boy if he remembered where the cemetery was located, and Johnny Boy responded with, "Yes, sir." Zip then asked him if he would take us to the graveyard, and Johnny Boy nodded his head yes.

But before we left the house, Zip retrieved an 8.5" x 11" spiral-bound, laminate-covered booklet with a picture of a hand-drawn tree on the front. It was a Zipperer family tree. He and my dad conversed back and forth about various Zipperer ancestor names, trying to find a grandfather in common, until my dad mentioned Charles Robert Zipperer was the son of Theophilus Zipperer. Turning a few pages in the book, they found the name Theophilus. Zip's family line had descended from Theophilus' brother, so we did discover where we were directly related via Theophilus' parents. Reading the sketch on Theophilus, my dad and I felt we had uncovered why our downline of the family had been forgotten. Zip's book listed Theophilus and his wife Marie as having four daughters and no sons, when in fact, they had two sons and one daughter, one of the sons being Charles Robert Zipperer. Zip told us to keep the Zipperer family tree book. Said he could get another one. I still have it thirty-five years later among my stash of family history paperwork.

Walking toward a pickup truck parked in the front grass, Johnny Boy told us to hop in the back. I'm not sure why we were in the back bed of the truck. Maybe Zip came along with us and rode in the front cab, or maybe the young man had some dogs in the front seat, but I specifically recall riding in the back. Rolling along down a sandy fire break trail densely wooded on both sides, we crouched down behind the cab, springing at the knees like shock absorbers, countering the bouncing side to side sway of the truck bed, dodging encroaching tree branches as they whipped back towards us from the side mirrors. Coming to a stop, we saw a small cemetery, just a few graves, red bricks stacked up on the ends in triangular shapes, like two-dimensional pyramids a couple feet tall.

Stepping over the tailgate to the rear bumper and swinging down to the ground, we walked to the burials. The backs of the headstones were towards us, so we had to walk around to the opposite side to look back at the etchings. All Zipperers, four of them, Charles

Robert next to Eliza Ann, and Theophilus next to Marie. Four of my ancestors, the men who gave me my last name, out there in the middle of those woods, the middle of nowhere. I was young, but I got it, immediately, the gravity of it, the connection, the significance of that place.

We never again crossed paths with Zip or Johnny Boy, but they are lifelong memories for me. Those two small acts of kindness the family tree book, the ride in the back of a truck out into the woods were indelible. It was just one single old cemetery, but a seed had been planted, a seed that would thirty-plus years later grow into a very big tree. I'm sure Lake Park is still talking about those two strangers who plugged their U-Haul extension cord into electrical outlets on the sides of their buildings.

Using the Zipperer family tree gift from Zip, and my dad's knowledge of our immediate family, my dad wrote out a Zipperer lineage on a piece of paper starting at the top with the first Zipperer in America down to me at the bottom. The name Robert had passed down six continuous generations to me, from that man buried in the South Georgia woods. Every man in descending order had three names, except for one, Grandpa Tony. He had four names: Charles Robert Lovett Zipperer. I found that odd, out of place, but it was what it was, life moved on, and the family tree book went into a box somewhere, for another day.

The next thirty-three years went by quickly. Memories of significance were high school graduation, four years in the Navy, accepting Jesus, getting married, starting a lawn business, graduating from UCF, having a son, graduating from Harvard Business School, working at ServiceMaster, buying a home on the water, selling real estate, and having a daughter. We went boating. We went fishing. We vacationed in the Keys. I took my daughter to every National Park between Glacier and the Grand Canyon. We became scuba divers and blue belts in karate.

I lost my first close family member during my late thirties when cirrhosis of the liver claimed my dad in 2005. For 15,000 consecutive sunrises as an adult, nothing and nobody had been reason enough to quit drinking. But he quit cold turkey when his eyes turned yellow, his stomach distended, and concentrated dark yellow fluid began to ooze from his swollen legs. Six months later, my ninety-nine-year-old great-grandmother passed away. I had taken for granted still having all four of my grandparents. I was well into my late forties when my maternal grandmother, my Muffy, died in 2015. The man who inspired aspirations of Harvard, Eldon, my mom's husband, died in 2016. In February 2017, my paternal grandfather, my Papa, died in his sleep a few hours before my flight was scheduled to land. But I still had my ninety-two-year-old grandfather Gigi, my ninety-four-year-old grandmother, Nanny, and my mom. Living ancestor ranks had thinned.

My daughter's Spring Break 2017 was approaching, and choosing a trip to Washington D.C. to experience the Cherry Blossom Festival was unanimous. The spreadsheet itinerary I created included trees in full bloom, the marching band parade, the Smithsonian Museum, and an epic Civil War history road trip. Robert E. Lee's Arlington House was the first stop, followed by Manassas, Harpers Ferry, Antietam, Gettysburg, and Monocacy. I had made what I felt was a best effort to bring history to life by taking my daughter to as many National Park sites as possible before grades counted in high school. We'd already been to more than sixty. Battlefields weren't her thing, but for me, hallowed ground was powerful, especially Civil War sites.

I knew my maternal grandfather, Gigi, had been wounded in combat during WWII at Cherbourg, France just after D-Day, and again somewhere prior to liberating a concentration camp. As a hunter, I witnessed what a hollow-point rifle bullet did to the body of a pig as it entered the diameter of a pencil eraser only to mushroom, expand, rip flesh, push mass, and exit out the opposite side, producing a hole the size of a golf ball. An understanding of ballistics was necessary to fully appreciate what soldiers faced and endured. A bullet's path of destruction through a body was the shape of a funnel. A projectile shot from a cannon took an entire leg, arm, or head clean off.

To be candid, if my dad had taken me 10 miles to an actual battlefield where one honorable man died, I would have gotten out of the car at every opportunity and taken it all in. I would have read every historical marker, marveled at every monument, and imagined what it must have been like to have actually been there during the fighting. A seven-day, 2,400-mile round trip tour to pay respects at Arlington, Manassas, Harpers Ferry, Antietam, Gettysburg, and Monocacy where tens of thousands of casualties occurred would have meant the world to me as a boy.

Upon arrival at the hotel adjacent to the battlefield, I decided to take a solo walk to prepare myself. The next day, I would be introducing my daughter to the largest battle ever fought on American soil.

Desperately desiring to transfer my passion for history to my next generation, an actionable question came to mind at Gettysburg. It was a catalytic thought setting into motion what would be the greatest adventure of my life. I will never forget standing at the stone wall, near The Angle, looking toward the setting sun horizon in the spring of 2017 on the 11th of April. Alone in my mind, and there physically at the site of Pickett's Charge, I could see those 12,500 honorable Southern men in mile-long formation standing shoulder to shoulder in voluntary obedience. Was one of my grandfathers among them?

Pickett's Charge Sunset at Gettysburg

American historical recollection describes the Civil War as one of brother vs. brother, so if not a Confederate soldier at Gettysburg, possibly a lineal ancestor there in blue. Could one of my grandfathers have been among those with Joshua Chamberlin at that critical moment on Little Round Top when out of ammunition, he commanded his men to fix bayonets before sounding the charge downhill?

I knew I had an ancestor who was a Confederate soldier, and another who was a soldier in the Revolutionary War, because my grandmother, Myrtle Ellen Mathis Surgnier, had discovered these two men while researching her family tree. She had provided to me copies of her applications to United Daughters of the Confederacy (UDC) and Daughters of the American Revolution (DAR). My grandmother's tree was my tree, so I, too, was a son of both the Confederacy and the American Revolution.

I pondered. Was my grandmother's Confederate great-grandfather here at Gettysburg? What was his name again? I recalled him being attached to General Robert E. Lee's Army of Northern Virginia, stationed in Columbus, GA, and surrendered at Appomattox. What was my ancestor doing in Columbus, GA? Was he guarding a railway hub? When did he join the army? When was he sent to Columbus? How long was he in Columbus? When did he rejoin Lee's army in order to have been surrendered at Appomattox? He was attached to the Army of Northern Virginia, and the Army of Northern Virginia was here at Gettysburg. The sun had set, darkness was enveloping, and I marched quickly back to our nearby hotel room.

There in the hotel bed with laptop and WIFI, I began to type names into Google. Jency Gibbons? No. Jincy Giddons? No. Jimpsey Giddens? There he was, a member of Company I, 50th Georgia Infantry Regiment. Was the 50th Georgia in fact here at the Battle of Gettysburg? Another quick Google query and yes, the 50th was engaged at the Battle of Gettysburg. Oh my! I thought, *It's quite possible one of my direct grandfathers was here, in July 1863, in combat, participating in what is recognized as a most pivotal moment in American history.*

I interrupted my daughter's focus on her electronic device and pointed out it's quite possible one of her grandfathers was here during the Battle of Gettysburg.

"Really?" she replied somewhat enthusiastically.

As soon as the Visitor Center opened in the morning, we would be there to see if Jimpsey Giddens was among the list of those brave men, both North and South, who gave it their all at Gettysburg.

"We don't have a list of names," the National Park Service Ranger stated at the information desk.

I thought to myself, *What do you mean you don't have a list of names of the men who fought here? This massive visitor center, millions upon millions of visitors, countless books written about Gettysburg, 154 years to put together a list, and you don't have a list of names?*

He directed us to the location of a research room at the other side of the building where volunteers may be able to assist us. Upon entering that room, a row of cubicles with computer workstations sat vacant of inquiring minds except for a lone female volunteer waiting patiently for an opportunity.

"May I help you?" she said.

"Yes," I replied, "I'm looking for a soldier who may have fought here."

She explained they didn't have a list, but she could perform a search online to see if she could find my ancestor's muster rolls.

I thought to myself, *What's a muster roll?* I gave her his name, and we sat down in front of one of the computers together. She went to a web page and typed in, Jimpsey Giddens. Within an instant, his name appeared on the screen. The anticipation was indescribable. She clicked on the file, and up popped a vertical rectangular shaped card. On the card was his name, his regiment, his company, his rank, his enlistment date, where he enlisted, present or absent, and the time period for which the record documented.

"What is this website?" I asked.

"FOLD3.com," she replied.

There were more of those rectangular shaped cards for Jimpsey Giddens. Columbus, GA, detached service, Shoemaker. What? Shoemaker? Other muster roll cards described his services as "Pegging Shoes." Confused is an understatement, more like bewildered, as I stared at the computer screen. During the most famous battle of the Civil War, while his regiment, the 50th Georgia, was engaged in mortal combat with the fate of two nations hanging in the balance, my grandfather was cobbling shoes, out of harm's way, in Columbus, GA?

Not one to move on from a subject prior to mastery, I had to know more. But we were here at Gettysburg with another full day of exploration, reflection, and knowledge gathering ahead of us. I had been to several Civil War sites, including Chickamauga, Shiloh, Olustee, and Andersonville, and as a Southern boy I had been interested in the Civil War most of my entire life, but on this day, things changed for me. From this new perspective of possibly having an ancestor involved in an historical event, the minute details suddenly became significant and memorable. For example:

- Where was the 50th Georgia positioned on the battlefield?
- Who was in command of the 50th Georgia?
- Does a monument at Gettysburg recognize the 50th Georgia?

The details of what transpired at this place 154 years prior now took on a greater level of importance, because I could feel a real sense of connection with events. We drove slowly within the battlefield park boundaries stopping to read signs, markers, and monuments.

We took a horseback trail ride through the actual battlefield narrated live by a certified professional guide. Somewhere during his analysis of the battle details, I heard what would be dismissed by others, but to me personally was absolutely incredible. He said, "Half the Confederate soldiers marched away from Gettysburg barefoot." Bam! That's why my grandfather was in Columbus, GA pegging shoes.

Turns out, General Robert E. Lee had issued special order 243 to detach a couple thousand soldiers to government factories for the purpose of producing shoes. The Union navy had blockaded the South, so importing shoes was not an option. An army marched hundreds of miles, tromped through all types of terrain, and shoes in the 1860s certainly didn't last as long as a pair of combat boots today. The end result was an insatiable appetite for handmade leather shoes. Dozens of small factories were eventually consolidated into two large factories one in Richmond, VA, and you guessed it, Columbus, GA. There they slaughtered the bovine to feed the armies, tanned the hides to make leather, cut the leather into shoe patterns, whittled shoe pegs out of wood, and pegged the cut pieces of leather into shoes for soldiers' feet.

Then I found Jimpsey's State of Georgia Confederate Soldier indigent pension application. This was a man who lived and raised children to adulthood, so that I might one day have life. Segments of his DNA possibly survive within me and within my children. To read the hand-written words of my then eighty-year-old, 4th great-grandfather essentially begging for food from the state government was heartbreaking. He had been a widower for seven years, had not been able to work for ten years, and had no assets. The doctors' evaluation of his physical condition was as follows:

"We find him almost blind. Can hardly walk and can't walk without sticks. Has a trembling and jerking all the time. Kidneys and bowels both in bad shape. Running off mouth all the time and really a physical wreck."

In addition to all I learned about my 4ᵗʰ great-grandfather, Jimpsey Byrd Giddens, I also found a photo of him attached to my grandmother's UDC application. She had discovered the photo within *Pioneers of Wiregrass Georgia "POWG"* published by the Huxford Genealogical Society located in Homerville, GA. Fortunately for me, and many other people descended from ancestors residing in southern Georgia and northern Florida, *POWG* was an invaluable reference source for identifying my ancestors.

Viewing the image of Jimpsey Byrd Giddens was deeply meaningful. A name was something. An image was a connection. Unlike too many who never give the past a second thought, I comprehended my direct connection to the face in the photo who was once alive, making his way, just like me. This was a man who literally gave me life.

Had the man in the photo not survived childhood, married Nancy Kirkland, and raised a daughter named Mary Ann to adulthood, I simply never exist. The man in the photo was born 190 years ago. The man in the photo has been buried in the cold ground 110 years. But, the passage of time does not erode his contribution to my being, nor should it afford me the convenience to avoid acknowledging his role.

Jimpsey Byrd Giddens

My 4ᵗʰ great-grandfather Jimpsey Giddens was not at the Battle of Gettysburg, but I had other grandfathers who were alive during the Civil War period of 1860-1865. Maybe they were living in America during the war. Maybe they were of military age. Maybe they were soldiers. Maybe they wore blue. Maybe they wore gray. The only way to find out if one of my grandfathers was at Gettysburg would be to build a family tree.

As soon as our flight returned us home to Florida, I renewed my expired Ancestry.com account. I couldn't recall the specific reason why I had sparsely populated a family tree ten years before this urge to find Civil War soldiers. An unexpected plus, now aware of muster rolls, they were offering a special package membership including access to FOLD3.com. I dug through dresser drawers, pulled down cardboard boxes from the attic, and sifted through plastic storage bins to gather any old manila envelopes or file folders containing family records I had held onto over the years.

Chapter 2

A FAMILY TREE IN FORTY DAYS

Vividly envisioning a picture of my family tree not yet having any of the to-be-found names of ancestors attached, it was devoid of a canopy, as if a giant sharpened blade had sliced a horizontal path just below the foliage line. No canopy, no leaves, no small branches, no twigs, just the thick hardwood foundation parts of a tree were visible. I could see myself as the ground level base of the tree, a stout trunk represented my parents, and four massive branches protruded outward and slightly upward from the trunk representing my grandparents. The four structural branches, live oak, each big around as a small car, possessed incredible strength, enough to hold thousands upon thousands, millions of ancestors, like a four-armed Atlas holding up the world. Each grandparent arm branch soon forked, as if two muscular forearms anchored at a locked elbow, creating a total of eight load-bearing extremities.

Knowing I needed to construct a solid foundation upon which to discover my family tree, I carefully carved the names and dates of my parents, my grandparents, and my great-grandparents into the trunk, arms, and forearms, respectively. First name, middle name, last name (maiden name), birth date, and death date (if applicable) were entered exactly, accurately, without error. By accomplishing this reasonably achievable task, I built a solid foundation from which to grow my entire tree. I contacted relatives who knew my great-grandparents well enough to share vital information, recollections, and stories. These people with first-hand knowledge were able to point out my great-grandparents' faces in old family photos.

To ensure a solid foundation for my family tree, I knew accuracy was paramount, including correct spelling, exact dates, and confirmed locations. I made sure to add Grandma's first name, middle name, maiden name, and birth date perfectly. She was Granny Haynes to members of my family, but her real name was Ruth Amanda Self, and she was born on June 26, 1893. She simply married a man named James Monroe Haynes, which is why we called her Granny Haynes.

While pursuing the adventure shared in this book, I remembered those times spent with loved ones since gone and wished with all my heart for just one more day. I found old photos in my great-grandmother's final possessions, perfectly focused, studio quality, someone in their Sunday best, in the prime of their life, but the photo bore no name. The person in the photo was significant to my great-grandmother, significant to me, but she was the last living person who could identify that special person.

My grandfather on my mom's side, Gigi, was just days away from his ninety-second birthday in the spring of 2017 when I set out in earnest to honor my DNA. I had started into my family tree ten years prior, but this time was different. It was different because I had a sense of urgency. My grandfather, my Gigi, my World War II hero, was dying.

In hindsight, I had only six months, but I worked on my tree, on his tree, with a focus and level of endurance, as if tomorrow might be too late. I worked with a clear sense of purpose, because tomorrow had been too late just two months prior when my other beloved WWII grandfather passed away in his sleep at ninety-four. The Lord took him home literally a few hours before I was scheduled to board a flight to Atlanta to visit him.

Every spare moment was spent interviewing family members, searching online, studying census records, or digging through reference books in my local library's genealogy room. My normal bedtime became 3am, sometimes 4am. The sand in my grandfather's hourglass was slipping away, and after forty-eight years of having access to him, procrastination was no longer an option.

Something I observed and found interesting was that none of my ancestors were famous. They weren't famous, but all were extraordinary in my eyes, because they were my grandparents. I didn't choose them, just as they didn't choose me, but we are connected by blood, by DNA no different from the unconditional bond of love I have with family members I have known during my lifetime. Without any effort on my part, I instinctively took ownership of each deceased ancestor no different from if they were alive right now and able to wrap my arms around.

Always one to be honest, a reason why I hadn't pursued researching my family tree sooner was because I had been dissuaded by Charlie Sphincter quite a few years ago. During a conversation, I mentioned to him how excited I was to learn about my heritage and discover my roots. Before I could finish my sentence, Charlie interjected. His Uncle Marvin, Marvin Sphincter, had researched the Sphincter family all the way back to 650 B.C. He continued stating he was related to Julius Caesar, George Washington, one of his great-great-something-grandmothers was a full-blooded Cherokee Indian, and one of his great-great-grandfathers invented the first steam engine. Truth be known, Charlie had probably never taken the time to really look at his Uncle Marvin's family tree work, so I should have taken his unsubstantiated boasting with a grain of salt.

I did my own work, scrutinized each person I added to my tree, and am now able to speak with authority about the incredible people from whom I inherited each and every part of my DNA signature. Thoughts of digging up family member names from 1,000 years ago worried me, overwhelmed me, discouraged me, but I had the time of my life just going back 175 years. The discovery of a church named after my 5th great-grandfather in honor of him and my 5th great-grandmother taking in orphaned children as their own brought on a feeling of pride I had never known. George Washington does not hold a candle as compared to my great-grandfather who volunteered as a civilian pilot in 1942 to fly "The Hump" across the Himalayan Mountains in the U.S. Army Air Corps during WWII. They called him the "Old Man" of the squadron.

Honoring my DNA, I first identified the finite list of people who contributed the genetic sequences living within me today. One by one, generation by generation, I traveled back in time, opening dust covered pages and chapters of my personal history. Names not recognized, with no connection, with no familiarity, suddenly took on an importance no less significant than the last name I had identified with my entire life. Surnames like Tomberlin, Blair, Dansby, Alderman, Clopton, McCranie, Varnes, Dasher, and Ihly became my own. Each grandparent had parents. Who were they? What were their names? As I added each name to my expanding tree, their individual stories began to emerge, as if they were alive once more. They were remembered.

First-hand knowledge is perishable, because it lives within the minds of those who can recollect and share verbally. Stories can be passed down from generation to generation, but someone has to know the story, and someone has to care enough to listen. I pray others will experience their catalysts, set their goals, and acquire a sense of urgency quickly, while they still have access to their priceless family members.

While sifting through my stash of family tree documentation, I noticed several photocopy pages sourced from *Pioneers of Wiregrass Georgia "POWG,"* including the photo of Jimpsey Giddens. I thought to myself, *Maybe the local library has a copy of POWG.* I had driven by the library countless times, but the internet had eliminated any reason to utilize the resource. So, I jumped in my truck and struck out to the library, feeling like I was back in school.

Steering off Gladiolus Drive at Bass Road, I navigated the bending curves to an open parking space. Across the parking lot, up the walkway, and through the doors, I felt a welcomed cool burst of conditioned air. Stopping at the reference desk, I inquired.

Trae: Excuse me. Where might I find *POWG.*

Staff: What is *POWG*?

Trae: It's a book with family information in it.

Staff: Turning toward his computer monitor and typing a few key strokes, he said, *POWG* is a twelve-volume set, and the library system does have a copy, but it's not here at this location.

Trae: I'm thinking, *Why wouldn't you have a copy at each library branch building?*

Staff: The *POWG* set is stored at the downtown Fort Myers branch, in the genealogy room.

Trae: Genealogy room?

Staff: Yeah, they store all the genealogy related resources in a single room at the downtown branch building.

Looking down at my iPhone, I could see the branch was closing in about forty-five minutes, and it was about a thirty-minute drive to the downtown branch. Of course, it was Saturday, and all library branches were closed on Sundays, so I'd just have to wait until Monday. When Monday came around, I was able to break away to downtown and reach that library's front desk.

Trae: Excuse me, I'm looking for the genealogy room.

Guy: It's upstairs, turn right, go to the far end of the building, and you'll see the door. There should be someone in there, but if the door is locked, just come back and I'll unlock it.

A nice lady greeted me upon entry into the genealogy room. I explained I was looking for *POWG*, and she led me to the aisle and shelf.

Lady: Go ahead and pull what you want. Leave the books on the table when you leave, and we'll re-shelve them.

Only allowing library staff to re-shelve helps keep books from getting lost in the wrong place by well-intentioned visitors.

Lady: What else can I help you with?

Trae: What all do you have here?

She patiently walked me throughout the room, pointing out various sections and explaining that books, binders, and folders were arranged alphabetically by state from left to right.

Lady: We close in a little less than an hour, so I'll leave you to your *POWG*.

Unbeknownst to me, *POWG* was a twelve-volume set of books published by The Huxford Genealogical Society, Inc. based in Homerville, GA, which was the brainchild of one Judge Folks Huxford. The Wiregrass is a geographic area east to west from the Atlantic Ocean to Alabama following the Florida Georgia state lines. The northern boundary extends to approximately Macon, GA, and the southern boundary extends south into Florida just below I-10. Judge Huxford began documenting the people who pioneered this land area, and through the help of contributors, amassed a repository of genealogical history priceless to those of us who proudly descend from these successful people of grit and determination.

The resource of *POWG* alone accounted for a bulk of my initial family tree, branching out to the Revolutionary War and beyond. I had no idea how deeply rooted I was in the Wiregrass region of South Georgia and North Florida. Along the way, someone would

research and document a specific man who lived in this region. Information included his full name, where he was born, his parents' names, his wife's name, his wife's parents' names, his children and their vital information, who his children married, etc. The section in the volume set pertaining to a specific person and covering about a page or two of content is known as a sketch. The sketch includes a paragraph or more of written text essentially sharing a summary of that person's life story. Sketches written about my ancestors were incredible to read.

My wife must have assumed I had a girlfriend at the library downtown, because I was slipping over there during my spare hours most every day. I actually had not one but two mistresses: Ann Sestry and Jeannie Aloe Jee. One sketch would take me to another sketch, and then another, as my tree continued to expand throughout the Wiregrass. And then I remembered. My grandmother, Muffy, had purchased her own set of these priceless books. One call to my grandfather, and those books showed up on my doorstep in a UPS box about five days later.

Pioneers of Wiregrass Georgia:
seven volume set purchased 1978

Opening the cover of the hardbound, blue denim-colored and textured VOLUME 1, I was greeted by a cleared bank check taped to the inside front cover. The check was made out in my grandmother's handwriting PAY TO THE ORDER OF Judge Folks Huxford, $110.51, dated 10-2 1978. At the top right-hand corner of the first page is written October 10, 1978, just eight days after she wrote the check. She was forty-eight years old. As I wrote this sentence, I started crying, realizing I, too, began my ancestry adventure at the same age of forty-eight. It was a type of raw emotion I hadn't expected when I dug into my origins and discovered these connections that moved me.

I sensed her excitement on that fall day in 1978 when she turned to that page containing the first sketch of a great-grandfather. I bet she was combing through those books until 4 o'clock the next morning, never pausing to acknowledge the hour. Throughout her seven-volume set, she wrote notes that would—thirty-eight years later, and two years after her death serve as her participation in my journey of genetic discovery. And to think she did it without computers, internet, assistance from her grandmother's research notes, or DNA technology.

I share *POWG* as an example of resources discoverable at a genealogy room containing various pieces to family puzzles. I found things there I hadn't anticipated, such as resident directories, yearbooks, newspaper articles, and more. While there certainly exists a vast amount of content digitized and easily searchable online, library genealogy rooms still contain treasures beyond imagination. Buried on page thirty-three of a blue, side-bound report binder tucked out of sight between two non-descript books and never cracked open by any curious soul since inserted on the shelf sixty-seven years ago, I found an abstract of a last will and testament for my 3rd great-grandmother, Mary Ann Smith Surginer. In addition to my local genealogy room, I visited several located in counties where my ancestors once lived and died. Pulling from the shelves any resource I felt may be relevant to my family members, I skimmed through the pages and found arbitrary nuggets of genealogical gold.

In my peripheral vision, several books, binders, and folders were arranged in two stacks of unequal heights on either side of my laptop as I peered into pixelated 1870 Manatee County, Florida. There were places like Braden Town, Pine Level, and Sara Sota. There were cowboys, saloons, murders, and citrus groves. The county was massive in size, encompassing an area since divided into at least six separate counties, each of which is relatively large even by today's standards. Pioneer residents, excluding ancient populations, numbered 1,931, so to say it was sparsely populated would be an extreme understatement. Turns out six of those 1,931 people were my 3rd great-grandparents, my 2nd great-grandfather, 1 great-aunt, and 2 great-uncles.

My intense focus was interrupted by the sound of two whispering female voices emanating from the microfiche area two tables behind me. One mentioned having two Confederate soldier ancestors. The other said she was hoping to find a Confederate soldier grandfather, but so far, she had only found one Union soldier. We were in the genealogy room at the downtown Fort Myers location of the Lee County Library System.

Nonchalantly, I threw it out there. "I have nineteen." There was a pause.

"What's that?" one of the ladies responded.

I remained in my seat, facing away from the two listeners and stated matter-of-factly, "I have nineteen Confederate soldier grandfathers." The room was quiet. While the two seemingly envious genealogists digested the plausibility of nineteen, I went on speaking aloud, adding, "Forty-three of my grandfathers fought as Patriots during the Revolution." I could sense the intrigue, so I couldn't resist proclaiming, "I'm also a ninth generation Floridian." Light footsteps approached.

Halting beside me, one of the polite retirement-aged ladies asked, "How long have you been working on your family history?"

"About five weeks."

Her response was memorable when she replied, "I've been doing this for twenty-five years and haven't compiled that much information."

What I had considered to be low hanging fruit apparently resulted in a sizable family tree quicker than I had realized.

Leaving the library, I called my ninety-two-year-old grandfather and asked him what he knew about early Manatee County. He said, "You know the county seat wasn't always in Bradenton. It was way inland near Arcadia. My grandfather [my 2nd great-grandfather] used to carry the mail on horseback. He'd have to ride his horse way out east to where the Manatee River narrowed enough to ford the river. Then he rode all the way to Tampa to get the mail. There certainly weren't any paved roads and no bridges across Tampa Bay. It was a long way."

Chapter 3

PREPARING FOR 3 DAYS AND 16 CEMETERIES

I visit my mom. I visited my dad. I visited my grandparents. I visited my great-grandparents. So, why wouldn't I visit my great-great-grandparents? Because they were forgotten within three generations, that's why. Their names, their faces, their stories, when they were born, where they were born, where they lived, when they died, where they were buried, all forgotten. "There is no remembrance of former things, nor will there be any remembrance of things that are to come by those who will come after" (Ecclesiastes 1:11).

Memorial Day weekend 2017 was just a few days away when I thought to myself, *Why not just get in your truck and go pay your respects?* During the previous forty days, I had gone from my family tree quest catalyst on April 11, 2017 at Gettysburg's climactic Pickett's Charge upon Cemetery Ridge, to research Civil War soldier grandfather Jimpsey Giddens, to working toward my personal goal of identifying all my grandfathers of military age during the Civil War period. My tree had expanded significantly, as night after night I journeyed back in time via internet and reference book searches to identify my people.

Longing to meet them, to visit them, I recalled my father taking me to Lake Park, GA near Valdosta to find the grave of his namesake, Charles Robert Zipperer, when I was fifteen years old. I had never forgotten that meaningful trip, the U-Haul truck, the ice-cold Yoo-hoo bottle in my hand, the sign Zip's Tire Service, or the back pages of the phone book attached to the pay phone booth where countless Zipperers were listed.

I now had a family tree work-in-progress on Ancestry.com with names, dates, places, and Findagrave.com memorial links. My plan was to map out the burial sites of each of my ancestors and create a route linking each cemetery, so I could follow the route from cemetery A to cemetery B, and so on. Starting with my eight great-grandparents, I used an Excel spreadsheet to organize burial site information, such as first name, last name, maiden name, cemetery name, cemetery city, and cemetery state. One by one, I searched Findagrave.com using names, birth years, and death years to find each ancestor's grave.

At Findagrave.com, each grave was assigned a memorial number. The memorial number was associated with a cemetery. And each cemetery had a map link. So, I found a memorial, I clicked on the cemetery link, I clicked on the cemetery map link, and then zoomed out to discover and identify where the cemetery was located.

Cemeteries do not have physical addresses, and most older cemeteries are located in remote areas, so finding a cemetery was not as simple as plugging an address into my GPS system, or Google maps, or Apple maps, or MapQuest.com. My process was to zoom out on the Findagrave.com map to the point where I could see a nearest town, crossroad, landmark, etc. I then performed a Google search for the name of the town nearest the cemetery. Google search results for a town includes a map on the right side of the search results page. I clicked on that map and zoomed out until I recognized the point of the cemetery location red pin on the Findagrave.com map. Next, I clicked on the Satellite map link square in the corner of the Google map. Then, I zoomed in to the cemetery location on the Google Satellite map to see if the cemetery was visible. In most cases, I could clearly see a cemetery in the zoomed in satellite map view, because headstones cast shadows creating parallel rows of evenly spaced darker spots. Another common landmark from space was the roof of a church building along an edge of the cemetery.

For my first cemetery road trip, I printed a screenshot of a Florida state map on an 8.5" x 11" piece of paper. I later joined AAA and obtained free, large-sized state maps for plotting my ancestors' cemeteries. I received discounts on hotel stays during my ancestry road trip adventures when I mentioned being a AAA member.

In my spreadsheet, I assigned a number to each cemetery and then assigned the appropriate cemetery number to each ancestor. With multiple ancestors in a single cemetery, this system made it easier for me to write one number on the map to designate a cemetery location, and then reference my spreadsheet to see which ancestor, or ancestors, were buried in that cemetery. In addition to having the cemetery designated numbers in my spreadsheet and assigned to each ancestor name, I also wrote a list of numbers and cemetery names on the map itself for quick and easy reference. For example, 1. Empire Church Cemetery, 2. Sunset Hill Cemetery, and so on.

Not all cemeteries were visible from a satellite map view because they were old, small, remote, off the beaten trail, under tree canopies, or simply overgrown from neglect. These cemeteries were the most memorable, because I had to work for them. And honestly, it was an adrenaline rush to turn off a paved road 20 miles from nowhere, drive a mile down a dirt road, step out of my vehicle, and then trod 50 feet into the woods through knee-high brush meandering along an undefined path rarely, and not recently, traveled. I knocked on a door to ask permission if a house was nearby, but local people were aware of a cemetery's existence, so they knew why a vehicle was parked near the access point. In my limited experience, descendants have rights to access cemeteries on private property. From a practical standpoint, most people respected that someone was interested in taking the time to visit a cemetery and were more than willing to help and enable access. Many people near a cemetery knew who owned the land and were willing to call that person for me. Meeting people and hearing their stories of what they knew about the cemetery was a relevant part of my journey of ancestral discovery.

Sixteen cemeteries, designated numbers 1 through 16, were plotted on my Florida state map. The Florida section of my spreadsheet contained the names of forty-three grandparents and Memorial Day weekend 2017 was just one day away. I thought about what I might need, put together a list, and started loading my truck. My wife recognized the importance of what I was doing, so she took it upon herself to visit our local Dollar General to purchase some artificial flowers to place on my grandmothers' graves and American flags for my veteran grandfathers. She also secretly left a box of tissues for me in my back seat next to the flowers and flags.

I stopped into a Dollar General to see what they had to offer as far as supplies I needed during my cemetery visitations. Many of my ancestors' cemeteries were located in small, rural towns because pretty much everyone was a farmer, and I found Dollar General stores almost everywhere I went. Most small towns aren't big enough for a Walmart, but Dollar General filled the niche supplying locals with essentials. I purchased dozens of $1 artificial flower bouquets and $2 American flags, along with gallons of water, scrub brushes, paper towels, and bags of ice for my cooler of drinks. I have returned to gravesites six to twelve months later and found my $1 flowers and $2 flags a bit faded, but still displayed. Well done, Dollar General!

I carried with me whatever supplies I thought I'd need during my gravesite visits, because there weren't any resources available onsite. Sometimes I found a water spigot in the cemetery but learned not to count on it. That's why I brought at least six 1-gallon jugs of water to each cemetery and refilled them along the way to my next cemetery. I used the water to wash and rinse my ancestors' headstones, grave markers, and footstones. Most importantly, I needed drinking water and protein snacks, because again there wouldn't be any resources nearby, and I was bound to get thirsty and hungry, especially during summertime. I had spent upwards of two hours working up a sweat at a gravesite cleaning, raking, sweeping, trimming, scrubbing, and sometimes digging to reset leaning headstones and footstones. A cold drink and healthy snack enabled me to remain onsite and finish whatever I found needed to be done. The following is a list of supplies I carried along with me during my cemetery visitation road trips:

- Cooler full of ice
- Lunch if I thought I wouldn't be near food sources
- Drinks such as bottled water and Gatorade
- Protein snacks such as nuts and Cliff Bars
- Six 1-gallon jugs of water for refilling
- A large Rubbermaid plastic bin
- Three 5-gallon standard plastic buckets
- Rake, hoe, shovel, trowel, broom, dustpan
- Garden shears, loppers, hedge trimmers
- Rubber gloves, various size bath brushes
- Cleaning rags, paper towels, trash bags
- Artificial flowers, American flags
- Digital camera or smart phone w/camera
- Bath towel and change of clothes
- Hat, sunglasses, sunscreen, bug spray
- 10'x10' basic blue tarp for moving debris

Noticing a few of my ancestors' gravesites were located near Palatka, FL, and knowing my buddy from business school grew up in Palatka and lived in nearby St. Augustine, I called him up.

"Hey, Ted, I'm sure you'll find this hilarious, but like you, apparently I'm from Palatka, too."

Ted laughed and asked me to explain, which I did. I told him I would be in Palatka on Sunday to visit some cemeteries where my ancestors were buried and asked if he would be available to escort me around the greater Palatka metropolitan area. Palatka is a small, rural north Florida town, so of course he laughed and let me know he was available and would love to join my adventure.

Ted asked me which cemeteries I would be visiting. I gave him the name of the first cemetery, Union Grove Cemetery.

Ted said, "Oh sure, I know where that's at. It's up there off Bardin Road. What's the next cemetery?"

I said, "Etoniah Cemetery, it's also known as Bardin Cemetery."

Ted didn't say anything, and the line just fell silent.

I asked, "Ted, you still there?

Ted's voice came back on the line. "My dad's buried there."

It was at that moment when this new ancestry adventure took on a very odd life of its own. The first of many strange unexplainable occurrences, Ted would meet me at Etoniah Cemetery. We would visit his dad's grave, and we would find the grave of my 5th great-grandfather, George Varnes, not more than 50 feet away. The two seemingly unrelated men were buried more than 100 years apart. This was an old rural cemetery in northeast Florida attached to a Primitive Baptist Church. What was the probability of this happening?

Chapter 4

ALL THEIR GRAVES FACE EAST

Memorial Day weekend arrived, and I was chomping at the bit to leave my driveway and point my truck toward Sarasota and cemetery #1 on my list of sixteen to visit over the next three days. I didn't know how long I would be at each cemetery, and I didn't know how far along my route I would travel by nightfall, so my plan was to find a hotel room at the end of each day.

I had been to Sarasota many times, but never knew the location of ancestors I had heard mentioned being buried there. Specifically, my grandfather had told me his grandmother died of cancer at a very young age, and she was buried in Sarasota. Her untimely death became very real to me while I stood next to her grave reading the dates and calculating her age at twenty-nine. My grandfather also told me of his grandfather having died from accidentally drinking kerosene out of a clear glass jar. Desperately thirsty while picking vegetables for day wages in a field near Clewiston, FL, the job foreman told him a water jug was in the bed of the work truck. Twenty-seven years separated the two tragic deaths, but their children transported his body the 130 miles to lay him to rest next to his first love.

Next to Grandpa and Grandma Surgnier were her parents, James Jackson Holland and Lutishua Blair Holland. I cleaned each of the four gravesites and took photos to upload to my family tree and Findagrave.com. When I showed my grandfather the photo of his grandparents' grave, he said, "Oh, I remember my daddy pouring that concrete ledger himself one day after work."

My next stop was Manasota Memorial Park Cemetery just up the road in Oneco, FL. I had stopped by this cemetery several times over the years to visit the graves of three of my eight great-grandparents. WWII pilot Ray Mathis had been there since 1971. Arthur Paul Surgnier had been there since 1974. And I had attended the actual burial of Blandena Estelle Helms Surgnier in 2002. But no one had ever shared with me, or maybe I wasn't paying attention when it was mentioned, that my great-great-grandparents, Charles Branson Self and Eleanor Jarratt Self, were buried there, too. Time and again I drove into Manasota Memorial Park, got out of my car, walked to three different gravesites, and had no idea I was within just a few steps of another two extremely significant people in my life. Five grandparents in one cemetery.

Unlike the flat bronze markers pinpointing the burials of Ray, Arthur, and Blandena, the Selfs had been buried in a section of the cemetery where above ground headstones were allowed. They had a fine, large, upright granite memorial with only SELF etched on the front and nothing on the back. Ground-level flat granite footstones for Grandma and Grandpa Self were chosen to inscribe their names and dates. I found those stones literally black with thick algae, so I spent more time scrubbing stubborn organic growth than I had anticipated. Finishing up, I loaded my cleaning supplies and headed toward Fort Meade.

Backtracking to I-75, then north across the Manatee River to east on Highway 301 through Ellenton, I turned east onto Highway 62 or Wauchula Road. At Duette, I took the left fork in the road. A right onto 630 would point me toward Fort Meade, where future Confederate General Thomas Jonathan "Stonewall" Jackson served in the U.S. Army during 1850-1851 in efforts to rid Florida of the threat to settlers posed by Seminole Indians. The fort was named after U.S. Army officer George Meade, who would one day lead Union forces at the Battle of Gettysburg. In 1864, Yankees burned to the ground all structures comprising the town of Fort Meade.

Turning south onto Peeples Road to reach New Hope Cemetery, I couldn't have known several months later I would learn of a Confederate Captain R. A. Peeples from Valdosta, GA, who would lead the militia unit of my grandfather James A. Wisenbaker in 1864 and lead my grandfather Charles W. Haynes into battle in 1865.

I haven't confirmed it yet, but I suspected New Hope Cemetery was once affiliated with a Primitive Baptist Church. Looking at the satellite Google map image, I saw where a segment of New Hope Road at some time in the past was consumed by phosphate mining, as evidenced by a lake where what appears was once a continuation of New Hope Road to the cemetery. Surrounded by land previously mined, the cemetery had been protected from the landscape-altering activity. Once an island in a sea of strip mining, it was now all quiet. I felt at peace there and distinctly remember a Bobwhite quail trotting, weaving, walking along the interior of the perimeter chain-link fence.

Only my third cemetery, arriving after high noon with the sun dropping toward the west casting shadows toward the east, it was the first time I experienced the challenges of photographing headstones in the afternoon. The light source from the sun shining toward me flooded my camera lens while attempting to capture the shaded etched side of the vertical marble slab. Exacerbating the problem, the marble stone selected 115 years before I arrived on the scene provided almost zero contrast between surface and etchings. Frustration ensued, due to the photographic lighting difficulties.

Eventually, I correlated the timing of the lighting frustrations to afternoon headstone photo shoots. Then the common denominator became apparent to me. All the headstones were facing east, all of them. It wasn't by accident they all faced east. My ancestors, all Christians, buried their dead face up, feet toward the east. They believed Jesus would return from the east with the rising sun. They wanted to be facing their Savior when they stood up out of their grave. Collectively, the cemeteries containing millions of our ancestors all buried facing east created an archeological wonder no less significant than the discoveries of King Tut's Tomb, Machu Picchu, or the Rosetta Stone. These weren't terracotta soldiers. These were my ancestors.

Buried here were my 4ᵗʰ great-grandparents Willoughby Berrien Holland and Ellender Yeomans Holland. His stone read: IN MEMORY OF W. HOLLAND BORN OCT. 24, 1822 DIED OCT. 24, 1902. That's what others would know about him if they strolled by his marker and happened to pause, but I saw more. I saw the final resting place of a Confederate soldier, a cavalryman, a man who joined the 11ᵗʰ Georgia Cavalry State Guards at age forty-one following the death of his oldest son, Reddin Holland, a Private in Company G of the 50ᵗʰ Georgia Infantry Regiment. Willoughby was thirty years old when his grandfather, Revolutionary War soldier Henry Holland, died in 1852, so he would have known him well.

Next to Willoughby was his wife, Ellender, mother of ten children. I had just visited the grave of their second oldest child, and my 3ʳᵈ great-grandfather, James Jackson Holland, in Sarasota earlier in the day. Assuring them I would return, and I have, I needed to get moving toward Davenport if I was ever going to make it to Groveland with enough daylight left to visit with family and see three more cemeteries there.

I had driven through Davenport a few times each year my entire life, taking a specific route by a citrus processing plant emitting an olfactory stimulation distinct to these massive buildings. Truckloads of freshly picked fruit enter at one end, and frozen juice concentrate exits the other. As a child, I remember helping to load grapefruit into the bed of a truck fitted with tall wooden sides to extend the height and increase the capacity of a motor vehicle originally designed to carry significantly less weight. Squatted down with the tops of the rear tires rubbing the fender wells, I was too young to worry about whether or not the brakes could slow the momentum when we reached our local citrus processing plant. With no seat belts, who needed the ability to stop? I assume my dad coasted in for the last quarter mile, bleeding off enough speed to allow the undersized brakes to prevent us from smashing into the docks where conveyor belts hoisted the liquid vitamin C to, I had no idea where. That smell unique to Florida has been imprinted ever since.

Behind the processing plant in Davenport, and just a short way down Lee Jackson Highway, was Evergreen Cemetery. Never once as I passed through this little town did I have an inkling my family members had been employed by the landmark citrus industry employer. It never dawned on me the source of 6.25% of my DNA, 25% of my Gigi's DNA, was buried less than 400 yards west of Highway 17-92 as I whizzed by heading towards Winter Haven from Kissimmee. I had been oblivious, hadn't asked, hadn't cared, and nobody pointed it out. Gigi's grandmother, Amanda Louise Bass Helms, my great-great-grandmother, was there surrounded by three of her children and two daughters-in-law. I know now three of her children were with her, because one grave, for a Janie Lee Smith, seemed to be situated within the Helms family section, so I took a picture. Listening to Gigi talk about his Aunt Janie and her husband, Norman Smith, the grave of Janie Lee Smith spoke to me.

Oneco, Fort Meade, Davenport, and Groveland. These are Florida city names you've probably never heard of, but they're where I come from. I was way behind schedule by the time I rolled into Groveland, but three living family members were still waiting on me. I had visited with them several times over the years, but this time was different. It was more meaningful. Having linked my family members in an organized tree, I was now keenly aware of their respective places in my familial web and felt a connection like never before. I now appreciated the common ancestors and DNA we shared on the inside.

They accompanied me to three different cemeteries to visit five ancestor gravesites representing three generations dating back to my 3rd great-grandmother, Sarah Conway Smith, born in 1867.

The first day of my ancestry adventure road trip was life changing. The feelings, energy, and emotions associated with being alone with grandparents I'd gotten to know through research, but never actually met, was impossible to describe. Visiting their graves, paying respects, and sprucing up their final resting places from a position of unconditional love was meaningful beyond words. In one day, I visited seven cemeteries, seventeen grandparent gravesites, and three living relatives. One day! It was pitch black dark when I started looking for a hotel room. Dog tired after such a fulfilling day of discovery, I finally found a room about forty-five minutes away and near cemetery #8 on my map of Florida.

Chapter 5

THREE SMILES FROM HEAVEN

Waking up in Bushnell and grabbing a quick bite to eat, I scooted over to Center Hill to find 2nd Great-grandma and 2nd Great-grandpa Mathis. I arrived to find a beautiful, wide-open manicured field of green bahia grass accented by handsome Southern live oak trees. Not knowing where to start, I chose a spot to park at the east end of the cemetery where I could walk into the rows of headstones with the writing facing me and the morning sun at my back.

It hadn't yet occurred to me that all my ancestors' graves were facing east. I started at the northeast corner and chose a first swath where I could see all the names for a distance of about 20 feet on both my right and left sides for a total observation path of 40 feet in width. To and fro, to and fro, 40 feet at a time, until under the shaded outstretched arms of a mature shade tree, I spotted the name Mathis. Ocie Ann James Mathis had a granite headstone sitting upon a poured concrete ledger. Beside her, William Walter Mathis' headstone had been placed directly on the ground and appeared to be approximately 8 inches shorter. On a hunch, I started digging around the base of his headstone. As I suspected, his stone was identical in dimensions as hers, but the weight of his without a concrete ledger foundation had steadily pulled the stone down into the soil over a period of sixty years.

Mathis graves at Center Hill, FL after thorough cleaning

After cleaning up the Mathis gravesites, I couldn't help but notice an adjacent headstone covered completely in algae, moss, lichens, and grime. I was really worn out from scrubbing and cleaning my grandparents' graves, but I stepped over with my broom and took a few quick swipes across the face of the illegible stone. Recognizing the name Mathis, I put forth a little more effort to reveal the name William Glenn Mathis born 1900 and died 1921. He was only twenty-one years old. And then it hit me. This was my grandmother's uncle, the one she had told me about who got struck by the rattlesnake! Cleaning his entire stone informed me he had a wife and child when he died. When I told my grandfather, Gigi, I had found Uncle Glenn's headstone, he told me what had happened.

2nd Great-grandpa Mathis was a watermelon farmer. Back in those days, people would clear a piece of land for the owner in return for the right to plant a crop of watermelons. Supposedly, the newly cleared land could only grow one crop of melons. Anyway, 2nd Great-grandpa Mathis had his boys working with him to clear a field. At lunch time, he told the boys to load up into the wagon for the trip home, but Glenn chose to walk instead. Apparently, he stepped over a downed tree, and a large rattlesnake struck his leg.

Rattlesnakes were everywhere in Florida back in those days, and they were big, really big. Glenn lived a few days after the venom entered his body, but it took too long to send for and fetch a doctor from Gainesville via train. The story goes that 2nd Great-grandpa Mathis went out of his mind over the death of his son. It was said he would catch every rattlesnake he could find, put them in barrels, and provide them to the University of Florida for antivenom research. Gigi remembered walking over to 55-gallon barrels out by the barn at 2nd Great-grandpa Mathis' house. Approaching carefully, leaning forward, stretching his neck, chin out with eyes looking downward, and peeking over the rim of a barrel, he would regularly see six to ten long, fat, live, intertwined diamondback rattlesnakes.

Leaving Center Hill, I worked my way toward Umatilla and then an hour north to Palatka. Ted was waiting for me when I arrived at Etoniah Cemetery. Together we paid our respects at his father's grave and my 5th great-grandfather's grave before pulling out onto Bardin Road and heading north a couple of miles to Union Grove Cemetery. We made a left turn onto Union Grove Cemetery Road, a dirt road with deep ruts from recent rains. As we made a right turn pointing north toward the cemetery at the dead end, we saw a woman riding a large mower blowing a cloud of sand, dust, and mulched plant growth. Seeing us on her road rarely traversed by outsiders, she turned off her blades and pulled to the side. Being neighborly, we stopped next to her, rolled down the passenger side window, and engaged in friendly conversation.

Trae: Hey. Howya doin?

Lady: Fine. How you?

Trae: Pretty good. I see you mowing the sides of the road. Do you maintain the cemetery at the end of the road? We're here to see some ancestors buried there.

Lady: No, but my husband Addison Moody does.

Ted: Your husband wouldn't be Addison Moody who graduated Palatka High School in 1983 would he?

Lady: Yes, sir, that's him.

Ted: Does he still play a guitar?

Lady: He plays any instrument you put in his hands!

Once a Primitive Baptist Church cemetery, the church building where dinner on the grounds filled the country setting with joyful activity on Sunday afternoons had long since disappeared. But sixty-seven graves, all facing east, stood witness to what these people believed. There at the end of that quiet dirt road where time is suspended and birds chirp in the gently rustling oak canopy, not one, not two, but three of my grandmothers, unknown to me forty days earlier, sleep. This was my first pioneer cemetery.

Etoniah Cemetery was old, a Primitive Baptist Church cemetery on a main paved road, but this place, Union Grove Primitive Baptist Church Cemetery, was different. Off the beaten path, small, quiet, peaceful, this was a place of reflection devoid of distractions. These three women, now mere names and dates etched into marble in a mostly forgotten half-acre of land demarcated by a chain-link fence, are mine. Combined, these women contributed 3.125% of the DNA residing inside of me. Lucinda, Mary, and Sarah had been here for 108, 107, and 102 years, respectively, patiently waiting for appreciative descendants to stop by and pay a visit. There were no flowers at the base of each headstone, but I had my Dollar General bouquets and generated three smiles from Heaven.

The second strange occurrence of this initial ancestry adventure road trip happened as Ted and I followed our internet map directions toward the next Primitive Baptist Church cemetery where Sarah's husband was assumed to have been buried in 1880. As we approached the area where the map pin designated the cemetery location, we were traveling north beside a tall, imposing fence protecting the boundary of a military base. Finding a locked access gate near where we assumed a road would lead toward the cemetery, a warning sign read "Camp Blanding." I recognized the name. Camp Blanding was where my grandfather, Gigi, was inducted into the army during World War II before eventually landing at Normandy. What is the probability that one of my ancestors would be buried in a cemetery within the confines of the army base where my grandfather entered World War II?

Attempting to gain access at the main gate, we parked at what turned out to be a museum where I was able to learn details about not only my grandfather's service, but my great-grandfather's service as an Army Air Corps Pilot. Happenstance? No, it was not.

Leaving the WWII museum heading toward Middleburg, a suburb just west of Jacksonville, we made a quick U-turn and parked alongside four-lane Highway 16. Findagrave.com had a pin designating the location of Old Conway Cemetery as being a few dozen yards into the woods. An overgrown path crisscrossed with spider webs and downed trees seemed to be in the right place to lead toward the cemetery. The dense treetops in the late afternoon/early evening timeframe created a rather dim environment in which to search for a less than well-marked set of burial sites holding the remains of my 5th great-grandfather.

Ted and I slowly worked our way back into the wooded area about 100 yards or more, looking both ways into underbrush on either side of what seemed like a pathway. In a hurry with the sun dropping fast, I chose not to spray myself with DEET before walking away from my truck. It turned out to be a poor decision, as I looked down to see a flat tick spider-crawling up my leg. Quickly dispatching her, I alerted Ted, and we agreed it was a good idea to call off our search. While we didn't find the cemetery, and I turned out to be a tick magnet, tromping through the woods in search of an ancestor burial site proved to be somewhat exhilarating, exciting, and adventuresome.

Grateful 9th Generation Floridian

Hurrying to Middleburg, we found my 6th Great-grandfather Isaac Varn's Florida Pioneer headstone, grabbed some Taco Bell, and parted ways. My next cemetery stop would be near LaCrosse, FL. The only hotel along the route from Middleburg to LaCrosse was in Starke, where I would call it a night at the Best Western. After a much-needed hot shower, I kicked back on the bed and reflected on my second day of ancestor cemetery road tripping. What a meaningful, memorable day. One of the best days of my life, it seemed like a week had passed, but I had woken up in Bushnell only thirteen hours ago. In a single day, I had:

- Traveled 170 miles
- Visited five cemeteries
- Placed flowers at five grandmother gravesites
- Introduced myself to three grandfathers
- Cleaned nine headstones, including Uncle Glenn Mathis
- Made a lifelong memory with a close friend
- Met a lady on a riding lawn mower
- Attempted to find two other cemeteries
- Visited a WWII museum
- Stood where my grandfather entered the army in 1943
- Fended off an attempted tick attack

My level of anticipation for morning to arrive with the rising sun was shear giddiness. I closed my eyes and imagined what God had in store for me on Memorial Day. Within seconds, I was fast and sound asleep.

Chapter 6

MEMORIAL DAY 2017

Alarm, shower, brush teeth, sunrise, dew, flexed nostrils, deep breath, fresh air, train tracks, coffee, breakfast, fill my six, one-gallon jugs, and steer my truck toward La Crosse. I'd never heard of La Crosse, FL, let alone been there. The map showed it 15 miles due north of Gainesville. I would drive through Brooker to get there. Having run out of flowers, the yellow Dollar General sign up ahead was a welcome sight, so I pulled in to replenish. I found beautiful $1 bouquets in yellow, pink, red, and white. Each had six flowers, and I spread each apart, just so, to optimize their appearance. Honestly, they looked pretty darn good.

As I drove near and through the rural town of La Crosse, I couldn't help but notice the beautiful expanses of pasture lands, huge oaks, and pleasant homes. Not many people or cars stirred on Memorial Day morning in Alachua County, especially 3 miles north of the town I'd never heard of despite spending most of my life traveling scenic route backroads of the real Florida. The ride to New Hope Primitive Baptist Church Cemetery was picturesque. Mickey Mouse had never been here, and it showed. I could see the sign, then the opening, then the traditional-style church building with wood siding freshly painted white, then the rows of headstones beyond the chain-link fence. The setting was absolutely perfect, beautiful, old Florida, so I parked there under the oaks for a few minutes to take it all in.

It was time, so I gathered my stuff, the five-gallon buckets, the one-gallon jugs, the rake, and I walked into the cemetery not able to read the headstones as I was entering from the west side of the burial grounds. After a few minutes to and fro, I found her under the central focal point oak tree just inside the gate not far from the church, Lydia Anderson, a 3rd great-grandmother and one of my favorites. Directly on the other side of the tree, her son, Elijah Newton Anderson, the Reverend Elijah Newton Anderson, my great-great-grandfather, had been buried beside his first wife. So, I set up my supplies around Lydia's headstone and got to work.

I tilted a gallon jug of water directly above the stone, slowly pouring back and forth watching the water cascade down all sides wetting and softening everything in its path. I kept the stone wet for several minutes and then used my bathroom scrub brush to begin removing the algae and other organic growth from the ninety-eight-year-old monument of marble. Scrub and rinse, scrub and rinse, the water clear from the jug gathered dislodged grime and darkened, as if tobacco juice spit, on its gravity induced journey toward the thirsty tree roots below. The darkened water gathered within the etchings, making more legible the letters carefully chosen by her children to memorialize her in anticipation of my arrival this Memorial Day.

LYDIA ANDERSON
BORN
APRIL 18. 1843
DIED
APRIL 18. 1919
She is gone to the land where
the weary enjoy the sweet
rapture of sacred repose.
Gone but not forgotten.
Her children

My aloneness ended as I noticed a full-sized pickup truck with bed canopy steadily creep into the church grounds rolling slowly over unmown bahiagrass seed stalks until coming to a halt between the cemetery gate and the white church building. A long way from nowhere, by myself, in an unfamiliar setting, I had the advantage of the morning sun at my back in the event things went sideways. A concealed loaded Kimber, my daddy's marksmanship training, and routine visits to the weight room prepared me for situations such as this. I continued with my work, scrubbing, rinsing, studying the details and craftsmanship, but vigilantly alert to the pickup and testing various assumptions in my mind as to the purpose of those intruding upon my moment.

Crouched down with one hand on top of the stone and the other working the moistened bristles, a man approached from my right side. I wasn't looking at him, but I could sense his presence.

A voice broke the silence. "Do you know this person?" the man asked.

"Yes, I do. This is my 3rd great-grandmother," I responded to his question.

"She's my 2nd great-grandmother," he replied.

Looking up at him, I said, "Who are you?"

This was the third out-of-the-ordinary occurrence, and most surreal, encountered so far during my three-day cemetery trek. More than 825 people were buried across more than four acres of land, yet this guy comes here to this specific cemetery, to see the exact same person, on the exact same random day, at the exact same time. I literally looked around to see if this was really happening, or if I was still in my hotel room experiencing rapid eye movement.

"My name's Bob Holder. Lydia Anderson is my great-great-grandmother. My aunt died recently and left me a piece of property not far from here, so my wife and I came over this morning to look after it and decided to stop by here. How are you related to Lydia? Her daughter, Sarah Amanda Anderson Conerly, is my great-grandmother. Some of Lydia's children are buried all out through here," he said, as he turned and scanned the expanse of the cemetery.

I pointed to Elijah Newton Anderson's headstone a few feet away and shared that Elijah was Lydia's son and my great-great-grandfather. I shared that Elijah's daughter, Lydia Louvinnie, was my great-grandmother.

Bob said, "She married a Zipperer didn't she? Are you a Zipperer?"

Now it was getting beyond weird, because how in the world did this guy know about my great-grandmother, who she married, and my last name? He went on to tell me his daughter recently died from cancer and that he was currently battling stage-four cancer himself. He shared that Lydia's parents and grandparents were buried not too far away in Lake Butler. I let him know that's where I was going next after I finished cleaning Lydia's and Elijah's headstones. He then explained how to get there from here and why his route was the easiest. Bob asked if I needed anything and offered his contact information, which I accepted when he handed me a business card of some sort. He and his wife had places to go this day, so he said goodbye, and the pickup truck rolled around the other side of the church building, out the driveway, and down the road void of traffic.

I did reach out to Bob Holder, and we became quick friends. As it turned out, Bob and I were 3rd cousins 1x removed and DNA matches on Ancestry.com sharing 62 centimorgans across 3 DNA segments. He had been working on his family tree for many years and had added nearly 17,000 names. He was a wealth of information and kind beyond words, even going so far as to travel to a cemetery at my request to place flowers at a seven-year-old child's grave (my great-aunt Alcy Anderson) and take photos to upload to her memorial at Findagrave.com. Months later, I called Bob and arranged to meet him in Brooker, so he could guide me to Alcy's grave. It was during that visit when he showed me his large tumor protruding from his lower abdomen.

Standing just the two of us at Rock Primitive Baptist Church, I said to him, "Bob, I believe God brought us together."

Bob replied, "I know that to be true. My wife and I talked about it yesterday."

He offered to lead the way back to the main highway where he would turn left back home to Starke, and I would turn right, southbound, toward home. As I pulled beside him at the stop sign where he waited to cross to the median, something told me to look down at my dash. As I rolled forward to a stop, my fuel gauge distance to empty changed from 317 miles to 316 miles. I immediately knew what that meant. 316 is John 3:16 from the New Testament of the Bible. You may say that's just a fluke, but the digital clock there on my dash read 3:16 p.m.

Trae Zipperer and Bob Holder

From La Crosse, it was north to Lake Butler to Swift Creek Primitive Baptist Church Cemetery, where Lydia Douglass Groover Anderson's parents and grandparents, my 4th and 5th great-grand-parents, are buried. Knowing that Lydia's first husband, Coleman Groover, was killed in battle during the Civil War, I couldn't help but notice the surname Groover on headstones near those of my Douglass ancestors. Observing the gravesites with now familiar names that had never before been significant to me prior to forty days ago reinforced my internalization of ownership and connection to the family tree I was building.

As I drove away from Swift Creek, about a mile, I passed a blue sign pointing toward Douglass Cemetery. Now aware of my Douglass roots, and that I was in the land of my Douglass heritage, I turned around, took a right, and parked my truck outside the gates to Douglass Cemetery. As my footsteps carried me past headstone after headstone, I didn't recognize the specific people, but the name Douglass in this neck of the woods left no doubt these people and I, although separated by time, shared DNA sourced from common ancestors long ago. Knowing I had many more miles and several more cemeteries ahead of me this Memorial Day, I closed the gate behind me.

My dad's mother's maiden name was Haynes. Prior to the turn of the century in the late 1890s, her Haynes grandparents Daniel and Martha migrated with their children, including her father James, to Dover, FL east of Tampa, from Madison County situated in far north Florida. Surnames of 3rd great-grandparents hailing from Madison, FL include Haynes, Lindsey, Dansby, and Loper. The common thread bringing these four family names together in Florida appears to have been the Seminole Indian Wars in the mid-1800s, as all four grandfathers of military age were Indian fighters. One of the four, Charles W. Haynes originally from New Hampshire, enlisted in the U.S. 3rd Infantry Company K in Albany, New York on 7 Sep 1837 was deployed to the Florida Wars and was listed as deserting the army on 5 Jul 1838. The 1840 census shows him living with his first wife in Lowndes County, GA, a few miles north of the Florida Georgia line.

Apparently, he blended right in and married a local girl. As I made my way through downtown Madison, past town square, and turned northward onto State Road 53 in the direction of the first of two church cemeteries, the name "Haynes" caught my eye atop a street corner stop sign. Looping back around a residential city block with two consecutive right turns, the sign confirmed "NE Haynes

St." The Haynes family wagons had rolled out of Madison 120 years before I paid attention, but a street named after my ancestors serves as a reminder of an honorable legacy.

Haynes Street sign in Madison, FL

At the first cemetery north of Madison, I found an abandoned church building falling into disrepair. Literature was still visible through the glass doors, but it was obvious a sad day had come several years before I showed up on the steps, when the last church member locked the doors and walked away. Exploring around the church structure, I couldn't help but imagine my ancestors here, worshipping, thinking about their crops in the field, and sharing thoughts with their neighbors. Someone still mowed the church grounds and cemetery, but oversized landscape plants steadily encroached, having already enveloped several markers.

The final address of my 4th great-grandparents, John and Susan Loper, was easy to locate thanks to a grateful descendant who had replaced their original aging markers with a substantial granite monument of modern design beautifully etched with the names and dates of their nine children, including my 3rd great-grandmother, Caroline Elizabeth Loper Dansby. The added names of their children left no doubt I had come to the right place.

A few miles away, in contrast, was Pine Grove Missionary Baptist Church. It was a well maintained stereotypical small Southern town house of God complete with cross-topped steeple and overwhelming evidence of an active and conscientious congregation. The large cemetery out back was manicured near perfection, but I could not find my 4th great-grandparents, Reason and Rebecker Dansby. I walked with purpose, scanning the entire burial grounds, but still I came up empty. I knew the shape of Reason's headstone from viewing photos at his memorial on Findagrave.com, but nowhere could I find his stone.

Pausing for a moment, I decided to pull up those photos online on my smart phone while standing right there in the cemetery. Fortunately, I had cell reception! Paying attention to the entire photo and not just the stone, I could see where the stone was located in relation to the church building, trees, and several uniquely shaped monuments in the background. Holding my position, with my arm outstretched, the photo displayed on my phone matched exactly the setting I saw in front of me. Still no headstone. Then I looked down to see a flat-to-the-ground, newer marker inscribed with the names Rebecker and Reason Dansby. As with my Loper grandparents, a caring descendant, or the congregation members, had lovingly replaced fallen and/or damaged memorials.

A replacement marker

Memorial Day, Monday, 2017, the third day of my ancestry cemetery road trip was beginning to run short on daylight. It seemed as though my alarm had gone off in that Starke Best Western hotel room days ago, but that was this morning. I met Bob Holder at Lydia Anderson's grave near La Crosse several hours ago, but it seemed as if I'd known him for years. Four cemeteries, first time visits to the graves of ten recently discovered grandparents, 125 miles, but I didn't want this day, or this trip, to end. There were a couple of cemeteries I wanted to stop at along I-75 near Tampa, but the distance was too far to cover before sundown. My only hope to keep this adventure alive just a little longer was to find James I. Mims.

James I. Mims was one of my nineteen Confederate soldier grandfathers. His death certificate said he died in Suwannee County,

FL, and I had found a Mims Cemetery located in Suwannee County, FL while looking through Findagrave.com. With only three Mims cemeteries in all of Florida, only one in the county where he died, and not another within 100 miles, it seemed like a logical place to find him. I mean, how many Mims could there possibly have been in Suwannee County, FL in 1918? Wouldn't they all be related and buried together? The map pin showed Mims Cemetery about 25 miles SE of Madison and not too far out of my way as the crow flies, so off I went to soak up every last minute.

One thing I hadn't anticipated was the limited, to poor, to no cell phone reception in the now isolated areas that my ancestors once called home. Looking at my phone, looking at my screenshots, looking at my truck navigation display, and trying to identify common layouts and contours of roads was difficult, because as I zoomed out to gain perspective, the street names disappeared. Eventually, I found the physical area where the map pin on Findagrave.com was marking. I drove slowly, scanned both sides of the road, but could see nothing indicating a cemetery. I pulled into the long driveway of a small farm that appeared to encompass the patch of land holding the Mims graves.

Florida Southern country people are good folks, but they're smart, they're tough, they're not naïve, and consider them armed. No one acknowledged my presence, for which I was relieved, so I drove around to the wooded area, got out of my truck, and started walking along the dirt road studying the edge of the densely wooded area for any indication of an access point.

A car came around the corner from the direction of the dirt road dead end, this being their only exit, so I knew they lived on this road. Of course, the window rolled down and the intimidating man in the passenger seat gave the customary Florida greeting, "How's it goin? You need any help?" What he meant was, "You don't belong here. I have a .357 on this side of the door. My wife driving this tank has a loaded 9mm, and she knows how to use it. I don't recognize you. You have thirty seconds to give a good explanation as to what you are doing here."

I told him I was looking for a cemetery and asked if he knew where I might find one along this road. He pointed to the woods and shared there were graves in the woods, but the last surviving people who cared stopped coming to maintain the cemetery quite a few years ago. In addition to the lack of trimming and nature's rec-lamation, vandals in the form of teenagers seeking a haunted thrill had visited and caused significant damage every Halloween or any other random night when a dare or scare seemed like a harmless activity. The man also shared with me the property owner on the other side, the small farm where I had tried to ask permission, ran his cows on the land and wouldn't take too kindly to me trespassing. We talked a little more, and they eventually drove away. My guess is they immediately called the owner of the small farm.

Observing the downed fencing wire, nearly flat to the ground in several places, I could tell no farm animals had been held in this parcel for a very long time. The wooded area was relatively large, and so thick with trees and scrub, there would be no way for anyone on the other side to observe me looking for headstones. If they did take a shot at me, the odds of a bullet traveling through this thicket without a ricochet deflection off target were slim to none.

Picking up a long, spindly stick, I twirled and swished the spi-derweb catcher in front of me as I kept my head and eyes down, alert for the presence of a coiled rattler. Growing up an outdoors-man in Florida, I knew how and why to slowly and cautiously place each and every step.

Reaching the center, I found the first headstone leaning up against the base of a tree. Another was actually wedged in between two trees, which had lifted the memorial off the ground 18 to 24 inches as the trees grew steadily without interference. Seeing evidence of a third marker and ledger, I swept away a thick accumulation of fallen leaves and detritus, uncovering components of a burial now not positioned as originally intended. Witnessing firsthand the devastation of neglect, nature, and intentional destruction, thickly coated with dead leaves and fallen twigs, I thought to myself, *If James I. Mims is in here, there's no way I'm ever going to find him.*

Discouraged that I hadn't found Grandpa Mims, but never beaten, my first initiative to honor my DNA by paying respects at the gravesites of my ancestors had run out of three-day holiday weekend. The sun was casting long shadows toward the east, shadows stretching steadily with hope of reaching the horizon, desperately hanging on to this day as if it were the last, but faithful, as their form faded away to darkness, a new day would come.

Possibly the most meaningful three days of my life, thoughts immediately shifted to the realization that my adventure had not ended this evening. These were my Florida ancestors, and I still had several more cemeteries to visit within my home state. Expanding this concept beyond, to Georgia, to South Carolina, to Alabama, to North Carolina, my next road trip would be even better, now knowing what I didn't know about ancestry road trips just seventy-two hours ago. Something of great importance was happening to me, a spiritual journey, an awakening, a force moving me to seek, find, and acknowledge the origins of my inherited DNA and place in this world.

Chapter 7

HEADSTONES

Erected all sizes, expenses, and shapes.
Most plain succinct, yet some cared ornate.
Flat to the ground, six feet towered tall.
Erosion, ants, gravity, ensure all will fall.

Descendants few visit, lichens algae splatter.
Vases hollow empty, weathered flowers matter.
Intended long remembered, forgotten in three.
Final address marker, no coin, flag, or wreath.

Seconds tock hours, minutes days weeks.
Years decades centuries, nobody speaks.
Wood marble granite, they represent ceased.
Awaiting their Savior, all facing east.

Tangible, visible, lasting, a headstone pinpointed the site of burial for a specific human enabling demarcation of physical remains. I envisioned in my minds' eye a three-dimensional area below ground two feet wide by six feet long by six feet deep (2' x 6' x 6'). The headstone of course represented the top of the deceased's head, with the 6 feet in length extending away from the headstone toward the deceased's feet. Some gravesites included a footstone etched with the deceased's first, middle, and last initials. A headstone signified hallowed ground, a place for remembrance, a place to pay respects, and most importantly, the repository of that person's DNA.

My appreciation of headstones was acquired during my first two road trips to honor my DNA by way of visiting each of my ancestors' gravesites. I had been to a few cemeteries during my life prior to beginning what would become my epic journey of genetic adventure, but during those initial visits to cemeteries, I hadn't really paid close attention. In hindsight, those earlier visits to cemeteries didn't have the same context. I was either attending a funeral with mourners, or the cemetery visit wasn't the primary purpose of my travels. In summary, I hadn't been alone, I hadn't been in a mindset of quiet reflection, and I hadn't experienced the sensation of placing my hands upon a 105-year-old marble monument etched with the name of my great-great-great-great-grandmother.

The first task upon arriving at a cemetery where one of my ancestors was buried was to locate their grave. I looked for a name, but sometimes I had a photo of their headstone. Among sometimes hundreds or thousands of graves, landmarks or points of reference were extremely helpful. If I had a photo of the headstone, obtained from a Findagrave.com memorial, I looked for the shape of the headstone or things in the background. Maybe there was a tree. Maybe there was a unique tall headstone nearby. Maybe there was a road. Next, I looked around the cemetery to see if I could identify anything viewed in the photo. Sometimes I just had to choose a starting point at one corner of the cemetery and then walk the rows one at a time, from one end to the other, headstone to headstone, looking for that name.

During these slow and steady searches, I witnessed literally thousands of headstones. Certain things began to stand out. Children's headstones were smaller and sometimes adorned with a lamb. Many young women who died, most likely did so while giving birth, a torn uterus or breach birth having been the cause of death. The saddest graves contained the remains of both mother and child. Commonly viewed epitaphs became familiar. Certain stone shapes were popular in 1912. Older stones were made of white marble, tall, narrow, thin, leaning, tilting. Newer stones were granite, grey, not so tall, thick, wide foundations, straight, level, plumb. White marble is soft as compared to granite, causing marble to erode at a faster pace. Not only does marble erode, making lettering difficult to read as the once sharp edges of etchings slough off, but the white color of the stone itself provides little to no contrast, making it extremely difficult to read. They learned from experience over time what not to use, what not to do. I learned, too.

As I walked slowly, stopping at each headstone to ponder the lives of those once no different from myself, a stone would be lying face down, toppled by gravity yesterday or possibly forty-five years ago. I experienced an urge to right the stone, to see the hidden etchings, to perform a good deed for the departed. I instinctively reached for the stone but did myself a favor. I squatted down with knees bent and spine vertical to avoid a debilitating back muscle injury. Headstones are unbelievably heavy!

Careful observation during time invested admiring burial antiquities will provide evidence of various common causes of toppled stones.

- First, a lack of sufficient foundation capable of bearing the massive weight load per square inch when the headstone was originally positioned in place.
- Second, ants, notably fire ants, excavated nests beside and below headstones, weakening foundations.
- Third, as noted, the stone itself was flawed in design being too thin to withstand top-heavy leverage applied by gravity.
- Fourth, a tree or perennial shrub sprouted and grew uninterrupted in close proximity.
- Fifth, an accident occurred, such as a falling tree limb, careless visitor, or mower.
- Sixth, unfortunately vandalism inflicted a heavy toll on these sacred artifacts.

While a person's grave was an obvious last opportunity to share their story, on the majority of headstones, information provided for posterity was limited to first name, last name, birth date, and date of death. For the loved one who selected, paid for, and erected the monument, it was probably their first attempt, likely their last, and they simply couldn't know the longevity and impact of their choices. These kind-hearted, well-meaning people did their best, with, in many cases, limited means, to honor the memory of some-one close to them. One hundred years later, with so much surface area underutilized, I wished the stone could have answered more questions.

With the benefit of having visited dozens of cemeteries, having viewed thousands of headstones, having witnessed common gaps in my ancestors' personal stories, and having seen what happens to headstones over time, my headstone will be erected to specific standards. The grey granite stone will be quarried in Elberton, GA. The shape will be obelisk, standing at least 6 feet tall. All sides of the stone will be polished smooth as glass, and etchings will be cut at the maximum depth possible without compromising the structural integrity of the stone or etchings themselves. The base stone will be engineered to carry the load taking into account proper thickness, surface area, and sufficient footer. Etched into the stone will be adequate information, clues, and corroborating evidence to leave no doubt as to my identity and share details that a visitor may find helpful or interesting.

An obelisk, like the Washington Monument, is conspicuous without appearing as ostentatious, gaudy, or uppity. It has a proud look about it, like a sentinel possessing military bearing at attention. Its shape invites exploration of all sides, bottom to top. Standing tall an obelisk is easy to spot from a distance and will remain visible above ground well into the future taking settling and sediment into consideration. Algae rarely takes a foothold on polished granite as compared to roughhewn stone, where algae can establish an almost tar-like substance essentially impossible to remove entirely. Fifty-year-old polished Elberton, GA granite looks like it was delivered last week.

Erosion persists, and granite is not immune to the relentless effects of water, temperature, wind, and particulate. Eroding at a rate of approximately $1/10^{th}$ of one-inch every 1,000 years, attention to detail regarding the depth at which etchings are cut into granite is of paramount importance. When all human verbal history of my existence is gone, all written evidence disappears, and all digitalized history is erased, the headstone of granite and the story upon it will be lasting hard evidence.

A grave ledger is a rectangular-shaped slab of granite, marble, or concrete covering the entire dimensions of the burial site. Ledgers protect the grave contents, they command attention, they maintain a kempt appearance, and they provide substantial surface area for etching additional life details. With stone cutting technology available today, large-scale photos of the deceased, or any image desired, can be etched into a granite ledger. A ledger can be the actual grave marker itself, but in most cases, the ledger is incremental to the headstone. Combining the polished granite surface areas of the entire headstone and ledger, a person's identity and life story can be communicated for literally thousands of years.

Ledger my great-grandfather poured for his parents.
Morning shadow shows they face east.

What do I want my descendants to know about me 100 years, 250 years, 500 years from now? It's an interesting question to noodle on. Speaking from my grave to one of my future descendants, what information and words of wisdom will they find I chose to convey to them on my granite monument? With 100% certainty, some will come to pay respects. No matter my faults, no matter my perception of myself, they will love me. The same as I feel about my ancestors, I will be important to them, and I will be significant.

Etched upon my granite will be my first name, middle name, last name, birth date, death date, and the following information I wish my ancestors would've left for me to find and enjoy.

- My wife's full maiden name.
- My father's full name.
- My mother's full maiden name.
- My sister's full maiden name.
- My children's full names.
- My birth state.
- The address I considered to be home.
- Name of my highest-level school attended.
- My military service.
- My most significant job description.
- My favorite Bible verses.
- The name of the God I believed in.
- My five favorite hobbies, interests, or accomplishments.
- Events that defined me.

Chapter 8

DNA FUNDAMENTALS

How important is DNA testing? It's so important, you're hearing it here first: I'm calling on lawmakers to require by statute that all funeral directors and morticians must provide decision makers for the deceased with a standard written form offering DNA testing services. My sense of urgency to complete this book is based on DNA testing awareness for the living and mandatory DNA testing for the newly deceased. Once they seal that casket, or God forbid cremate the body, the invaluable one-of-a-kind DNA capable of enabling time travel to the past is irretrievable. And, who knows what future breakthroughs DNA research might uncover and the benefits those discoveries might provide to our descendants tens, hundreds, or thousands of years from now.

You are special, unique, important, and perfectly designed by your Creator. Your one-of-a-kind DNA sequence is God's custom set of blueprints He used as His guide to construct your earthly tent to exact specifications with purpose. The opening of the Bible at Genesis 1:26 confirms it: Then God said, "Let Us make man in Our image, according to Our likeness."

DNA is of much greater importance and more remarkable significance as a physical and visible connection to God than we mortals have acknowledged. Why do you think God specifically used the plural pronouns Us and Our in this verse?

It's hard to believe, but in the not-so-distant past there were no:

- Written languages
- Church records
- Etched headstones
- Census records
- Birth certificates
- Death certificates
- Family Bibles
- Photographic images
- DNA testing services

Each of these potential contributors to your posterity have been passive on your part, except for DNA testing, because DNA testing is something you must personally take the initiative to do while you are living. DNA testing is easy, it's affordable, it's readily available, and it's fun. Take it from me, do yourself and your loved ones a huge favor, and order a DNA test kit today. From someone who has had to sit down awkwardly with family members to educate them about DNA testing and then ask them to participate, please stop what you are doing for ten minutes and order your DNA test kit. And, when the test kit arrives, spit in the tube and mail it back immediately the same day. If it's your first DNA test kit, or you plan to only do one DNA test kit, I recommend you use Ancestry.com DNA testing, because they focus on genealogy and integrate DNA test results with your family tree.

When I began my ancestry adventure, I knew very little about DNA. I remember talking with my buddy about DNA testing and recall him mentioning his sister was big into genealogy. He had taken some DNA tests for her. She told him she would give her left arm to have their father's DNA. That statement struck me as powerful from someone on a mission. So, I read a book on DNA, *The Family Tree Guide to DNA Testing and Genetic Genealogy*, by Blaine T. Bettinger to learn more.

In summary, there are three types of DNA you will want to understand when it comes to building your family tree. The three types of DNA are as follows:

- **Autosomal DNA**, or atDNA, is the most common type of DNA talked about by people you know who have taken DNA tests with companies such as Ancestry.com and 23andme.com. Autosomal DNA is not gender specific, so Autosomal DNA test results from males and females can be compared to discover matching segments of Autosomal DNA. Autosomal DNA is measured in centimorgans. We measure distance in inches, or centimeters. We measure weight in pounds, or kilograms. We measure Autosomal DNA in centimorgans. A quantity of matching Autosomal DNA as measured by centimorgans indicates a likelihood that two people have a common ancestor. The probability of a common ancestor increases as the quantity of matching Autosomal DNA increases as measured by centimorgans. Examples of Autosomal DNA matches include the following:

  - 3,500 centimorgans: parent and child
  - 1,600 centimorgans: grandparent and grandchild
  - 150 centimorgans: 2nd cousins w/common great-grandparents

- Y-DNA is male specific and is passed down exactly 100% from father to son. Therefore, all brothers from the same father will have identically matching Y-DNA. I call Y-DNA the male-last-name-DNA. As a man, our last name is important to us, because it's our family name, and we have a desire to pass down the family name. We pass down our family name via only our sons, because our daughters have historically taken the last name of their husband. As a man, as far back in time as you can document your last name lineage, that grandfather who passed down his last name to you 145 years ago would have had the exact Y-DNA as you. All the males you know, or can find, who share your same last name, should have the exact same Y-DNA.

- **Mitochondrial DNA**, or mtDNA, is passed down only by females to both sons and daughters. Therefore, a daughter will pass down their Mitochondrial DNA received from their mother, but a son cannot pass down their Mitochondrial DNA they received from their mother.

Sure enough, I now understand why my buddy's sister wanted their father's DNA. A mother and father each randomly pass down approximately 50% of their atDNA to their child. Your father has 100% of his atDNA, but you only have 50% of his atDNA, so when you want to find relatives via your father's branch of your family tree, there are people out there who would match with your father, but not you, because they share atDNA with the 50% of your father's atDNA that wasn't passed on to you. The same goes for your father's mother and father, because your father only received 50% of each of those people's atDNA.

I know what you are thinking. You're thinking about your grandparents instead of your parents, and you are correct. You're also thinking about your great-grandparents, and yes, you are correct. If you seek an atDNA match with fellow descendants of Great-grandpa Smith, the number of matches will double with each generation you travel up your tree.

Siblings do not have identical atDNA, because each randomly received 50% of each parents' atDNA. The 50% one sibling received from the mother won't be the same 50% received from the mother by another sibling (same with the father). That's why only identical twins have exact atDNA matches.

I used a jelly bean analogy to explain the concept of DNA to a family member. Imagine your father as a five-gallon bucket filled with jelly beans, where each jelly bean was a uniquely different color and flavor. Now imagine your mother as a separate five-gallon bucket filled with jelly beans, where not only was each jelly bean uniquely different, but none of your mother's jelly beans were duplicates of your father's jelly beans. Yes, that was a lot of jelly beans with no two exactly the same. To make you, God thoroughly stirred the jelly beans in your father's bucket. He then thoroughly stirred the jelly beans in your mother's bucket. Then God set out a new five-gallon bucket and randomly poured half of your father's jelly beans into the new bucket. He then randomly poured half of your mother's jelly beans into your bucket and thoroughly stirred the one-of-a-kind combination of different jelly beans to create you.

To conceptualize how you and a sibling share DNA, but not exactly the same DNA, you have to imagine your father and mother as once again full, five-gallon buckets of jelly beans just like we started when God began to make you. The same original jelly beans were in your father's bucket and the same original jelly beans were in your mother's bucket. To create your sibling, God thoroughly stirred the jelly beans in your father's bucket and then thoroughly stirred the jelly beans in your mother's bucket. Setting out a new five-gallon bucket, God randomly poured half of your father's jelly beans into the new bucket and then randomly poured half of your mother's jelly beans into the new bucket. He then thoroughly stirred the jelly beans in the new bucket to create your sibling. Each child received 50% of each parent's jelly beans, but not the exact same combination of jelly beans. A jelly bean test would tell you and your sibling exactly which of your parents' jelly beans you share in common!

Chapter 9

AMANDA LOUISE BASS HELMS USING DNA

Inevitably, I reached some dead ends and faced some curveballs while building my family tree. I utilized all known available resources in search of Great-great-grandma Amanda Louise Bass Helms' parents' names but came up empty. There were no census records. There was no death certificate. There was no birth certificate. There was no family Bible. Another tool for a possible family tree breakthrough was DNA matching thanks to people who did their part by participating in DNA testing.

Using DNA for genealogy is a group effort, so I submitted a DNA test kit to Ancestry.com, joining millions of others who had contributed their DNA to the central repository. The pool of data had exceeded critical mass, enabling comparison analysis. Each participant had some amount of DNA in common with hundreds or thousands of fellow test takers. The genealogical power of DNA testing was unleashed when test takers each built best-effort family trees within Ancestry.com. With DNA linked to a family tree, the Ancestry.com service:

- identified which of the contributors to the data pool had an amount of their DNA in common with my DNA (Match),
- ranked all of my DNA Matches from highest quantity of DNA in common to least quantity of DNA in common,
- overlaid my attached family tree with the attached family tree of a Match to show where our family trees intersected at a common ancestor,
- provided a list of surnames (last names) I had in common with a Match's family tree, and
- searched my list of Matches for those who have a specific surname in their family tree.

In the case of one of my eight great-great-grandmothers, Amanda Louise Bass Helms, I was searching for the names of her parents. My grandfather had shared with me the story of his mother's family migrating to Florida from North Carolina in the early 1900s soon after the death of his mother's father. My grandfather recalled his mother's family traveling to Charlotte, NC in a wagon pulled by a mule. During a phone call, while looking at a map, I called out to my grandfather each city name surrounding Charlotte, NC.

When I said, "Matthews?"

He said, "That's it!"

So, I knew they had lived in Matthews, NC in Mecklenburg County. My grandfather knew his grandmother, loved her very much, and he told me his grandmother's maiden name was "Bass." Her maiden name is also confirmed by her daughter's death certificate, where it states MOTHER'S NAME as "Amanda Louise Bass." The informant on this death certificate was her daughter, my grandfather's sister. Their mother had resided with his sister for many years, so his sister would have had plenty of opportunities to hear her mother mention the maiden name of her mother.

*My 2ⁿᵈ Great-grandmother
Amanda Louise Bass Helms*

I had exhausted all means of finding the names of her parents using traditional methods, so I turned to my grandfather's DNA test results that I managed on Ancestry.com. I searched his Matches for any containing the surname "Bass" in their linked family trees. Seven out of the top eight DNA Matches on the surname Bass only matched on the surname Bass, while one Match had three surnames in common. Ruling out the one Match with three surnames in common, the other seven Matches were managed by five different people, so there were five independent family trees linked to DNA Matches with my grandfather's DNA on the surname Bass. All five of the independent family trees had one name in common, who could have been the father of my Great-great-grandmother Amanda Louise Bass Helms born in 1869. His name was William Jasper Bass, born 1849 and living within 2 miles from Matthews, NC in the 1880 census.

Amanda Louise Bass was not listed among the children of William Jasper Bass and his wife Martha J. Sharp Bass in the 1880 census when Amanda Louise would have been eleven years old. Until more is revealed via future DNA Matches, my best theory is that the mother of Amanda Louise Bass was either William Jasper Bass' yet to be discovered first wife, or she was born out of wedlock to a single mother who knew William Jasper Bass was the father and gave Amanda Louise her father's last name. She must have grown up in the household of her mother, or her mother's parents, which could explain why she was not residing in the household of her father. Her mother's maiden name and possible married name are still unknown at the time of writing this book, but there exists strong atDNA evidence linked to multiple independent family trees pointing to her father as being William Jasper Bass born 1849 in NC.

Through atDNA via Ancestry.com, I was able to identify a high probability father of my Great-great-grandmother Amanda Louise Bass. With no family stories or historical documentation linking her to the wife of William Jasper Bass, and no insights as to her biological mother's maiden name, it would seem her mother's identity is lost forever. But there is another way to identify Amanda Louise's mother 149 years after her birth. To solve this mystery, we turn to mtDNA for a potential breakthrough.

As I shared earlier, mtDNA is passed down from a mother to all of her children, both male and female. However, males cannot pass down mtDNA to their children, so we need to follow the family tree down through female offspring to a living son or daughter at the end of the chain of mother to daughter descent. In the case of Amanda Louise Bass, the mtDNA of her yet-to-be-determined mother still lives within several known descendants of one of her daughters, Blandena Estelle Helms Surgnier. Blandena had five sons and one daughter, each of whom inherited the mtDNA of the unknown mother of Amanda Louise Bass. Sadly, Blandena's only daughter, I'll call her Caroline, had already passed away prior to this adventure of discovery, but Caroline had given birth to daughters, and those daughters had children, all of whom inherited the identical mtDNA of our yet-to-be-determined mother of Amanda Louise Bass. In addition to Blandena's only daughter's descendants, two of Blandena's five sons were still living. Each of these relatives had inherited the priceless mtDNA that may someday expose the identity of the woman who gave birth to Amanda Louise Bass back in 1869.

One of those two surviving sons was my ninety-two-year-old grandfather, Esly Paul Surgnier. He had previously taken an atDNA test with Ancestry.com a few weeks earlier and authorized me to manage his Ancestry.com DNA test results, so I was hopeful he would be willing to provide an additional DNA sample. The additional DNA sample would be for testing with FamilyTreeDNA.com (FTDNA), because they offered testing for Y-DNA and mtDNA in addition to atDNA. Ancestry.com only offered atDNA testing.

My grandfather seemed sincerely interested in my efforts to build out his family tree, but you have to remember, he was literally dying. And this is a prime example of why you need to personally take the initiative, order the DNA test kits, provide the DNA samples, and mail in the completed kits while you are alive and of sound mind. Otherwise, I hope you can see how awkward it will be for your loved ones to respectfully ask you to provide DNA samples before you die. Do yourself and your loved ones a favor, please.

- Order your DNA test kits today.
- Get it done!
- Enjoy the results for yourself while you're alive.
- Let your family know what you've done.
- Share your usernames and passwords with trusted family members so they can access your DNA results in the event of your death.

Despite the somewhat awkward conversation where I had to tactfully explain to a dying man how he would benefit from providing a DNA sample to a second testing company, my grandfather agreed. I ordered and paid for two bundled DNA test kits from

FamilyTreeDNA.com (atDNA, Y-DNA, and mtDNA): one for me and one for my grandfather. I took the test myself first to become familiar with the process of swabbing the inside of my mouth cheeks as opposed to spitting in a tube. Of course, it was super easy, just different. My grandfather's younger 1st cousin agreed to help my grandfather complete the kit, so I explained the process and enclosed an additional Y-DNA test kit for him as a thank you and a way to confirm our Helms paternal lineage.

As of the writing of this book, I do not yet have an actual success story to share where I was able to identify an ancestor using mtDNA, but it will happen in time when I get to it. However, obtaining my grandfather's mtDNA prior to his death was a success story in itself, because I have it, in storage so to speak, when I need it somewhere along my genetic journey. My grandfather entrusted to my care his stories, his recollections, his family memories, his atDNA, his mtDNA, and his Y-DNA. Honestly and truthfully, I'd rather have his DNA than his house. I share this personal experience to emphasize just how important your DNA will be to your loved ones when you, too, depart from this Earth.

Chapter 10

ORAL HISTORY VS. REALITY SURGNIER FAMILY

When I was growing up, my grandfather, Gigi, my mom's dad, would tell the story about how his family on his father's side came to Florida from Mississippi. The story included a terrifying event whereby the wagon train was attacked by Indians and everyone was killed except for a few people. I can vividly remember as a child screaming in the middle of the night as I woke from a recurring dream where Indian warriors on horseback, faces covered in war paint, galloped their horses, circling round our single-wide mobile home. My father, having proclaimed our home sat atop an old Indian trail, fueled my fears. And, all those cowboy movies where pioneers circled their wagons, and the cavalry bugler, yellow neckerchief slightly to the side, standing tall in the stirrups, sounding the cavalry charge, served to interrupt an imaginative boy's peaceful slumber.

Watching a recorded interview of Gigi taken in 2005 during his eightieth year, he began telling the Surgnier family story, beginning with the migration to Florida from Mississippi. I assume his father told him the story, which had been told directly to him by either his father, Benjamin Harvey Surgnier (Gigi's grandfather), or his uncle, Henry Wise Surgnier. From the videotaped interview, I transcribed it, exactly the way he said it. In his own words, this is the Surgnier family history, as told by my grandfather, Esly Paul Surgnier.

"My father's family migrated to Florida from Mississippi just after the Civil War. And they came to Florida as a group. It was a wagon train pulled by oxen. They didn't have horses, they were pulled by oxen, which you know oxen are real slow. It took 'em a year to get from Mississippi to Florida, because, well, a little girl got sick on the way, and they had to bury her in a trunk, you know, and uh, I think they had to stop somewhere one time to grow some corn, or something. I think they were running out of feed. Anyway, they got to North Florida, in the camp, that night, and the Indians raided 'em. Well, the only ones in my father's family, there's only three that got away. And that was my grandfather [Harvey], his brother Henry, and a sister, one sister. The three of them were the only ones that got saved from his family. And, I don't know how many other people got away, you know, I don't, you know, I don't know that. I only know about my own family, but those three got away, and they made their way, to uh, Sarasota. They settled in Sarasota, and at that time it was just a tiny little fishing village. And they were basically farmers, you know, out in Mississippi. They were, we think they were, they were French descent. And we think maybe they might have been Cajuns that came down from uh up you know in Canada down the Mississippi River. And they settled in Mississippi."

The story above is all Gigi knew about his surname of Surgnier, pronounced /Sir-gin-er/, the gin being pronounced like the alcoholic beverage. His family tree went back only as far as his grandfather, Benjamin "Harvey" Surgnier. Apparently, Gigi's father, Arthur Paul Surgnier, never asked his father, Harvey, or his uncle, Henry Wise Surgnier, any details about their parents. Having been told they died in an Indian massacre during a wagon train migration was probably a wound not to be re-opened.

Gigi told me about his grandfather Harvey carrying the mail from Sarasota to Tampa on horseback, having to ride many miles inland from the coast to reach a point along the Manatee River where he could ford it. As a toddler, Gigi had learned to walk, took his first steps, in front of the courthouse in Arcadia, FL. During a conversation we were having one day, I shared with Gigi that I had learned Manatee County was once the size of six counties. He said, "Oh yeah, it was really big, and the courthouse was way out near Arcadia." Tucking that tidbit toward the back of my brain, I later Googled Manatee County Seat Near Arcadia to discover a rare piece of Florida history, a town called Pine Level. Googling Pine Level, I learned Gigi was in fact correct about there having been a county seat for Manatee County way inland near Arcadia.

According to what I read, Pine Level was very much like a town you'd see in a movie set in the wild west—complete with wood-frame, porch-front structures, saloons, cowboys, shootouts, cattle roaming around, and plenty of alcoholic beverages consumed. The town was now a ghost town, which is probably why I'd never heard of it. The town's real claim to fame was a capital murder case tried in its courthouse revolving around a murderous gang known as the Sarasota Vigilance Committee. The trial was so significant, it made front page news in *The New York Times*, and the judge presiding ultimately became the governor of Florida. The sheriff of Manatee County, named A. S. Watson, rounded up a gang of more than twenty men who had created a secret society. The gang had targeted five local men to assassinate and successfully carried out the killings of two before getting caught.

Gigi's health condition was declining rapidly, so I had no time to waste. If I was going to build his family tree for him, it was now or never. He had given me the names of his mother's parents, Cyrus

Helms and Amanda Louise Bass. He never met Grandpa Cyrus Helms because Cyrus had died in 1918 from diabetes. He knew his grandmother Amanda very well and knew her maiden name was Bass. On his father's side, he knew his grandfather Harvey Surgnier, but he never met his grandmother. She was a Holland and died young from cancer. Both were buried in Sarasota. With the names of all four grandparents, I figured I'd have a well-developed Surgnier/Helms tree in short order.

First, I targeted Cyrus Helms, actually J. Cyrus Helms. The problem was the first name, because conflicting information varied between Joseph and Josiah. Worse yet, I learned the only two names suitable for a baby boy born into the Helms family around Charlotte, NC were Joseph and Josiah. Second, I searched all the way to the end of the earth for the parents of Amanda Louise Bass, but found not a single trace. To describe my efforts as extensive and exhaustive would be a total understatement. I had even been on the phone with the actual analyst at the Florida Department of Health: Office of Vital Statistics in Jacksonville going through every possible iteration of the name Amanda Louise Bass Helms. Adding to the challenge, she was known to go by the names Amanda, Manda, Mandy, Louise, Lulu, and Lula. Having died in 1944, it made no sense a death certificate could not be located.

Third, I discovered the name of Gigi's father's mother who had died young from cancer. Her name was Ellender Mirandi "Ella" Holland. After failing to document even one generation beyond the first two grandparents, building out Grandma Ella's tree was a breeze. I quickly raced all the way back to not one, but two Revolutionary War Patriot grandfathers.

Next, I turned my attention to the Surgnier surname. My first observation, and my mother agreed, was the spelling and pronunciation were incongruent. The "i" and the "n" were in the wrong positions. Gigi would sometimes pronounce his last name with a

French flair as /Surn-yay/ followed by a laugh, because it sounded absurd. During my initial searches, I found the name spelled Surginer, Surgoner, Surgener, Sergener, Surgenor, even Sojourner. But, rarely, if ever, did I find the name spelled Surgnier unless affixed to someone in our immediate family. Phonetically, the spelling just didn't make sense. And then, something else didn't make sense.

I found one-year-old Grandpa Benjamin Harvey Surgnier in the 1870 census living in the household of his father, Benjamin Surgoner, along with his mother Mary, brother Henry, sister Mary, and brother William, located in Manatee County, FL. While I should have been ecstatic about having found Gigi's great-grandparents, I was more fixated on the fact that the entire family, including an additional brother, was living far southward into the central peninsula of Florida. Oral family history described an Indian massacre in North Florida resulting in only three survivors, but an attack didn't happen and the 1870 census lists six Surgoner family members alive and well in Manatee County, FL.

Moving forward ten years to the 1880 census, I found forty-five-year-old Mary Surgener, now a widow, with six children at home, and her eighteen-year-old daughter, Mary Alpene Surgener, living next door with her fifty-year-old husband, Stephen Goings, and his nine-year-old son, John Goings. An eighteen-year-old girl, one of seven children living within the household of a forty-five-year-old widow, marrying a fifty-year-old man sounds like an escape from financial hardship to me. And the location of the census page is noted as Pine Level, Sarasota, Manatee County, Florida.

The 1870 census did support the oral family history of having migrated from Mississippi, because the three oldest children are listed as having been born in Mississippi. However, the family recollection fell short regarding the other three family members with father Benjamin noted as being born in North Carolina, mother Mary in Florida, and Gigi's grandfather Harvey's birth place also

Florida. So much for Grandpa Harvey being born in Mississippi and the family having migrated from Canada. The timing of the family's migration occurring just after the Civil War was accurate based on Harvey being born in Florida in approximately 1869 and his next oldest brother, William, being born in Mississippi around 1865.

Another part of Gigi's family history story was very specific regarding a little girl who died along the way to Florida and was buried in a trunk. Looking closely at the Surgoner family unit in the 1870 census, the children's ages were nine, seven, five, and one. A three-year-old child is missing in the sequential order of a child having been born every two years. It's important to pay attention, listen, and remember what your elders share with you. Great personal satisfaction can be attained when you're keen enough to connect disparate bits of seemingly irrelevant details to fabricate missing pieces while working the intricate puzzle of your heritage. Using several clues, I was able to find a long undocumented aunt.

1. I remember Gigi mentioning, during one of our conversations about the "olden days," how women would have a baby about every two years, because nursing a baby served as a form of birth control until the baby was weaned.

2. I noticed a four-year gap between Surgoner children in the 1870 census.

3. A five-year-old child, William Surgoner, born 1865, was born in Mississippi.

4. The Civil War ended in April 1865.

5. Gigi said his Surgnier family migrated to Florida from Mississippi just after the Civil War.

6. A three-year-old child missing in the 1870 census would have been born in 1866 or 1867.

7. A young girl got sick and died during the migration to Florida and was buried in a trunk.

8. A one-year-old child, Benjamin Harvey Surgoner, born 5 Oct 1868, was born in Florida, so we know the Surgoner family had reached Florida by 5 Oct 1868.

9. Assuming the missing three-year-old child was born near the end of calendar year 1866 or beginning of calendar year 1867, she would have been a toddler during a Surgoner family migration just after the Civil War in 1868.

Based on Gigi's oral history of his Surgnier family, along with details of the Surgoner family found in the 1870 census and Grandpa Benjamin Harvey Surgnier's headstone, I was able to deduce the Surgoner family most likely departed Mississippi in early 1868. A little girl born during the summer of 1866 would have been a toddler recently weaned when the oxen-pulled wagons rolled out of Shubuta, MS headed southeast. Grandma Mary Ann Smith Surgoner's natural birth control no longer effective, she would have conceived Grandpa Benjamin Harvey Surgnier around 29 Dec 1867, resulting in his birth 280 days later on 5 Oct 1868 in Florida. Somewhere along the route between Mississippi and Florida, the little girl toddler became sick and succumbed to her illness.

Cold, rain, mosquitos, a wagon as their only shelter from the elements, contaminated drinking water, and contact with countless disease-carrying others from points unknown converging along the same migration trail to the post-Civil War hopes of Florida any of these could have hosted her cause of death. With no better option, the grieving family emptied the best of their traveler's trunks, converting it to an improvised child-sized casket for proper burial. A collateral cost of Southern Reconstruction, placing her lifeless body in the ground must have challenged their boundaries of sanity. Climbing up onto the wagon, releasing the wooden brake, encouraging the oxen forward, and slowly pulling away from the handmade wooden cross fixed in place beside the trail must have been unimaginable.

I named the little girl Tabitha Surginer, after her maternal grandmother, Talitha. Surgnier family history passed down verbally for five generations kept her memory alive until 151 years after her death, when I was enabled to confirm her existence as a member of our family. The little girl who died during the family's migration to Florida, now known as Tabitha Surginer, born 1866 or 1867, was my 3rd great-aunt, worthy of my efforts to remember her. While I may never know exactly how her birth, life, and death directly affected me, I acknowledge her existence, significant enough to those who knew her that a memory of her would endure five generations. Honoring my DNA, I added her to my family tree, documented her story, created a memorial for her on Findagrave.com, and linked her memorial to those of her parents and siblings.

I mentioned earlier in Chapter 2 a blue, side-bound report binder I discovered at the Fort Myers branch of the Lee County Florida Library System containing an abstract of a last will and testament for Mary Ann Smith Surginer. It was one of those report covers into which a high school or college student would choose to insert a finished term paper, one with a rectangular-shaped slight-indention in the upper middle section of the front to label the contents. The white label affixed to the front of this particular report binder read,

Manatee County, Florida, Selected Records, Extracted from *South Florida Pioneers*. It was one of maybe a dozen items I pulled from the Florida section of the genealogy room's collection sorted on shelves alphabetically by state. Having no idea what I might find, I started at the beginning of the Florida section and skimmed through the titles of each book, folder, binder, etc. until I reached the first book attached to the Georgia section.

My immediate family was from Manatee County, so I thought maybe I might learn something. Flipping open the flimsy binder and looking at each page, I hit pay dirt on page twenty-five in the section titled Manatee County: 1870 & 1871 Tax Payers. The fifth name above famous Florida cattleman Jacob Summerlen was my 3rd great-grandfather, Bin Surgurner. In 1871, he was listed as Benj. Surgener just two names below J. Summerlen. I know the name Summerlin quite well, because I live just off Summerlin Road, which leads to the Sanibel Causeway and the historically significant cattle docks at Punta Rassa where Jacob Summerlin and other Florida Crackers drove large herds of cattle to board ships bound for Cuba in return for payment in gold.

Considering Ben Surginer was a cavalry horse soldier during the Civil War, it's possible he served as a drover for Jacob Summerlin on one or more of his cattle drives to Punta Rassa. In 1872, he was simply Serginer. J. J. Summerlins had 5,500 head of cattle while Serginer had no cattle. His lack of livestock pales in significance compared to that portion of my DNA he carried in his body to Manatee County from Mississippi, from Alabama, from North Carolina. By 1873, Benjamin Sergenier was taxed based on the two horses he owned.

Near the very back of the blue report binder, the name Mary A. Surginer caught my eye, setting off a chain of events that would open a chapter of my family's history long since buried by accusations, charges, trials, witnesses, murders, lies, and deceit. I saw on the page an abstract, or summary, of the Will of Mary A. Surginer of Sara Sota, Manatee Co. dated 23 Oct 1883. Her children's names were each listed, along with the names A. S. Watson & Harrison T. Riley to be executors. With Mary Surginer's name missing from an 1885 Florida State Census, I was able to narrow her date of death to sometime between late 1883 and 1885.

Assuming Mary Surginer's complete last will and testament may have been recorded in Manatee County, FL, I reached out to the Manatee County Library located in Bradenton, FL via email. A quick response suggested I contact the Manatee County Historical Records Library located a few blocks away in the old Carnegie Library building. Within three hours' time, a handwritten transcription of Mary's original last will and testament arrived in my email inbox. It was Friday, November 17, 2017, and I immediately forwarded the document via email to several Surgnier family members. In the body of the email containing the attached three-page last will and testament, the sender included, "There is a probate file on Mary containing a couple dozen pages maybe more, the original will is not in the loose paper file but was recorded in Probate Book #1." I replied to the email stating that I was willing to pay the $1.00 per page for the probate file contents. Considering it was a Friday afternoon, I would have to wait until Monday.

My grandfather Gigi was in his final days. I was pushing along as hard and fast as I could go, researching, hoping I could share with him just a little more while he could still hear me. On Sunday, November 19, 2017, I sent out the following email:

Hello Surgnier Family Members,

If you read page 3 of Mary Ann Smith Surginer's will that I emailed to you, you will see she named two men as the executors: A. S. Watson and Harrison T. Riley.

During my research, I learned about the ghost town of Pine Level, FL that was once the county seat of Manatee County. I read about Pine Level and the story mentioned a famous murder case involving a secret gang, how the members were rounded up, most escaped the jail, and nothing really happened to the murderers.

Last night, I was googling the 79th Infantry Division, which was Gigi's division during WWII. I googled 79th Infantry Surgnier to see if maybe Gigi's name would show up. Instead, the name Mary Alpine Surgnier, married to a man named Goins, was in about the third result. I recalled her as being Benjamin Harvey Surgnier's older sister. Don't ask me why her name came up in the results for the 79th Infantry. In hindsight, this was just another example of Divine intervention during my ancestry adventure.

Anyway, while researching Aunt Mary Alpene Surgnier, I ended up on someone's family tree profile for our grandma, Mary Ann Smith Surginer. In their list of family members for her, they showed a second husband as being Harrison T. Riley. I clicked on his profile and found some documents telling the story of his murder in 1884 by a secretive gang from Sara Sota. One of the documents posted by someone mentioned one of the potential motives for his murder was that he was living with the widow Mary Surginer, out of wedlock, and that the vigilantes thought Harrison T. Riley was trying to steal the widow's money.

I have to dig into this story for more details and support, but the name Harrison T. Riley is in fact an executor of her will. Another twist is that the other executor, A. S. Watson, was the sheriff of Manatee County. Sheriff A. S. Watson's name is also listed in a document pertaining to his obtaining evidence in the killing of Harrison T. Riley.

The will I sent you is dated 1883. Harrison T. Riley was murdered in 1884. I have not yet found the date of death for Mary Ann Smith Surginer, but it was sometime between 1883 and 1885.

This true crime murder case drew national attention, and someone affiliated with the case eventually became the governor of Florida. I may as well have entered the Twilight Zone! Now I'm really wondering what happened to Grandpa Benjamin Surginer when he died sometime just before 1880 in only his late fifties.

Love,
Trae "Surginer" Zipperer

The next day, Monday, November 20, 2017, between 1:30 p.m. and 2 p.m., I received several emails containing forty-eight attached pages representing documents housed in the recorded probate file for my 3rd great-grandmother, Mary Ann Smith Surginer. It was a family history treasure trove. Each piece of yellowing paper was dated between the years 1883 and 1891, making the documents, receipts, and memos on average 130 years old, all pertaining to the aftermath of Mary Ann Smith Surginer's death. Most importantly, the documents revealed 18 Nov 1883 as the date she died. Comparing her death date to the date of her last will and testament, she was dead within twenty-six days of the will being written. At only forty-eight years old, I found it suspicious she would decide to write a will and then be dead only twenty-six days later.

Her daughter, Mary Alpene Surgnier Goins, had her husband, Stephen C. Goins, contest the last will and testament naming Sheriff A. S. Watson and Harrison T. Riley executors based on a legal loophole of there having been only two witnesses instead of the minimum of three witnesses required by Florida state law. The court ruled in favor of Stephen C. Goins. The last will and testament was ruled to be null and void. Sheriff A. S. Watson was ordered to cease and desist from any further duties as an executor of the estate of Mary Ann Smith Surginer. And Stephen C. Goins became the executor of the estate.

Receipts in the file showed Mary Ann Smith Surginer was a citrus grower. She owned at least one orange grove, and memos describe trees being pruned, fruit being picked, and fruit being shipped as far as New Orleans. Three of her children, Henry Wise Surgnier, Mary Alpene Surgnier Goins, and my 2nd great-grandfather, Benjamin Harvey Surgnier, received portions of the small profits generated from operations. Payment receipts for services rendered also show the children worked on the grove from time to time, along with several other non-related workers. An added bonus is that some of the slips of paper show my 2nd great-grandfather's detailed services and fees in his own handwriting, including his signature.

Reading through all forty-eight items, I didn't find anything related to a relationship with Harrison T. "Tip" Riley. Google search results mentioned accusations and charges of adultery committed by Harrison T. Riley and widow Mary Ann Surginer. One informative and credible search result was page ten of the book *Manatee County Sheriff's 1855-2005 150th Anniversary History and Pictorial* where both Harrison and Mary are mentioned. However, the text focuses primarily on the murder of Harrison T. Riley by the Sarasota Vigilance Committee and how the gang eventually killed again before being caught by Sheriff A. S. Watson, tried, convicted, and sentenced in the most famous crime spree of the 1800s in Manatee County. A key point, maybe someone not related to Mary Surginer might miss, was the line, "Mary died prior to the resolution of the case."

As a direct descendant of Mary Surginer, and therefore being most interested in her story, I tuned right into the fact that her death at an early age received no attention. I also found it very odd Sheriff Watson failed to investigate the murder of Harrison T. Riley, a man ambushed on Bee Ridge Road, shot off his horse, and throat slit.

Despite my lack of training as a crime scene investigator, the following facts concerned me:

- Harrison T. Riley and Mary Surginer were involved in an unresolved "case" prior to her death. The case most likely pertained to a charge of adultery.
- As the law man in Manatee County, Sheriff A. S. Watson would have been involved in the case of Harrison and Mary, either serving a warrant or arresting them.
- Mary Surginer's last will and testament dated 23 Oct 1883 listed A. S. Watson and Harrison T. Riley as executors.
- Twenty-six days later, on 18 Nov 1883, Mary Surginer died, but Sheriff Watson didn't investigate.
- Harrison T. Riley recorded Mary's will and filed with Manatee County as the executor of Mary Surginer's estate. I assume Sheriff A. S. Watson would have been notified.
- Sometime later, Harrison T. Riley was brutally murdered, but Sheriff Watson didn't investigate.
- At some point after Harrison T. Riley's murder, Sheriff A. S. Watson took over as executor of Mary Surginer's estate, because the judge specifically ordered him by name to cease as executor when Stephen C. Goins successfully contested the will. Or, maybe A. S. Watson was acting as co-executor with Harrison T. Riley prior to and at the time Riley was murdered. The accounts I've read say Sheriff Watson did not investigate Riley's murder, which seems unexplainable if the two were acting as co-executors of a will written twenty-six days prior to Mary Surginer's unexplained and uninvestigated death at only forty-eight years old.

- Sheriff Watson did not seek justice for Harrison T. Riley until the killers of Charles Abbe confessed to having also killed Riley, thereby forcing Sheriff Watson to look into the murder of Riley.
- Sheriff Watson did not seek justice for Mary Surginer, ever, despite being involved in her adultery case, being listed as executor in her will, and being an active executor for her estate.

I wondered what I might find at the Manatee County Library and the Manatee County Historical Records Library, so I added to my calendar a road trip to Bradenton, FL. Traveling two hours north from Fort Myers, my first stop was the county library where the genealogy room was located. Near downtown, the large multistory library building overlooked the Manatee River flowing west to Tampa Bay, its source far to the east where Mary's son, my 2nd great-grandfather, Benjamin Harvey Surgnier, would ford the river on horseback carrying the mail between Manatee and Tampa. My main objective was to learn what resources were available to me there, because Manatee County had eventually divided into multiple counties. One was Sarasota County, where the Sarasota County Library system would potentially house some helpful family history from its geographic Manatee County days. Another county cut from Manatee County was Desoto County, where Arcadia is now the county seat.

An unanticipated resource in the genealogy room were yearbooks going as far back as the 1940s for all the high schools in Manatee County. If you attended a high school in Manatee County, I can tell you your yearbooks are there. Another interesting find were old local directories printed prior to home phones. Similar to a phone book, these directories listed the names of adult members for each household, their address, and their occupation. For example, Charles Platt might be listed "Platt, Charles, 4771 Webster St., driver, Holmes Dairy."

As is always the case, the library staff members were extremely helpful going the extra mile to assist with whatever they could do to enable my research success. For several of my inquiries, they directed me to the Manatee County Historical Records Library located a few blocks away. Looking at the time on my iPhone and noting the day quickly slipping away, I exited the building, cranked my truck, and followed directions to the old Carnegie Library. When my mother was a girl, my grandmother would take her to this very library, but in those days, it was the main library building.

I parked at the back of the building, eventually working my way around to the front entry doors. Stepping up to the reception desk, I introduced myself. They remembered me having earlier requested the will and probate file contents for Mary Surginer. I had also given them the names of Mary's husband, Benjamin Surginer, and my 2nd great-grandfather, Benjamin Harvey Surgnier. The lady told me she had dug around through some of the old records housed there and actually found a few things labeled either Surginer or a variant spelling of the surname. I asked her if they would have court case records from the 1880s. "We do. What case are you searching for?" she asked. I told her I was looking for an adultery case involving a Harrison Riley and Mary Surginer sometime between 1880 and 1884. She pointed to some filing cabinets behind me, over my right shoulder, and let me know, if they had anything, it would be over there.

She and I walked to the file cabinet area. She did the searching, and I watched. As each file drawer opened, she sifted through the nineteenth-century court case folders of old Manatee County looking for the last names of Riley or Surginer. My eyes latched onto the folder at the same time she said, "Found it." It was the case file for the 1882/1883 criminal trial of my 3rd great-grandmother on the charge of adultery. It immediately brought back images of high school English class reading *The Scarlet Letter* by Nathaniel Hawthorne, but this was not a fictional character in the 1600s. This was my ancestor, my grandmother, my DNA, and I could sense her anguish all these years later. I followed the librarian back to the reception desk, where she allowed me to open the folder and view its contents.

Inside were the original pieces of paper, legal documents, surprisingly in excellent condition for their age and easily legible except for a couple hastily drafted examples of severely poor cursive handwriting. There they were, Harrison T. Riley and Mary A. Surginer, charged with and being tried in a court of law, accused of living in an open state of adultery. For the next hour, I reviewed each page, interpreting the letters and words etched by swooping pen strokes, unraveling a family's shameful act set into motion in 1882 and hidden from the next four generations by cleverly crafted deceit. The shameful act was not adultery.

Important missing puzzle pieces from this section of my family story were the circumstances surrounding the death of Mary's husband, and father of her eight children, Benjamin "Ben" Surginer. Based on the birth year of their youngest child in 1878, and Mary being identified as a widow in the 1880 census, Ben had to have died sometime between the end of 1877 and the beginning of 1880. Based on his birth year of around 1819, Ben would have been approximately fifty-nine years old at the time of his death. Not an old man, he was also not a young man either, and therefore probably not out running around causing trouble the likes of which might get him killed. But he did have a beautiful wife sixteen years his junior, aged forty-three, and a sixteen-year-old daughter.

Florida after the Civil War was a wild, ruthless, open range relatively lawless expanse of pines, wetlands, palmetto, and oak hammock where men made fortunes rounding up scrub cattle free for the taking simply adding their brand to claim ownership. Google search results for the Barber Mizell feud provided a quick study about what it was like to navigate tough living conditions literally scratching out sustenance within a deadly competitive environment.

The taxpayer records for Manatee County years 1870, 1871, 1872, and 1873 showed Ben Surginer owning no livestock except for eventually two horses, so I deduced he was not a cattleman. My research revealed widow Mary Surginer owned at least a forty-acre orange grove as of 1882. From this information, I gleaned Ben Surginer was a citrus man, having invested his entrepreneurial spirit into the acquisition of suitable land, his labor into the back-breaking clearing away of native fauna, and his mindshare into the art of grafting citrus trees. It took a long time to clear forty acres and five to eight years for seeds to grow into citrus trees large enough to produce a profitable harvest. Cultivating a productive forty-acre orange grove out of 1870s Florida with bare hands, determination, and long-suffering patience would have resulted in a most desirable cash cow asset, an asset someone just might have wanted to take away from him. Men have certainly been willing to kill for less.

I suspected someone killed my 3rd great-grandfather to get at his grove, which took him ten years to develop. If so, the culprit made one critical error in their dastardly plan. They underestimated Ben's wife, Mary Ann Smith Surginer. Assuming she would sell out the grove and move on, the perpetrator soon realized his flaw when he stopped by to check on the widow Surginer only to find her manning a hoe leading her older children by example. Ben's killer hadn't known about the precious little girl Mary was forced to bury in a trunk along the trail to Florida. Having sacrificed an eighteen-month-old child and ten long years of toil in the most difficult of circumstances, nothing on earth would deter Mary Surginer from success. Maybe Ben's killer didn't have to travel far to witness Mary's determination. Maybe he just had to look across the fence.

The 1880 census shows the household of Mary Surgener, widow, age forty-five, with her children Henry, Thomas, Harvey, Clara, Sharp, and Curry. The three sons, including twenty-year-old Henry, were listed as "work on farm." Mary's recorded will later accurately identified the two youngest children as Charles and Carrie, not Sharp and Curry probably the census taker's misinterpretations of Mary's strong Southern accent. Living adjacent to Mary's family was the household of fifty-year-old Stephen Goings whose wife was now Ben and Mary's oldest daughter, eighteen-year-old Mary Alpine Surginer Goings. In the same blue report cover where I found the first evidence of Mary Surginer's will, I also found the marriage record for Stephen Goings and Mary Alpene Surgener dated 25 Jun 1880.

My list of suspects in the murders of my 3rd great-grandparents, Benjamin Surginer and Mary Surginer, included Stephen Goings (Goins), Harrison T. Riley, and Sheriff A. S. Watson. Stories I'd read about the Sarasota Vigilance Committee mentioned that the gang had compiled a list of five men targeted for assassination. Two of the five named were Harrison T. Riley and Stephen Goings, both closely linked to Mary Surginer. Sheriff A. S. Watson was in and around the obviously suspicious deaths of Ben, Mary, and Harrison, but did nothing, and then acted as an executor for Mary's will, which was eventually found to be null and void. In my opinion, the motive for the murders of my grandparents was the newly matured forty acres of orange trees. Close attention to every word and every letter in the adultery criminal trial case folder provided the evidence needed to reach my own conclusions.

A letter written from Ocala, FL and dated 21 Jun 1882 set in motion the criminal charge of adultery, the death of Mary Surginer, the murder of Harrison T. Riley, the murder of Charles Abbe, the discovery of the Sarasota Vigilance Committee, the national press coverage of the assassination society of Southern murderers, and the legacy of Manatee County Sheriff A. S. Watson. The letter was written by Idell Riley in response to a letter from a Mrs. goins inquiring as to whether or not Idell Riley was the wife of Harrison T. Riley. Idell wrote the following:

Ocala June the 21 1882

Mrs goins
you wanted to know whether I was the wife of Harrison T. Riley I am his Lawful wife or at least was married to him if he had another I didn't know it he lived with me one year and five months we was all sick I was very Low at the time he left me he taken my mare and colt off and sold the colt and bought him a buggy and left far south I have never seen him since we are not Divorced neither he left me in a helpless condission I have seen a great deal of trouble since thank god My health is tolerable good now I am getting along verry well My little children has all got good homes and doing well Mrs. goins will you be so kind as to answer this letter as soon as you can and let me know the particulars about this subject you will ablige me verry verry much in so doing

yours respectfuly
Idell Riley

We know now Mrs. goins was Mary Surginer's oldest daughter, Mary Alpene Surginer Goins, wife of neighbor Stephen C. Goins. In probate documents, she wrote her last name with a lower case "g," which was consistent with Idell Riley addressing her as Mrs. goins with a lower case "g." Based on the contents of this letter, it sounded like Harrison T. Riley must have been living at the grove property with Mary Surginer and her children. However, records indicated

Harrison did have a sixteen-year-old son, Marcus Riley, living in Manatee County in 1884, who would have been fourteen years old in 1882, so more needed to be learned about the Riley family unit to shed light on peripheral details potentially relevant to the court case.

Alpene and her husband Stephen Goins must have suspected a sexual relationship between Mary and Harrison, so Alpene began her own investigation into Harrison T. Riley, discovering Idell Riley in Ocala. Or, was it possible fifty-two-year-old Stephen Goins influenced his twenty-year-old wife Alpene into suspecting more was going on next door than simply a grown man providing much needed manual labor for her widowed mother's forty-acre orange grove, an orange grove Stephen Goins may have wanted to get his hands on?

A separate document dated 24 Jul 1882, just a month after the letter was written by Idell Riley, S. C. Goins filed an accusation with Justice of the Peace A. J. Adams that Harrison T. Riley and Mary Surginer were living in an open state of adultery. A warrant for the arrest of H. T. Riley was issued by A. J. Adams to Constable A. P. Curry. Curry arrested Riley the next day on 25 Jul 1882 and delivered him to the court on 27 Jul 1882. The witnesses for the State of Florida listed on the arrest warrant were none other than Mary's two oldest sons: Henry and Thomas Surgenior. Mary's three oldest children, Henry, Alpene, and Thomas, had sided with neighbor Stephen C. Goins to accuse and seek conviction of their own mother on charges of adultery.

It appears both Harrison and Mary traveled the 40 miles due east to the Manatee County courthouse at Pine Level to stand before A. J. Adams and pleaded not guilty in the form of waiving examinations and each gave $300 bonds. Associated with the bonds, both Mary and Harrison each had to bring two men to vouch for their respective bonds. This appeared to be strong evidence supporting the innocence of the accused, because Mary and Harrison knew the witnesses were Mary's children and her son-in-law. Had they been guilty as charged, it would seem they would have pleaded guilty, paid their fines, or just simply gotten married. Instead, both were willing to face the humiliation and stigma within their close-knit community attached to adultery charges and stand trial in open court, with Mary's own children testifying against them on behalf of the prosecution for the State of Florida. Mary Surginer's bond paperwork was signed by none other than Sheriff A. S. Watson on 5 Mar 1883.

It's unknown when exactly, or if, Harrison T. Riley came to live on the Surginer grove property. Maybe he lived there as a laborer prior to Ben's death. Or, maybe he stepped in to lend a hand after Ben died. During the Civil War, H. T. Riley was a Confederate soldier, a Private in Company G of the 20th Georgia Infantry Regiment. However, his muster rolls stated he was unfit for field duty, so he was assigned to Macon, GA on detached service as a guard at a distillery related to medical supplies. The 1870 census showed Harrison living in Quitman, GA with his wife Julia, son Marcus, and son John. We know Harrison and Marcus ended up in Sarasota, FL, but the whereabouts of Julia and John are unknown. The letter from Idell Riley claiming to have been married to Harrison in Ocala, FL doesn't mention a son named Marcus.

Was Harrison T. Riley living at the Surginer property? It's unclear where exactly he was sleeping at night. Maybe he lived in the Surginer family's house. Maybe he lived in the barn. But what about his teenage son, Marcus? Where was Marcus living? Where were Marcus' mother Julia and brother John living? Considering Mary's twenty-one-year-old son Henry lived in the house, along with her seventeen-year-old son Thomas, her fourteen-year-old son Harvey, especially her nine-year-old daughter Clara Jane, her six-year-old son Charles, and four-year-old daughter Carrie, I find it virtually impossible to think Mary would allow a grown man to sleep inside the family home.

There was no reasonable scenario to suggest Harrison was sleeping in Mary's bed, because every person living in 1882 knew that was unacceptable. Were they lovers? Maybe. But the probability of a third-party eye witness to adultery would have been zero considering the vastness of Florida. Had they walked a quarter mile, there would have been no human within a quarter mile. Maybe Stephen Goins fabricated a story and told his wife Alpene he had witnessed something. As to whether Henry, Alpene, Thomas, Stephen, and another witness, Emmit Tucker, actually witnessed adulterous activity preposterous.

During the eight-and-a-half-month period between Mary Surginer's bond date of 5 Mar 1883 and the date of her death on 18 Nov 1883, the adultery case was not concluded in the court. Presumed innocent until proven guilty, until her death Mary never wavered from her claim of innocence. Mary Surginer did not commit adultery, but she did own an established orange grove.

Mary's last will and testament dated 23 Oct 1883 raised obvious suspicions. First, she died twenty-six days after the will was written. Second, it described notes payable by Harrison T. Riley in five separate installments of $400 each, one to each of her five youngest children, with the first payment due in three years and the last four payments due every two years thereafter. Third, Sheriff A. S. Watson was listed as an executor despite the fact that he was involved in her bond arrangements for a charge of adultery. Unless she already knew she was dying, it's improbable she would randomly die twenty-six days later as an otherwise healthy forty-eight-year-old woman. What was the purpose of the loan the will infers she made to Harrison T. Riley? Were the loan notes recorded at the county courthouse? Did she sell the orange grove to Harrison in return for him promising to pay $400 to each of her children when they reached approximately a certain age?

After analyzing each written detail, Mary's last will and testament actually made logical sense, assuming she knew she was dying. Her husband was dead. Her oldest son had been a witness against her in court on charges of adultery. Her oldest daughter had started the adultery case with her letter to Riley's wife in Ocala. Her son-in-law, Stephen Goins, had filed the original adultery charges with the Justice of the Peace. She had no family in Manatee County. Harrison T. Riley and the sheriff may have been the only two people available for her to have placed her trust as executors. Reviewing other abstracts, it wasn't uncommon for the sheriff to act as an executor for someone's will. Leaving only $5 to each of her two oldest children was logical considering they betrayed her. Leaving a $400 note payment to her son William Thomas Surginer seemed odd, because he was a witness against her. However, he was the youngest witness against her at just seventeen years old, so it's possible he had reconciled with his mother during the twelve months between the opening of the adultery case and her untimely death.

Another key observation was that for each of the five separate $400 payments to each of five children, the will specifically states in the event the dedicated child dies before payment is due, the money goes to the other four children listed to receive $400 payments. Never once does the will provide for any portion of the $400 payments to be transferred to either Henry or Alpene.

One of the two witnesses on Mary's will was William A. Bartholomew. I read one Google search result account where a William A. Bartholomew was noted as having been Harrison T. Riley's attorney during the adultery case. Mr. Bartholomew also showed up in court with A. S. Watson during the hearing held to determine the validity of Mary's will. Had the will not been legitimate, I found no rationale for Mr. Bartholomew to have shown up in support of it. He being an attorney explained the clearly written proper legal word choices within the will itself.

The other witness on her will was a J. T. M. Tippet, who must have been the John Tippet listed adjacent to Mary's home in the 1880 census. Asking William Bartholomew and John Tippet if they did in fact witness Mary Surginer signing her last will and testament would have been an easy confirmation of fact to complete.

According to a statement made in Manatee County Court by Mary Alpene Goins on 5 Aug 1885, "at the time of her said mother's death there was found in the possession of one Harrison T. Riley a paper purporting to be the last will and testament of Mrs. Mary A. Surgener." She goes on to state, "the said Harrison T. Riley presented the aforesaid paper to the County Court of Manatee County for probate and that it was so admitted and put-upon record." Mary Surginer died on 17 Nov 1883, so Riley would have recorded the will in his possession sometime soon after that date. Therefore, soon after Mary's death, her adult children and son-in-law, Henry Surginer, Mary Alpene Surginer Goins, and Stephen C. Goins, the ones who pushed hard the charges of adultery, would have been extremely bitter having been effectively cut out of the will with only $5 each for Henry and Alpene. Had the will been a fake, or had Mary Surginer's adult children suspected foul play surrounding Mary's death, the three ringleaders of the adultery charges would have immediately accused Harrison T. Riley of murder and contested the will. But those actions were not initiated. Not until after Riley's death did Stephen Goins contest the will.

Sheriff A. S. Watson doesn't seem to have suspected foul play in Mary Surginer's death. Had Harrison T. Riley murdered Mary Surginer, someone would have drawn a conclusion and alerted the sheriff. The sheriff would have investigated immediately, because he was directly involved with Harrison and Mary's adultery trial. He could have easily tied Harrison to Mary's cause of death, but Watson didn't. And another seemingly insignificant detail stood out to dis-suade murder as the cause of Mary Surginer's death. Her will states, "I desire my funeral expenses and doctor's bills to be paid out of my other property I may die possessed of..." She anticipated doctor's bills would need to be paid after her imminent death, because she was suffering from a terminal illness. The evidence suggested Mary Surginer died of natural causes, and the will entrusted to Harrison T. Riley's care articulated her final wishes.

On June 30, 1884, just seven and a half months after the pass-ing of Mary Surginer, Harrison T. Riley was riding his horse along Bee Ridge Road heading west toward the post office. Google search results provided various accounts of what happened, but he was riding into an ambush. From concealed positions within the thick palmettos bordering the sandy rutted path, multiple shotgun blasts erupted, pelting Riley with buckshot. Knocked from his saddle by the heavy impact of lead and flipped upside down by the bolting of his startled horse, Harrison crumpled with a muffled thud upon hitting Myakka soil. Dazed, surprised, in shock, and bleeding, he attempted to rise, staggering up to one knee, flesh damaged beyond repair. From behind, a firm grasp yanked at hair, pulling his head up and back; a large, sharpened blade grazed his Adam's apple as it parted his windpipe and jugular.

Written accounts suggested Sheriff Watson failed to investigate the assassination of Harrison T. Riley. The adultery case, the death of Mary Surginer, the co-executor of Mary's will, but he did not investigate. Rumor had it, Harrison had gotten what he had coming for stealing the widow's money and killing her slowly with poison. Old Florida Southern vigilante justice had been served. It would later be determined to have been the first assassination carried out by the Sarasota Vigilance Committee. The second murder by the gang targeted the postmaster, Charles Abbe, killed on the beach, his body dumped at sea.

Innocent until proven guilty in a court of law, if I had to guess who started the rumors about Harrison T. Riley, my prime suspect would be Stephen C. Goins. His name was included among the next three men chosen for execution by the Sarasota Vigilance Committee. My theory was the Committee found out they had been duped into killing an innocent man by a clever person wanting to even a score over being cut out of a mother-in-law's estate.

Without mercy, conflicting with the Bible's teachings, Goins had unleashed the harshest of salacious accusations against widow Mary Surginer. Someone orchestrated the destruction of Ben Surginer's family unit right down to the elimination of four Surginer children and the purposeful suppression of Ben and Mary's very existence for future generations. Maybe the gang went so far as having suspected fifty-year-old Stephen Goins of murdering Ben Surginer to get his hands on Ben's grove, or maybe Ben's sixteen-year-old daughter. God spent an inordinate amount of attention on the subject of widows in the Bible, leaving little doubt Deuteronomy 27:19 came into play: "Cursed be anyone who perverts the justice due to the sojourner, the fatherless, and the widow." Notice sojourner in this verse pertaining to Surginer.

The Surgnier family history, as told by Esly Paul Surgnier, described a wagon train massacre where only his Grandpa Harvey, Uncle Henry, and one aunt survived. Henry and Harvey never spoke of their parents Benjamin and Mary, never shared the locations of their graves, their memories expunged. Four siblings, William Thomas, Clara Jane, Charles, and Carrie, disappeared without a trace, sometime between the writing of Mary's will on 23 Oct 1883 and Mary Alpene Goins' statement to the court on 5 Aug 1885. With Mary's will nullified by a missing third witness signature legal loophole, and Henry and Alpene in position to receive a percentage of their mother's estate, fewer siblings meant larger percentage shares. Carefully crafting the wagon train story was their way of disassociating themselves from what they had inflicted upon their own mother, the disgrace they had brought to their father's good name, the disappearance of four siblings, and the gruesome execution suffered by Harrison T. Riley in the wake of their transgressions.

Somewhere in your personal family tree, a Mary Surginer silently waits for redemption, counting on someone, someone like you, to care enough to honor your DNA and unearth evidence to exonerate, or correct inaccuracies. Unexpectedly restoring the honor of an innocent man like Harrison T. "Tip" Riley by lifting the burden of unjust clouds of suspicion from the shoulders of his descendants might just be the underlying purpose of your efforts. Pay attention, listen, and respect family lore, but seek supporting evidence and let truth be the Light that guides.

Chapter 11

HISTORICAL SOCIETY MUSEUMS

When I traveled to a place where my ancestors lived long ago, there was a chance they were some of the earliest residents of that area. If so, odds were I'd find mention of them at a local historical society museum. These groups served to record, preserve, and protect local history. In addition to objects and documents of local significance, the people who worked and volunteered at these organizations were the gatekeepers of the region's past. I posed my questions, and these amazing, ready-to-assist historians either knew the answers or pointed me in the right direction.

Setting out on an eighteen-day epic motorhome trip to visit twenty out of thirty-eight Civil War battlefields where two of my ancestors were engaged in combat, three battles that I looked forward to visiting most were Camp Bartow, Camp Allegheny, and McDowell. I know what you're thinking. "What country is he talking about?" Yes, these were three out of those hundreds of battles fought during the American Civil War you won't hear about in history class—or anywhere else for that matter. To the descendants of those soldiers who fought and died there, these battlefields are sacred ground.

When I discovered an ancestor who lived in the United States during the period 1861 through 1865, I wanted to know where they were, what they were doing, and how they were affected. Were they a Northerner? Were they a Southerner? Were they a slave? Were they a soldier? If they were a soldier, I wanted to know if they were in battle, and if so, which battles? There weren't diaries detailing personal movements, but I was able to follow the movements of their regiment. When I studied regimental history, rosters, and muster rolls, a chronological wartime story began to emerge. This particular wartime story I was following was that of the 12th Georgia Infantry Regiment.

The 12th Georgia's first assignment was Camp Bartow in western Virginia. West Virginia was still a part of Virginia at that time. Tragically, so many of the men died from disease at Camp Bartow, they moved to Camp Allegheny. Camp Allegheny wasn't much better, but conditions became exponentially worse at the Battle of McDowell. I considered myself fairly knowledgeable about the Civil War, having been to Gettysburg, Shiloh, Chickamauga, Manassas, Stones River, and a few other major battles, but battlegrounds that weren't national parks had never been on my radar screen.

We departed Staunton, VA heading west on the Highland Turnpike. Along the way, we stopped at a turnout with a sign that read "Confederate Breastworks" to discover fortifications built and manned by the 12th Georgia, including my ancestors. Moving on to McDowell, we stopped at Highland Historical Society. The historical society was essentially a museum inside an old, wood frame house, and they had a free informative movie explaining the Battle of McDowell. The kind gentleman manning the place started the movie for us. We later toured the museum and learned a great deal about McDowell, gaining a better understanding why the 12th Georgia suffered such a horrific rate of casualties there.

I asked the man, "What do you know about Camp Bartow and Camp Allegheny?"

Confederate breastworks west of Staunton, VA

The 12th Georgia Regiment

At the Battle of McDowell, the 12th Georgia was the only Confederate regiment involved that was not from Virginia.
Positioned on a small knoll at the center of the battle, the 12th Georgia suffered more casualties than any other regiment. One hundred seventy-five men, or more than one fourth of the Georgians engaged, were killed or wounded.
Six companies lost their Captains and the seventh its First Lieutenant.

"I felt quite small in that fight the other day when the musket balls and cannon balls was flying around me as thick as hail ad my best friends falling on both sides, dead & mortally wounded. Oh, Dear, it is impossible for me to express my feelings. When the fight was over & I saw what was done, the tears came then free. Oh, that I never could behold such a sight again. To think of it among civilized people: killing one another like beasts. One would think that the Supreme Ruler would put a stop to it, but weev sined as a nation and must suffer in the flesh as well as spiritually: those things wee cant account for."

Captain Shepherd G. Pryor, 12 GA Regiment

Information cards displayed at Highland Historical Society pertaining to Battle of McDowell.

His expression was immediate, looking as if I had just informed him we had been listening in on his private conversations for the past four years. It was almost a stunned look. He was speechless for about three seconds as he gathered his thoughts privately in his mind, choosing his words carefully before uttering, "I actually know quite a bit about Camp Bartow and Camp Allegheny, why do you ask?"

"Well, we had some ancestors who fought there with the 12th Georgia, and we'd like to go to those places to pay our respects. Can you tell us how to get there?"

He sized us up, determining whether or not we were to be trusted. It was obvious these places were deeply important to him. We would have never found those two battlefields if it weren't for the helpful historian at the Highland Historical Society, who entrusted us to be respectful and leave no trace of our visit at these hallowed grounds. His directions were spot on, and more importantly, his narrative descriptions of the landscape were visible upon arrival. He even directed us to a great place to eat along our route. From then on, I made sure to stop in to visit with the local historian at the historical society or museum wherever my ancestry travels took me.

Chapter 12

JOTTING DOWN MEMORIES

I asked my Nanny, my dad's mama, if she knew her dad's parents, her paternal grandparents, and she said, "Oh yes, we kids would take turns staying with them in Dover during the summer. Grandpa would sit in a chair on the front porch and spit tobacco juice between our toes when we walked by. He had a biiiig belly. If we got too close, he'd grab us by the head, smash our faces into his stomach, and make a suckling sound like we were nursin' a pig or something. Oh, he thought that was reeeaaally funny. Grandpa had a little road front business, a window ledge really, in the building across the road from the house, where he sold necessities and vegetables and such. He would gather eggs, put a layer of salt in a barrel, put those eggs on the salt, cover the eggs with salt, add another layer of eggs, and keep doing that until he had a barrel of eggs. The salt preserved 'em somehow. Anyway, Grandpa would take those eggs to town and trade with 'em.

"Grandma was always workin in the fields. They were farmers. She would always make us rake the sand yard. We couldn't leave anything, not even a leaf or twig, just sand, white sand. Helped her see any rattlesnakes getting near the house. She'd make us tote that white sand into her kitchen and scrub it into the wood floors to fill in the grooves and make her wood floors look nice. I guess it polished them or somethin'. One time, my brother James thought it would be a better idea, faster, to wet the sand first. Made a muddy mess all over Grandma's kitchen, and she just about rung our necks.

"They moved to Dover east of Tampa from north Florida around Madison in a covered wagon. My dad and Uncle Tommy would run ahead of 'em and shoot game for supper during the trip. Several of their daughters married Simpson boys and had lots of children. Grandma would smile when she'd say the devil owed her a debt and paid her off in Simpsons."

Martha Jane Dansby Haynes and Daniel Thomas Haynes

Their names were Daniel Thomas Haynes, born 29 Nov 1863, and Martha Jane Dansby, born 18 Feb 1873. I had never heard of them until I was forty-eight years old and my Nanny was ninety-five. Nobody ever talked about them. It never occurred to me my grandmother had grandparents and felt the same about them as I felt about her. I'd lived in Florida most all my life, but I'd never heard of a place called Dover, until I found Daniel and Martha Jane's graves on Findagrave.com. Zooming in to Dover on Google maps, I couldn't miss noticing Haynes Road running east to west. Just like where they came from in Madison, FL, the Haynes family was significant enough to have had a main road in town named after them.

Their son, James "Jim" Monroe Haynes, my Nanny's daddy, carried on the family's good name for a third generation, as evidenced by his being elected a Manatee County Commissioner. When I visited their graves, Martha Jane's parents were buried directly across the access path. Uncle Tommy was there, so was a row of Dansbys, and those daughters who had married Simpsons.

When my Nanny passed away, she was the sole survivor, the longest lived of her generation, the last to remember Daniel and Martha Jane Haynes. While going through her final possessions, I found an envelope addressed to her from her brother, Uncle Earl Haynes, who had died more than eight years ago. Inside the envelope were a few separately folded, type-written pages. One group of folded pages was titled "My Sister," and it was a story Uncle Earl had written about his sister, my Nanny. Another was a poem he wrote describing another sister, Aunt Ruth. A six-page story in poetic form was titled "DAN'L and MA'A'THY JANE." Someone else may have tossed it, but I knew exactly who the story was about. The title was special to me, because I could hear their voices and accents as Uncle Earl's choice of spelling revealed pronunciation of their terms of endearment for one another. I won't share the entire story, but I will provide some of my favorite parts of our family history that would have been lost forever had Uncle Earl not sat down in front of his keyboard and lovingly captured his recollections of his grandparents.

Excerpts from "DAN'L and MA'ATHY JANE" by Cecil Earl Haynes

They filled the covered wagon, pulled by horse and mule alike. Old Florida state consumed them, their trek became a plight. To gather food for all this crowd, Dan'l strove with all his might. But Jimmy helped with traps and gun and Tom with skillful sight.

They built a cabin by the creek, with dirt floor neat and nice. A mansion Ma'athy thought it was, e'en with the snakes and mice. Mosquitos buzzed their frenzied song, while panthers lent their cry. So Dan'l built a smoky fire, those critters to defy.

One day she followed Dan'l to cut their winter wood. He sharpened up his axes, the iron was honed and good. They labored all the morning, and felled enough to last. When that great tree fell on him, it pinned him hard and fast.

When Ma'athy ran to help him, she thought he couldn't live. With might and strength she lifted, that big tree wouldn't give. With sheer determination, and none would be so bold. She pushed the tree from off him, to free him from its hold.

A broken back he suffered, but they were not deterred. She nursed him 'til he walked again, she'd given him her word. Now what to do they wondered, she came with answer true. You open up a country store, and that will get us through.

Though Dan'l couldn't walk well, but shuffled as he went. He worked the store and Ma'athy Jane, she could not be content. With healthy boys and strong of back, and girls with ready hoes. They planted corn and 'taters, and how those seeds did grow.

They took to farmers' market, the produce that they raised. To keep them going day and night, she heaped on them her praise. While Dan'l churned the butter, and shelled the butter beans. The rest attended to the chores, thus living like a team.

Though those eight children were her care, she never missed her call. For midwives were much in demand, and she was best of all. She delivered near five hundred, including her own kin. Just when she thought that rest would come, they sent for her again.

An illness came to Dan'l then, it sent him to his grave. With most the children grown and gone, she knew she must be brave. Her Pa built well a new pine box, as Dan'l had desired. They buried him in that great state, where his bairns were sired.

Now what of all the children? The best that one can tell. They married set up households, and lived their lives right well. Did any love like Ma'athy, and Dan'l in his prime? My dad's the one named Jimmy, I think they did just fine.

CEH

Uncle Earl's story corroborated what my Nanny had told me about Daniel and Martha Jane Haynes while it also shared two significant new details about the tree cutting accident and Martha Jane having been a midwife. Daniel's back injury explained why he was always sitting on the porch and manning his roadside store, while Martha Jane was working in the fields. I was so grateful to have been able to find and read Uncle Earl's stories. Not only did the stories provide insights into Daniel, Martha Jane, my Nanny, and Aunt Ruth, they also told us a lot about Uncle Earl. He was everyone's favorite kind, loving, genuine, humble, fun, and happy. The fact he chose to write these accounts, and write them well, gives us a glimpse inside his heart and level of thoughtfulness. I noted he focused on telling the stories of others, putting the spotlight, praise, and admiration on someone else, going so far as using only his initials so as not to detract from his subjects. He realized what he knew inside his mind would do no good for future generations if he took it all with him to Heaven. Uncle Earl, thank you for sharing.

You don't have to write a book to share an ancestor story. It doesn't even have to be typed nor does it have to be on any particular size of paper. Just jot it down in your own words without worry of spelling, punctuation, grammar, or length. Critiquing your writing abilities is not even remotely in the realm of possibilities from those who will read whatever you take the time and effort to share. One sentence, one paragraph, one page, it doesn't matter. What matters is that something is recorded about someone who lived, because something, anything, is better than nothing when honoring your DNA.

Mark your calendar right now to dedicate an hour, two hours, or maybe even an entire day to just get something on paper about anything of interest you might know about people in your family, living or not. What may seem insignificant to you may just be genealogical gold for someone interested in that family member sometime in the future. If you want to continue working on your first draft later, that's fine, but ink your initial thoughts as soon as possible. If you never get back around to it, at least your initial efforts will be available to those who survive you. Start thinking about loved ones to write something about them and who knows how many happy times or special details you'll remember. If you don't write it down, it's likely no one else will either. And you know what that means.

Like Uncle Earl did, make copies and distribute them to your immediate family members. The process of sharing will inspire others to reflect and respond, adding to or enhancing what you started. If you know the person in your family who is the keeper of the family tree, be sure to provide a copy to them, because they will add what you wrote to the subject relative. Uploading the story to Ancestry. com and Findagrave.com are efficient ways to make recollections and facts readily accessible to people who have a mutual admiration for the story's main characters. Always remember, genealogy and honoring your DNA is a group/team effort with each participant enhancing the overall experience by contributing what they have, what they know, and what they find. Like most everything in life, getting is wonderful, but giving is rewarding.

Chapter 13

DISCOVERING JAMES I. MIMS

Leaving Mims Cemetery in Suwannee County, FL without finding James I. Mims, my determination escalated. His Florida death certificate stated he died in Suwannee County, FL, so I felt confident he would have been buried there, but no memorial existed for him on Findagrave.com. Seeking assistance, I reached out via phone to various agencies in the county seat of Live Oak, such as the library, historical society, and genealogical society hoping someone would have records of burials within the county. It didn't take long to get the information I was seeking. A lady on the other end of the line said, "You said you have his death certificate, the burial location should be on the death certificate."

Taking a second, more thorough, look, without distraction, I focused on the death certificate, top left corner to bottom right corner. At the top left corner were the fields for Place of Death with the cursive handwritten words Suwannee Co and McAlpin. Near the bottom right corner was a box labeled Place of Burial or Removal. In that box were handwritten the words and date, Crawford Lake 9/18/1918.

Using the key words Crawford Lake Cemetery Suwannee McAlpin in the Google search bar, the search results displayed Crawford Lake Primitive Baptist Cemetery located in McAlpin, FL within Suwannee County. He wasn't buried in the overgrown Mims Cemetery. He was buried, like so many of my other Southern ancestors, in a cemetery adjacent to a Primitive Baptist Church. I now knew the location of the cemetery where he was buried, but exactly where within that cemetery was an origin of my DNA resting?

I can't begin to describe the enjoyment and fulfillment I experienced during my search for my 3rd Great-grandfather James I. Mims. I wrote the following account to serve as a motivator that you can and will find the James I. Mims in your family tree during your adventure to honor your DNA.

James I. Mims was born February 26, 1837 in Laurens County, GA. At twenty-four and a half years of age, on September 1, 1861, he enlisted as a Private in Captain Francis Marion Jackson's Company E, "Alapaha Guards," of the 29th Georgia Infantry Regiment at Savannah, GA. Company E would later become Company H at the reorganization on May 7, 1862. We know he volunteered for service in the Confederate Army as opposed to being drafted, because the first Confederate Conscription Act wasn't passed until April of 1862.

James was good with a gun, and just what military leaders were looking for when they authorized a new fighting force known as Sharpshooter battalions. From the regiments locally stationed around Savannah, GA, the best marksmen were identified to create a concentration of accuracy on the battlefield. On August 1, 1862, James I. Mims was transferred from the 29th Georgia Infantry Regiment to the 1st Battalion Georgia Sharpshooters. Their first assignment was coastal defense at Fort McAllister on the Ogeechee River just south of Savannah.

On the morning of March 3, 1863, James Mims was among the Southern men at the earthen perimeter of Fort McAllister. Assigned to defend it, and with all Confederate States citizens counting on them, the men peered out across the open water to witness three ghastly dreadnaughts, known as ironclads, steaming steadily toward them. Soon, the big guns on the fortress walls and Union warship turrets roared to life. Confederate gunners accurately trained their guns, finding their mark time and time again to no avail as their projectiles literally dented the hulls and gun turrets of the armored nautical beasts. Union shells rained down upon the fort, burying 8 feet into the sand before exploding into clouds of sand and mud, leaving craters and destruction.

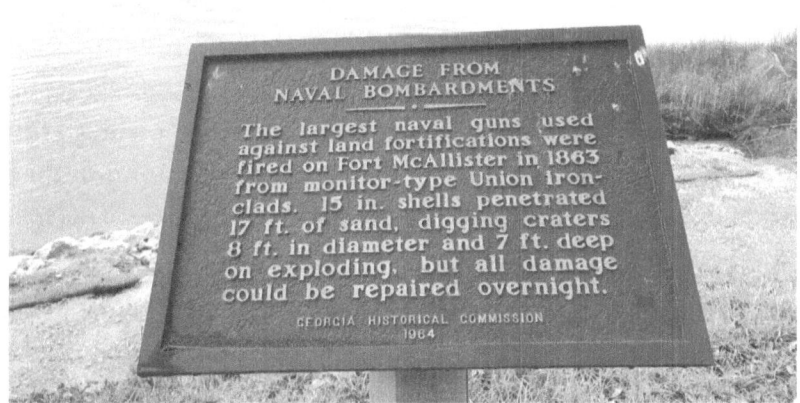

Fort McAllister historical marker, near Savannah, GA

You can read a detailed account of the battle in the book *Guardian of Savannah* by Roger S. Durham. The bombardment lasted all day. Wump, whistle, thud, BOOOOM! Union gunners gave everything they could hurl at the rebel soldiers in an attempt to pound the Southerners into submission. Slowly but surely, the earthen walls of the fort transformed from what first looked like a fort into some-thing more like a pock-marked, oozing flow of sand, grass, dirt, and debris. One of the Union shells found it's mark, slamming into the gun carriage of the eight-inch Columbiad nicknamed the Pet Gun by the fort's defenders due to its accuracy and dependability.

As the tide flowed out of the Ogeechee River in the late after-noon, the ironclads had to pull back to avoid being grounded at low tide. The Union commander knew the Southerners would rebuild the fort's protective walls at night by shoveling the sand back into position, so he planned a continual bombardment throughout the night to keep the Confederate soldiers inside the safety of their bun-kers. Every five minutes, all night long, one of two Union mortar boats would lob a large explosive shell into Fort McAllister.

Despite the mortal danger of shells falling every five minutes in the darkness of night, the men of the 1st Battalion Georgia Sharpshooters, including James I. Mims, were called into action. Inside and outside the fort, they went to work immediately and deliberately to make the necessary repairs in preparation for the next morning's immi-nent continuation of combat. A fresh supply of ammunition was transported in from Savannah, along with a new gun carriage for the eight-inch Columbiad. Some men shoveled sand into huge craters, some men distributed ammunition, and a few men began the task of remounting the Pet Gun into fighting position. Among the men repairing the big gun as the bombs rained down was James Mims.

The weights dealt with were tremendous. It was dark. There were no pieces of heavy diesel hydraulic powered equipment. Sweat cre-ated slippery conditions. Explosions were startling. Whatever the specific reason, one of the heavy timbers gave way, landing on the right leg of James Mims, crushing his ankle. He received medical aid and was sent to Savannah Medical College for treatment. "See page 95 in *Guardian of Savannah*."

As night turned to day with the rising of the burning star in the east, the fog cleared enough for the Union commander to see the results of his all-night harassment. Surely the Southern men had hunkered in fear as he had predicted. And, there it was in the light of day. Fort McAllister. Repaired, restocked, and ready to give 'em hell. Acknowledging further efforts to take the fort by naval force were futile, the Union fleet sailed away, defeated.

Word of Fort McAllister's steadfast resolve spread quickly throughout the Confederacy as an example for all Southern soldiers. Generals sent congratulatory messages, and the Confederate States Congress issued a joint resolution thanking the officers and men for their exemplary service. Duty, valor, bravery, and honor describe the actions of those defending the fort, including my 3rd great-grandfather, James I. Mims.

Assuming eight to twelve weeks for a broken leg to mend, James Mims would have just gotten back on his feet when the siege of Vicksburg, MS began on May 18, 1863. Defending the Gibraltar of the Confederacy, 650 miles west of Savannah, GA, General John C. Pemberton's 33,000-man Army of Mississippi was surrounded by 77,000 Union soldiers under the command of General Ulysses S. Grant. General Joseph E. Johnston gathered a force of 30,000 Confederate soldiers to rescue Pemberton's army. Among the units selected for the mission was the 1st Battalion Georgia Sharpshooters. We know James Mims was there, because he said he was, in his pension application, and one of his muster rolls shows him sick on June 30, 1863 in Canton, MS, just north of Jackson, MS.

But Johnston was too late. As he approached Vicksburg from the east at Big Black River, Pemberton surrendered his army. With Pemberton out of the equation, Grant was able to turn his army from facing west toward the fortifications of Vicksburg, to facing east toward the new threat from Johnston's 30,000 men. Union General William Tecumseh Sherman's 40,000 men began to march eastward, and Johnston decided to withdraw toward the recently burned capital of Jackson, MS. There, at Jackson, MS, from approximately July 10th to July 16th, 1863, the two armies totaling 70,000 men squared off in what James Mims described as "The Eight Days Fight."

The Eight Days Fight at Jackson, MS was effectively a siege by the Union Army. Facing a significantly larger force, with tens of thousands more Union soldiers in reserve around Vicksburg, and no Confederate reinforcements nearby, Johnston chose to skedaddle eastward before his last avenue of escape closed behind him. Combined casualties both North and South totaled just over 2,300 men killed, wounded, or missing. Statistics would be significantly different two months later along a meandering creek in the northwestern corner of James Mims' home state of Georgia.

Disease was the leading cause of death among Confederate soldiers, with approximately 164,000 able-bodied vibrant young men succumbing to dysentery, typhoid, and other deadly afflictions. Camp conditions were deplorable. Thousands of men gathered into close proximity for the first time as compared to relative isolation in sparsely populated rural Georgia. It was cold. It was hot. It was wet. It was muddy. It was stressful. It's fair to say it was downright miserable. And, the men in grey and butternut were continuously in desperate need of pants, shoes, shirts, jackets, blankets, tents, and food.

James I. Mims suffered greatly from sickness throughout the war. Six different muster rolls listed him as sick, or at a hospital. In his pension application, he described being "taken sick" and being sent home by doctors. With battles raging, and shortages of available Southern fighting men, James must have been extremely ill for doctors to have sent him home on furlough to recuperate. 1861 sick, 1862 sick, 1863 sick, 1864 sick. But there were no records indicating he was out sick during a fight.

The creek in northwest Georgia was Chickamauga Creek. On September 18, 1863, James Mims was there alongside 66,000 of his fellow Southern brothers-in-arms, facing 60,000 well-supplied Billy Yanks. The battle commenced on 19 Sep 1863 with a cavalry charge by none other than Confederate Major General Nathan Bedford Forrest. Repulsed by a hornet's nest of well-aimed, rifled-accurate lead bullets, Forrest called for immediate infantry support, which came at 9 a.m. from Wilson's Brigade comprised in part by the 1st Battalion Georgia Sharpshooters and James I. Mims.

Those three days in late September, now known to American history as the Battle of Chickamauga, would prove to be the second largest battle of the War of Northern Aggression, with only Gettysburg resulting in more casualties. In all, more than 34,600 men wearing blue and grey were killed, wounded, captured, or missing when the guns fell silent and the smoke cleared. It was a costly Confederate victory, as Union General Rosecrans hastily retreated to Chattanooga, TN.

1st Battalion GA Sharpshooters Monument, Chickamauga National Battlefield

General Braxton Bragg pursued the retreating Union Army to Chattanooga, taking up siege positions on the high grounds of Lookout Mountain and Missionary Ridge, TN. The 1st Battalion Georgia Sharpshooters were there, on Missionary Ridge, on November 25, 1863, as part of Wilson's Brigade forming the right side of Walker's Division of Hardee's Corps near the right flank of the Confederate Army of Tennessee.

General William Tecumseh Sherman committed only 4,000 of his 16,000 to attack Bragg's right flank, and Hardee's men held them off, counterattacked downhill, and routed Sherman's men.

But, to their left, Union General Thomas John Wood was ordering 23,000 Yankee soldiers to charge uphill, throwing themselves at the Confederate center. And, against all odds, they broke the Rebel line of defense. As the center collapsed, an all-out retreat was ordered, and the Rebels withdrew toward Dalton, GA. The strategic position of Chattanooga, with its supply and commerce routes of both river and railways, was lost. It was a death knell for Georgia.

The Confederate Army of Tennessee took up defensive positions at the mountainous and rocky cliff area of Dalton, GA, protecting the vital railroads to Atlanta. The First Battle of Dalton took place February 22-27, 1864. The purpose was to probe the Confederate defenses to determine their vulnerability to attack. The Atlanta Campaign of the Civil War began on May 7, 1864 near Dalton.

Pension application records for James I. Mims state that he left his command at Dalton. Specifically, recollections forty-three to fifty-one years later, between 1907 and 1915, were that he was taken sick at Dalton, GA, was sent to Atlanta, GA for medical treatment, and there doctors sent him home on sick furlough, where he remained until the end of the war. Dalton, GA was overrun on May 7, 1864 at the Battle of Rocky Face Ridge, so James Mims had to have departed Dalton, GA prior to May 7, 1864. A witness, S. M. Touchstone, states he was with James Mims all the time until June/July 1864. But he must have been slightly mistaken almost fifty years later. Some versions of the story are that James Mims was wounded in the leg, some say he was shot in the leg, and some say he had a broken leg. We know his leg was broken at Fort McAllister on March 3, 1863. In his first indigent pension application, James states he was taken sick at Dalton, GA. A soldier doesn't forget being wounded, so if he left his command wounded, he wouldn't have mistakenly stated he was "taken sick."

In any event, James I. Mims did not return to his command after leaving sick sometime prior to May 7, 1864. We know he married the widow, Mary Ann Allen McElhaney. Mary Ann's first husband, John T. McElhaney, was killed in battle serving with the 50th Georgia Infantry Regiment at Fox Gap near Antietam, MD on September 14, 1862. It's possible James Mims met Mary Ann while home on sick furlough and simply didn't want to leave her and her son. Or, maybe James had had enough, knowing the Confederacy's days were numbered. Or, maybe he was wounded and somewhat crippled in the leg, unable to soldier again. Maybe it was all of the above.

I found a clue in the birth date of Nancy Catherin Mims, the oldest child of James and Mary Ann. According to her headstone, Nancy Mims was born on October 12, 1865. A 280-day human gestation period resulted in a conception date of January 5, 1865. The 1880 census shows Nancy Mims as thirteen years old, which suggests a birth year of 1867, so the conception date is based solely on Nancy's headstone inscription. There would have been a court-ship of some time between James and Mary Ann, which could easily place their initial meeting sometime soon after James Mims came home on sick furlough, possibly near May 1864. Truth be known, Mary Ann was the reason James Mims did not return to his com-mand, which probably saved his life. She'd already lost her first love.

By the 1900 census, James Mims was a widower. Records from Bethel Primitive Baptist Church located in Echols County, GA state Mary Ann died June 24, 1895. Those same church records also document James I. Mims as a Christian believer, a church elder, and a man of God who regularly preached the gospel to the congrega-tion on Sundays. By 1907, at age seventy, we know he was struggling financially and applied for a Confederate soldier Indigent Pension.

Over the course of nine years, James applied multiple times to the State of Georgia for an indigent pension, being denied time and time again until 1915. In his application submitted on September 7, 1914, to Question #14, "Have you ever applied for the Georgia Pension and had it refused? and for what cause it was not allowed?" James Mims replied, "*I have made 1 or 2. But I got it rong some way.*"

He died on a Tuesday, September 17, 1918 in McAlpin, FL located within Suwannee County, just south of Live Oak. His son-in-law, Perry H. Hines, married to James' daughter, Martha Mims, was the informant for his death certificate. His grave would remain unmarked for ninety-nine years until 2017, when one of his 3rd great-grandsons, Trae Zipperer, traveled to Suwannee County, FL on Father's Day to attend a Primitive Baptist Church service, as many of his ancestors had done, and meet with the man who maintained the church cemetery, Mr. Holister. Immediately following a wonderful afternoon meal prepared by the loving hands of the women in attendance, known as dinner on the grounds, Trae met with Mr. Holister and walked to the edge of the cemetery. "What makes you think your grandfather is buried here?" Mr. Holister asked.

Trae shared the details of his research and the following observations:

- The death certificate for James I. Mims states he is buried here at Crawford Lake.
- In 1895, his wife, Mary Ann Allen McElhaney Mims, died in Echols County, GA and would have been buried there, not here, twenty-three years prior to the death of James.
- As of 1910, James was living in Echols County, GA.
- Two of his daughters, Nancy and Martha, are buried here in marked graves adjacent to their respective husbands.

- Census records, taken together, tell a story of his son, Hansford, being an unwed invalid.
- His unmarried son, Hansford Mims, is buried here in a marked grave, near a sister.
- My conclusion is that Hansford, single, who died in 1937, twenty years after his dad, would have been buried next to his dad by his sister, Martha.
- Therefore, my prediction is we will find an empty space next to Hansford Mims, and in that space will be the unmarked grave of James I. Mims.

Mr. Holister explained there were no burial records for the old section of the cemetery, but that they did have a map for the newer section. We didn't walk more than 20 feet before we spotted the headstone for Hansford "Hans" Mims. On the right side of his grave was an empty spot, just as I had predicted. On Hans' left was his brother-in-law, Perry Hines, the man who was the informant on the death certificate of James I. Mims. To Perry's left was his wife, sister to Hansford, and daughter to James. I had Mr. Holister's attention now. He walked over to the new section and pulled up a thin metal rod used to hold funeral bouquets. Stepping back to the empty spot next to Hansford Mims, Mr. Holister began to slide the thin metal rod into the ground. I asked him what he was looking for that would indicate an unmarked grave. He said, "If there's anything there, it will be about 18 to 24 inches down, typically the top of a vault." He probed in a few places with no results.

We walked away from that area, and he probed a few more empty spaces. Nothing. At the back of the cemetery, along a boundary fence, we found the graves of daughter Nancy and her husband. We walked back to the empty space next to Hansford Mims, and I asked Mr. Holister how he could tell where the old section of the cemetery ended, and the new section began. He pointed to a pvc pipe sticking out of the ground and said, "You see that pipe? That's the corner and edge of this old section. You see that fence post on that back fence with the jug on top of it? That's the other corner and edge on this end of the old section. You see this swath of grass? I made that path so I could drive my tractor between the two sections. On the other side of my tractor path is the new section." He handed me the thin metal rod and said he needed to walk back over to the church building to talk with some members.

I stuck the rod into the ground in the empty space next to Hansford, but hit nothing, so I started walking around the old section of the cemetery, sticking the rod into the ground here and there where I found an open space with no grave marker. In at least one spot, an old, worn-down piece of wood was sticking up, the remnant of once a wooden grave marker. I assumed that must have been what happened to Grandpa Mims. They must have used wood, it rotted away, and left his grave unmarked and forgotten over time. Then I got to thinking. How could Mr. Holister have known exactly where the boundary of the old cemetery was located if he didn't come onto the scene until fifty years after James I. Mims died?

So, I walked back to the empty space next to Hansford, and I stuck the thin metal rod into the ground about 2 feet deep. Nothing. I stepped back about 6 inches toward the assumed edge of the old cemetery section and stuck the rod into the ground. Nothing. I did this several times with no results until I stuck the rod into the ground about 6 inches beyond the assumed edge of the old section and inside the tractor path. About 18-20 inches down, the thin metal rod found it's mark with a "dunk, dunk, dunk." Moving around that area and sticking the rod into the ground, "dunk, dunk, dunk." I left the rod there, sticking up out of the ground, and went to my truck to retrieve the temporary granite marker I had purchased for $225 with James I. Mims' name, birth, death, and military service etched on it. That's how confident I was that I would find his grave.

Mr. Holister saw me at my truck and asked if I had found anything. I told him I think I had found something, so he followed me back to the cemetery. Mr. Holister bent down, took the metal rod in his hand, lifted it a few inches, and pushed it back. "Dunk." You should have seen the look on his face when he looked up at me and said, "There's something down there!"

*Using a metal rod, I found Confederate
soldier Pvt. James I. Mims*

I placed the temporary granite marker where I had found my 3rd great-grandfather. But my work was not yet finished. That week, I contacted the United States Veterans Administration "V.A." to inquire about a Confederate soldier V.A. headstone. I was directed to a person who handles pre-World War I veteran headstone applications. She explained the process and provided the appropriate V.A. headstone order application. In addition to the application, I had to find a local monument company to take delivery of the stone from the V.A. Once the local monument company received the stone, I had to pay them to deliver the stone to the cemetery and install it.

I asked the helpful lady at the monument company about having additional etchings made to the stone, and she informed me the V.A. would not provide that service. I would have to pay extra for any additional etching. She said another option would be for the monument company to cut a stone exactly like a V.A. provided stone, and I could have it etched however I wanted it. I thought about it, but decided I would rather my Civil War soldier grandfather have an authentic Confederate soldier headstone provided by the V.A. Unlike a standard United States military veteran headstone, which is rounded on top, a Confederate soldier headstone is the same dimensions, but the top is pointed instead of rounded. They were designed with a point on top to keep Yankees from sitting on them!

The only choice I really had was either white marble or gray granite. Based on the facts of him being from Georgia, wearing a grey Confederate uniform, granite eroding more slowly than marble, and granite being quarried in Elberton, GA, of course I chose gray Georgia granite.

So, I completed the application and attached required documentation, such as his Civil War muster rolls and death certificate. Within a short time, the V.A. notified me the application was approved, and the stone had been ordered. I let the monument company know to be on the lookout for James I. Mims' headstone from the V.A. Not having heard anything from the monument company, I gave the lady there a call. She said, "You're not going to believe this, but I just received a call from a person in Virginia. Their veteran son had recently died, they ordered his headstone from the V.A., and it was delivered a few days ago. Today, they lifted their son's stone and found your grandfather's stone underneath it on the same pallet!"

She called me a few days later to let me know the stone had arrived and emailed a couple of photos from their warehouse. During the time I had waited for the stone to be delivered, I decided to honor my Civil War soldier grandfather by etching on the back of his granite marker the names of battles in which he had fought. I sent her the lettering, she gave me a price, they etched the back of the stone, delivered the stone to Crawford Lake Primitive Baptist Cemetery, and set it where I had directed. Almost exactly 100 years after his death, and 153 years after the Civil War ended, I was able to honor my DNA by marking a Southern soldier's grave. A Christian soldier, he faces east.

James I. Mims headstone front. *James I. Mims headstone back.*

Chapter 14

CEMETERY MAINTENANCE

Mechanization of farming practices, mass migration from rural agricultural areas to diverse opportunities available in densely populated urban settings, and transition to a mobilized workforce have upset the historic localized family unit. The result has been the loss of that deep-rooted sense of belonging to a defined geographic area. Not long ago, Grandpa was buried at a church cemetery where his dad, too, was buried. Seventy years ago, within a five-mile radius, two dozen people with a DNA connection to Grandpa were able to watch after Grandpa's grave. Not only did they live nearby, they attended the same church where Grandpa was buried and volunteered on Saturdays to help maintain the church grounds.

Grandpa's children were the first in the family to move away to attend college. Finding work unrelated to agriculture, his children remained within their home state, albeit a hundred miles away in one of the state's three largest metropolitan areas, and never returned. His grandchildren followed job opportunities to far flung destinations throughout the entire country, resulting in a family unit no longer within proximity to gather together every Sunday after church for lunch. No longer connected to Grandpa, the place where their family comes from, the church where their ancestors worshipped, or the cluster of graves behind that church where each headstone bears their own last name, Grandpa's descendants are no longer concerned about cemetery maintenance.

I awoke Saturday morning, 14 Oct 2017, at the Holiday Inn Express in Waycross, GA, a seven-hour drive from home. The annual Ben James Church fish fry cemetery maintenance fundraiser was scheduled to begin at 12:30 p.m. As luck would have it, I had spent the previous few days visiting with my grandfather near Marianna, FL, so my drive time Friday night had been cut in half. Having left his house close to sunset, with moonrise not until 2 a.m., the trip eastward on I-10 and then north onto two-lane Hwy 441 at Lake City had been dark—really dark. Struggling to stay awake, reaching the hotel safely had come as a welcomed relief.

Waking for coffee and breakfast, and having a couple of morning hours unaccounted for, I decided to hop over to Kettle Creek Cemetery to pay respects to my 3rd Great-grandmother Julia Ann Tomberlin Deen. I had been there once, about six months before, so I knew the way and the exact location of her grave.

Parking near her plot, I noticed my $1 Dollar General yellow flowers were still there, weathered some, but it gave me a good feeling to see some color, her only flowers, that I had placed. After visiting and reflecting for a few minutes, with no rush for time, I scanned the cemetery looking at the thousands of headstones, wondering about the stories below each one. A wooden structure with a small roof atop it stood out of place about ten rows away. My curiosity took over as my legs involuntarily transported my eyes, fixed on what appeared to be some sort of information booth. Burned into the wood was "History of Obediah," and behind a plexiglass display cover were tacked up written accounts of the life and times of Obediah Barber: Legendary Swamp Pioneer. I would later learn Obediah was directly related to a very close friend of mine.

The cemetery having no visitors at that time other than myself, I couldn't help but notice a man arrive on a 4-wheeler ATV pulling a small trailer. He had a boy with him. A few minutes later, still reading about the Swamp Legend, the 4-wheeler had turned down my row of graves heading my way. Pulling up to where I stood, he turned off the ignition and we greeted one another. The boy sat quietly on the ATV watching us talk. I noticed a weed eater in the small trailer and asked the man if he helped take care of the cemetery.

"That's my job," he said. "That's what I do."

I told him what a great job he was doing, because the cemetery looked so nice. He motioned for the boy to remain seated on the ATV, and we walked to the grave of my grandmother.

I pointed out how the flowers I had left six months ago still looked pretty good and asked him how he could weed eat around all of these headstones without hitting the flowers.

"Well, I don't hit the flowers, because I remove each one. I then weed eat around the stone without hitting the stone. Then I put the flowers back the way I found 'em," is what he shared with me. Turning around, pointing, and walking to the next row of headstones, he said, "This here row contains my people. This is why I work here. That's my granny. That's my Uncle Roy. I treat all of these burials as if they were also my people, because they are somebody's people."

Considering I was in the area for a cemetery maintenance fundraiser, having seen dozens of cemeteries in various degrees of upkeep, and wondering how exactly cemeteries are maintained, I asked him how this particular cemetery's maintenance was structured. He shared that the cemetery was separate from the church onsite and that the cemetery had a board of trustees along with a maintenance fund for paying his salary and the salaries of other groundskeepers who worked there. He said they also have a big cleanup day once a year when they advertise the event in the newspaper, and a lot of people in town come out to spruce things up for a day. Volunteers also brought decorations for the graves of people they knew. He pointed across to the other side of the cemetery where a huge tree was toppled on its side with a large root system jutting upward more than 10 feet high. He let me know how much work it was going to be to remove that downed tree and repair the graves its root ball had damaged when it popped up out of the ground. "That there's at least a daggum thousand dollars not counting my time," he estimated.

His mentioning a one-day event to clean up the cemetery every year reminded me of a conversation I had with one of our neighbor friends, Carol. I had shared my DNA adventures with her, and she told me back in Alabama they had Decoration Day at the church where she grew up. Everyone came out that one designated day each year with their cleaning supplies, decorations, and flowers to honor their loved ones. She emphasized how important it was to her mother and how they never missed a Decoration Day. Her concern was whether the next generation would continue to care about the cemetery, or not.

It was getting close to noon, so I thought I'd better start driving toward Blackshear and Ben James Church. I couldn't help but feel a sense of pride that Ben James, the man whose name was on the church, was one of my sixty-four 5th great-grandfathers. I had to admit, a fish fry with hush puppies, French fries, potato salad, and sweet iced tea was sounding pretty good. However, the actual food was secondary to the primary purpose of raising money to maintain the cemetery for the coming year, a cemetery containing my 5th great-grandparents, Ben and Sarah Riggins James.

Arriving at the Primitive Baptist Church grounds, I could see there was a good turnout. On the front porch of the church, a couple of men were setting up a propane cooker to heat the grease where the battered catfish filets would be delicately but quickly drop-pushed into the hissing, rolling slippery boil.

The origin of my invitation was an American flag I had gifted to a lady there to pay respects to her military veteran husband during my first visit to the Ben James Church cemetery to honor my DNA. She had forgotten to bring a flag, and I had some extras to share. We were the only two at the cemetery that day, so we chatted, and she asked for my contact information. I never anticipated she would actually reach out to me and invite me to a fish fry. But she did, and here I was, walking into a dining hall attached to the west side of the main church building by a covered breezeway. Entering the room, I was greeted by smiling faces, registration nametags, and red Solo cups filled with ice cubes and sweet tea.

Before filling our plates, one of the organizers gave the blessing as we all bowed our heads. The ninety-four-year-old founder of the annual fish fry program stood to welcome the fifty-some-odd visitors. She shared her memories of attending Ben James Church her entire life and how honored she was to have lived a life of faith within a church named after a man she held in such admiration for his devotion and leadership so long ago. She continued to explain how she sincerely wished she were a direct descendant of Ben and Sarah James, but that there were some descendants in attendance. Asking any descendants to please stand, I rose to my feet and joined thirteen others, as we all looked around in amazement.

I learned the cemetery had a board of directors responsible for raising money to pay for maintenance. A third-party was paid to mow the grass, trim the limited landscaping, and spray herbicide at the base of the fenced perimeter. In years past, church members had volunteered to maintain the grounds. With membership dwindling, cremations negatively impacting burial plot sales, and interest in general on the decline, hired help had become a necessity. In addition to the annual fish fry attendees, some on the invitation list who weren't able to attend mailed in donation checks.

Probably my favorite part of the event was standing in front of the church for a group photo bound for insertion in the social column of the local paper. All fourteen direct descendants of Ben and Sarah James in attendance standing on the front steps together, cousins, blood relatives, each claimed at least 1.5625% of their unique DNA contributed from Ben and Sarah. Given sufficient time, the cousins could discover many instances where their historical pasts had crossed.

Ben James Church direct descendants attending
cemetery fundraiser fish fry. Blackshear, GA.

One of the women in the group photo asked from which of Ben and Sarah's children I descended. I told her William Thomas James was my 4th great-grandfather. She had descended from a daughter. I asked her the name of the James' daughter's husband. She gave me his name and told me she had heard he had died a soldier during the Civil War. Between conversations, I plugged her grandfather's name into FOLD3.com. My heart sank as I recognized his regiment, the 50th Georgia, and the place of his death, Fox Gap, a prelude to the Battle of Antietam. It was the same place my 3rd great-grandmother's first husband, John T. McElhany, had been killed in action.

You can read about the Battle of South Mountain, but in summary, the 50th Georgia eventually ended up pinned down in the sunken Old Sharpsburg Road with Union forces pouring down withering rifled musket fire from three sides. Our two men from Georgia knew what was at stake. As ordered, they held their ground at all cost. Accounts of what happened there included such horrors as Union supply wagons in haste literally running over top of wounded Confederate soldiers where they had fallen immobilized in the sunken road bed, crushing them through. The cost for my John, and her grandfather, was everything.

It had been another day of lifelong memories connecting with my ancestors on an ancestry road trip. I had randomly come into contact with a kind man who physically performs the tasks required to keep a cemetery looking like a cemetery. We pass by these places of somber reflection, hallowed ground, last addresses for deceased loved ones and ancestors, and never think about the special people who have a calling in life to care for them. It's not easy work.

Imagine if you owned a home on four acres and you had to mow it yourself. Now imagine distributed across that four acres of your own yard are 1,316 wine glasses standing erect and spaced every 6 feet. These aren't just any old wine glasses mind you, each of these were painstakingly retrieved from the bottom of the middle of the north Atlantic, 2.37 miles down, from the wreck of *RMS Titanic*. It's your job, every seven days, week after week, month after month, year after year, decade after decade, to navigate this obstacle course of antiquities with zero tolerance for as much as bumping into one with your mower deck as you zig zag, in and out, back and forth, all day, stopping every tenth wine glass to protect flowers or decorations.

I was also privileged to have met a core group of people who had taken it upon themselves to actively participate on a cemetery maintenance board to make sure the work gets done and done well. Each member of the board had effectively taken ownership of the Ben James Church cemetery, pledging their time, effort, love, and money to carry on where previous generations had ended their races. These remarkable people do whatever it takes to ensure the cemetery you drive by every day, twice a day, looks the same today as it did 125 years ago. All the while the grass, the weeds, and the trees perpetually grow. There is no timeout. The board members ask for help. They hold fundraisers. They interview caretakers. They hire sextons. And when necessary, they hop up into the driver's seat to mow, fire up the weed eater, or retrieve supplies.

I met dozens of like-minded wonderful men, women, girls, and boys who took time on a Saturday to attend a cemetery maintenance fundraiser fish fry. These were good people, and it was refreshing to be among them. Some prepared side dishes. Some caught the fish. Some cleaned the fish. Someone brought the cooker. Some fried the fish. Some set the tables. Some poured the drinks. And some cleaned up after the meal, leaving the Primitive Baptist Church dining hall as good or better than they found it. The food was delicious, fantastic, totally worth the drive, and thirteen newfound cousins was icing on the cake.

Unfortunately, some cemeteries, like the Wisenbaker Cemetery in Valdosta or the Zipperer Cemetery in Lake Park, GA have no full-time salaried caretaker nor board of directors. These final resting places of our DNA are like the homeless on a street corner, unshaven, disheveled, unbathed, with an empty plate on the ground in front of them. Sometimes a guy or gal like me pulls up on the scene, surveys the situation, recognizes the immediate need, and rolls up their sleeves. But it's only a temporary fix in haphazard fashion. It may be another year or more before the next charitable-minded person comes along.

These patches of hallowed ground mostly rely on good-hearted folks who live nearby. These neighbors literally see the need and feel the tug at their hearts, like when an abandoned dog wanders up to a doorstep desperately hungry. He sits patiently, communicating only with his eyes, sadly quivering with a steady focus on the door-knob, hoping to see it begin to turn, fearing rejection less than his stomach pains, surrendered to the probability of another mealtime unprovided.

Others, like the Mims Cemetery in Suwannee County, FL, have already gone back to nature, lost forever, like the last surviving mated pair of a species grown too old to reproduce, extinct. If you know of a cemetery or human gravesite on the verge of extinction, please notify authorities. Specifically, seek out your local library's geneal-ogy room and inform them of what you know about the location of concern. The people there will be knowledgeable and capable of taking action immediately, having contacts of various preservation resources and assets. Other places to contact are historical societies, historical museums, county offices, city offices, and funeral homes. It won't take long to find someone who cares. They will help you secure the area, document the site, and seek resources to save it if humanly possible.

Chapter 15

BURIAL VS. CREMATION

As one who has been fortunate enough to have visited the known graves of all my ancestors and experienced the inexplicable sensation of emotion associated with bringing one's self into close proximity with the final resting place of my DNA's origins, I am 100% unequivocally against the cremation of human remains. Allow me to be candid. Cremation is nothing more than the least expensive way to get rid of the body, period, end of story, no room for debate. Cremation is a shortsighted mistake. It saddens me now, but I stood by idly when my father chose cremation, because I didn't have the context of experience to form an opinion. I remember thinking, *Wow, my dad is really smart. He considered the costs of funeral vs. cremation and helped us avoid the grief and wasted expenses associated with burial.*

Three shifts in our contemporary societies, and one urban legend, have set into motion the death knell of historic private, family, and church cemeteries. While hope does exist, as humans capable of altering seemingly imminent outcomes, the cumulative effect of our individual choices can change our trajectory as a species, or not.

149

1. We've turned away from God.

2. We've embraced cremation as the cheapest way to dispose of their body.

3. We've allowed lobbyists to quash competition, thereby increasing the costs of burials.

4. And someone created an urban legend leading people to believe we're out of land.

I think we can all agree, as a collective people, God is no longer the center of our world as He once was to our ancestors. There aren't enough pages to describe and point out in detail the countless ways we go about our lives in exact conflict with teachings of the Bible. You know God is real, you know God exists, because you know you pray to Him for assistance during your most desperate of times. When your child is severely ill, you get down on your knees and you ask God to intercede. When that tornado or hurricane is bearing down on your home and family, you get down on your knees and you pray for God's favor. When you know God doesn't approve, you do it anyway. You might ask, "What does our sinful behavior have to do with honoring our DNA and cemetery maintenance?"

Had we not turned our backs on God, we'd still be attending church, living our lives as instructed by God in the Bible, and respecting human life for the miracle that it is. I am referring to all human life, regardless of age, regardless of color, regardless of race, regardless of insignificant differences in appearance. The probability of our births, our very existence, is so fragile and infinitely remote, yet we fail to appreciate how we got here in the first place. Without God, we have nothing other than a limited number of days to entertain ourselves while on this sphere hurdling through space at incomprehensible speed. Disassociation from God, at least in America, was how we initiated the erosion of our societal foundation originally built upon Biblical bedrock. We quit going to church. We quit burying our loved ones at the church cemetery facing east. We literally abandoned the church property, including the graves of our ancestors, the houses of God literally rotted to the ground. If not completely abandoned, the last two or three surviving members of the once robust congregation are desperately trying to maintain the church cemetery grounds by themselves. They are holding on in their golden years, hoping the next generation will turn back toward God, but so far that hasn't happened.

A church congregation, especially a growing one, assuming members were tithing, had the means to maintain the house of worship, the church grounds, and the adjoining church cemetery. Sales of burial plots within the church cemetery defrayed maintenance costs. Shrinking congregation sizes created a downward spiral accelerated by the adoption of cremation whereby the number of parishioners purchasing burial plots in the cemetery dried up. Without burial plot sales to defray the cemetery maintenance costs, the entire cemetery financial burden fell upon the now smaller congregation. Many of the church cemeteries I have inquired about have disconnected the cemetery from the church in the form of a separate entity, such as a trust, managed by a board of trustees. That ownership structure effectively removed the cemetery anchor from around the church congregation's neck, forcing the cemetery to stand on its own. How exactly is a cemetery expected to maintain itself without benefactors?

According to CremationAssociation.org, the percentage of deceased people being cremated in the United States increased to 51.6%, with ten states exceeding 70%. The five states with the lowest percentage of cremations were all located in the Deep South ranging between 22.5% and 33.1%. Wikipedia pegs cremations in America below 4% in 1960, so you can see just how far the cremation vs. burial pendulum has swung in less than sixty years. And the trend toward cremation seems to be growing unabated. Without worrying about what God thinks about it, not considering incinerated DNA as irretrievable, and not weighing the significance of future generations desiring to visit the burial sites of their ancestors, it seems like the lowest cost alternative to get rid of the body. What was once a deeply sacred ritual of paying last respects has been minimized to simply a financial decision based primarily on saving money.

The thought process seems to be, if we burn Grandma up for only $1,000, we won't have to allocate money from our inheritance to pay for her burial. She's dead, so who cares what happens to her body, right? She doesn't need that body anymore. No dead body means no money wasted on a cemetery burial plot, transporting her body home from Florida on a plane, embalming, hair styling, makeup, casket, flowers, funeral director, funeral home, travel expenses for all her descendants, and headstone. We can put her money to better use than some unnecessary, old school, traditional Christian funeral and burial. Now that we've turned away from God, we needn't worry ourselves with how death ceremonies were customarily handled within a church environment.

If you went to church, there was a good chance at some point you would have acknowledged the presence of God. If you believed in God, and He was important to you, you would have continued to go to church. While attending church and believing in God, you would have witnessed and learned how the church handled death ceremonies, specifically burial. If you attended funerals and burials for fellow churchgoers, burial would have been the norm, and you would not have been open-minded to the idea of cremation regardless of cost savings. Cremation was not the way bodies of believers in God were laid to rest by fellow believers.

It should come as no surprise that burials in America have de-clined from greater than 96% to less than 48% during the past sixty years. To find the reason behind the shift from burial to crema-tion in America, Google and research people's religious beliefs as a percentage of the overall population. The shift to cremation as a growing percentage has not been happening due to a desire to save money. More people are choosing cremation because less people go to church and believe in God, so those people are indifferent due to ignorance of Christian ways and are therefore influenced by cost savings. Many outright reject God and could care less how believers handle the remains of their dead.

With church membership numbers declining, and church congregations detaching themselves from adjacent church cem-eteries, it comes as no surprise new churches avoid establishing an adjacent church cemetery in the first place. If you do want to be buried, and your church has no cemetery, or you aren't too sure about the future of your church cemetery, you have to look outside of your church to identify a place for your burial. More than likely, your town has a large cemetery where most people desiring to be buried can purchase burial plots. The big cemetery in your town is probably owned by a large corporation operating within the funeral services industry. You most likely won't have many, if any, choices because of laws pertaining to minimum financial reserve require-ments and perpetual care requirements imposed by state and local governments upon any new cemetery.

These laws suggested and pushed by lobbyists, while intended to do good, created barriers to entry, stifled competition, increased existing burial plot prices, and pushed even more people to choose cremation. Effectively, the big cemetery in town became the only game in town, so they then had the ability to increase prices. As prices increased, more people chose cremation. As the number of burial plot sales declined, the big cemetery had to raise prices even higher, because they had to divide their fixed annual costs by the smaller number of plots being sold. As the big cemeteries raised their prices on the fewer plots sold, the momentum toward cremation accelerated. No longer was burial simply a more expensive option, burial as an option ceased to exist for many people who simply couldn't afford today's burial industry pricing structure. Burial became a luxury purchase, which seems ludicrous really, but it did.

What happened to grabbing a shovel, digging a rectangular-shaped hole in the ground facing west to east, lowering the deceased loved one to the bottom of the hole feet toward the east, shoveling the dirt back into the hole on top of the body, placing flowers, and installing a headstone? I'm sorry, but digging a hole isn't rocket science. Assuming a five-acre parcel of land on the outskirts of town costs $50,000 and at 3' x 9', there's plenty of room for more than 1,000 burial spaces per acre—the math equates to about $10 per burial space.

The dozens of church cemeteries I've visited do not have paved service roads, in case you're thinking about upfront costs required to establish a cemetery. I purchased an etched granite grave marker for $225 for an ancestor's grave. It was nothing elaborate, but it looked respectable, it's not going to blow away, and it'll be legible 1,000 years from now.

I inquired about purchasing burial spaces at two different for-profit cemeteries, and they each quoted $25,000 per space. That's $50,000 for two spaces—one for me and one for my wife, to be buried side by side! Oh, but that price included a headstone. Caskets would be extra. I thought to myself, *There ain't no way I'm gonna spend fifty-thousand dollars for two burial spaces. That just seems ridiculous to me.* The salesmen could sense my exasperation and tried to close me with pointing out the peace-of-mind that comes with perpetual care. One salesman held firm while the other called back to let me know they could do it for half price. I hadn't anticipated being prepared to haggle.

At the other end of the cemetery burial plot cost spectrum, I helped my mom select a place to bury her husband. He hadn't made the effort to handle his funeral planning responsibilities during his lifespan, including the eight years prior to his death when he should have been well-aware his passing was imminent. I know that last sentence sounds candid and harsh, but unfortunately, it's the truth for, I would bet, a majority of the deceased. He never came to grips with his mortality. He died without a plan, and he dumped the responsibility on his survivors. This mentality is another reason why cremations are outpacing burials.

We didn't know where to bury him, he left the burden of the expense to us, and we had no more than forty-eight hours to secure a spot. Not knowing where to start, the funeral director suggested three local cemetery options. The large for-profit perpetual care cemetery prices were hard to swallow, but another cemetery in town offered spaces for only $600 each. The funeral director made arrangements for my mom and I to meet the cemetery ambassador at the cemetery.

Arriving at the cemetery, situated on the crest of a hill abutting a well-traveled local street, we found the grounds to be in satisfactory condition with an overall good first impression. Scanning the graveyard, we observed evidence of recent burials along the very back row parallel to a fence separating the cemetery from a junkyard. The junkyard was out of sight behind the fence unless standing at or near the last row of plots. Other recent digs adorned with fresh flowers were located at the north end of the cemetery where the hill sloped steadily steeper down to the adjoining homeowner's property line. The adjacent property wasn't unsightly, but the slope concerned me, taking into consideration water runoff and erosion.

A car pulled up as we were standing near the center of the cemetery discussing how that particular area seemed to offer the optimal vantage point. A man and woman got out of the car. After exchanging greetings and confirming the roles of each party, it was determined the woman was a volunteer who looked after the cemetery. I pointed to a sizeable patch of grass devoid of headstones and asked if one of those spaces was available. She produced a rolled-up scroll of thin yellowing paper, opened what was essentially a cemetery map on the hood of the car, and we learned the cemetery and that map had been around more than 125 years.

The cemetery map was drawn as a group of squares, with each square representing an area the size of eight grave spaces. In the middle of each square was written the family surname of the person who had originally purchased those eight graves back around the year 1900. Inside each square were up to eight rectangular-shaped areas representing an occupied grave with the name of the interred scribed within the rectangle. Some of the squares only had two used rectangles within them, which is why certain physical areas of sod had no protruding monuments.

"How about this rectangle within this square here?" I asked. She informed us that the owners of that square, and others with unutilized grave spaces, had long since died off, and it was virtually impossible to determine the legal owners of unused spaces within said squares. "So what spaces do you have available?" I asked. She turned around toward the fence along the junkyard and pointed to the freshly dug graves we had seen upon our arrival. I let her know that area wouldn't work for us. She then pointed to the sloping area at the north end, and I shared my concerns about that area as well. Looking at the scroll, she pointed to a spot up by the street and said she had a couple of spaces available there. With an open mind, I asked if she would take us to the exact spot. Walking to the spot and surveying the lay of the land, the location was acceptable, and we gave her a deposit. She took out a pencil and wrote my mother's husband's name on the 125-year-old piece of paper.

Back then, I didn't know, or care to ask, how exactly the maintenance of that cemetery was handled. Maybe it was perpetual care. Maybe it was a former church cemetery maintained by descendants of those buried there. Maybe it was a cemetery maintained by the city using tax payer funds. I do remember the lady was kind, respectful, helpful, and considerate. And she was voluntarily there of her own choosing without pay and probably little to no recognition. But what I most remember was that 125-year-old scroll, because I've never seen another one since.

News flash… We are not running out of land! Someone created an urban legend, probably someone in the cremation industry, leading people to believe a shortage of land exists. Hogwash. Not true. I have traveled all over the United States, and there are plenty of wide-open spaces, millions upon millions of acres, and there are abundant acres available to set aside for cemeteries. Are there densely populated areas where we'll need to drive 2 miles beyond the beltway to find inexpensive acres? Yes, of course. Drive to the outskirts of any major city, and you'll find plenty of perfect locations for cemeteries to respectfully lay to rest our loved ones without resorting to environmentally insensitive incineration of DNA-rich ancestor remains.

After building out my family tree to almost 300 years and visiting more than 150 ancestor gravesites, I have two unfulfillable voids in my ancestry heart. I cannot make a DNA connection with my dad, and I cannot make a burial site DNA connection visit with one of my great-grandmothers. My instinctive genealogical urges are unattainable, because these two of my ancestors chose cremation instead of burial. Their DNA was forever destroyed by fire and heat. There is no specific place to which I can travel in remembrance of these two people in order to get close to my DNA. And, even if I chose to expend the resources to exhume their remains to obtain DNA samples for a purpose of which is unknown and unnecessary today, their cremation makes that future option absolutely impossible to achieve.

When is the last time you witnessed a funeral procession? A motorcycle policeman leads the way, followed by the solemn hearse carrying the body-filled casket for the recently departed. Close behind the hearse is a motorcade comprised of countless vehicles transporting loved ones from the funeral home service to the cemetery and gravesite. All headlights burn brightly during the light of day, to signal their participation in the funeral procession. Out of respect, ALL other vehicles pull to the side of the road and stop. People halt what they are doing, stand, and face the procession. Men remove their hats as the procession passes.

Today, more than 50% of uninformed and indifferent next-of-kin say, "Burn 'em." Soon, the mortuary informs the next-of-kin the ashes are available for pickup. Sometimes, nobody ever shows up, and the small particleboard box containing the pulverized ashes in a plastic baggy sits on a shelf in a storeroom, unclaimed. Once the statutory period of storage expires, the ashes are quietly discarded, as per standard protocol, the dumpster. No need to pay for a burial plot. No need to pay for a casket. No need to pay for a funeral. No need to be inconvenienced to attend a funeral. No need to pay for travel expenses. Flowers aren't necessary. Heck, there isn't even a need to pay for a motorcycle escort. And, 100 years from now, there's no need for any pesky caring descendants to go searching for a headstone. That's right, they even avoided paying for a headstone.

Unless the trend changes, or you plan for your own burial, odds are better than 50% your distraught loved ones will choose the cheap route, put you in a cardboard box, and slide you into a furnace. Fifty percent and increasing. Think about that.

Visit a few ancestor cemeteries, and you'll soon form an opinion as to where you'd rather be buried as compared to the types of places where you would rather not. Some are better maintained. Some are less uniform. Some have above ground headstones, while some allow only ground-level bronze markers. Some have lush, green, manicured turf as compared to weed-choked ground cover lacking irrigation. Some cemeteries are maintained voluntarily by private individuals, while others benefit from professional oversight funded by perpetual care or government budgets. Throughout the country, the United States federal government provides National Cemeteries for the purpose of providing military veterans and their spouses free burial plots, free grave markers, and perpetual care. There are reasons why some cemeteries will look and feel comfortable to you, while other locations will not rank favorably in your perception.

Perpetual care is the new terminology that means the following: We're going to set aside some money in an endowment investment whereby, based on actuarial mathematic calculations, there should be sufficient financial resources held in reserve generating enough income to fund the future costs of maintaining this cemetery forever, in perpetuity. The methodology of perpetual care uses a percentage of burial plot sales dollars to replace the benevolent care provided by a loving church congregation or a budget line item for a cemetery maintained at the expense of taxpayers.

A quick Google search provided two a la carte perpetual care prices averaging $1,100, or $75 annually, inferring a projected annualized return on the perpetual care investment fund of 7% annually. It's a solid plan provided the investment funds realize 7% annual income. But even if estimated annual returns were reduced to 3.5% resulting in an upfront investment of $2,200 per grave, that figure is still a bargain considering funding grave care for a hundred years, a thousand years, forever.

Cemeteries essentially exist in a variety of sizes, locations, and conditions, with each uniquely decorated by burial art antiquities. Lines of demarcation vary from ornate boundary barriers with historic grand entrance gateways, simple chain-link fencing, or none whatsoever. Landscaping varies, too, from mature shade trees with canopy-suspending structural branches outstretched, or void of any plantings from corner to corner. Some have thousands of graves while others have no more than three. No two cemeteries are the same.

I have yet to select my burial site, but I plan to do so in the very near future, because I am keenly aware of the fact that life on Earth is fleeting, and my departure date is not of my control. While I am living, I will select a final resting place meeting my personal criteria.

1. The cemetery will have in place a reasonable expectation of perpetual care. I have witnessed what happens to a rural private cemetery when the last person to care is no longer able to physically maintain the premises. Nature takes over, returning the plot of once hallowed ground into a dense canopied thicket of trees, undergrowth, vines, thick layers of annual fallen leaves, and decaying fallen limbs. Close observation reveals bits and pieces of grave markers long since broken and scattered from their original locations by vandals and years of expanding tree trunks.

2. The cemetery will allow above ground headstones. I just have more to share with my descendants than will fit within the confines of a 24" x 12" flat-to-the-ground bronze plaque. Ground-level bronze markers are required by some cemeteries for the sole purpose of simplifying grounds maintenance. Mowers skim across the tops of graves without obstructions, and tedious trimming around stones is non-existent.

3. The cemetery will not allow trees to grow near my burial plot. While shade from a tree sounds like a wonderful idea, there are four reasons why trees in a cemetery are a bad idea. First, trees and limbs will eventually fall. They don't live forever, and wind events happen. A falling tree has the ability to crush or uproot a grave marker. Second, trees shed leaves, and leaves bury grave markers in sediment. Third, shade is a perfect environment for algae and lichen growth. Fourth, trees have roots. Roots reach out to the drip line. And roots expand in diameter over time, undermining the foundation of stones and ledgers.

4. As a believer in God, my preference is to be buried in a church-affiliated cemetery.

5. Like the graves of my ancestors, the feet end of my grave will face an easterly direction.

6. My preference is to be buried within a cemetery where one of my ancestor's DNA is interred.

7. As a military veteran, I haven't ruled out burial at a National Cemetery, maybe Sarasota.

Choose a burial site for your remains and one-of-a-kind DNA, or one will be chosen for you. Or, maybe not.

Chapter 16

RESCUING OLD PHOTOS

It's often said, "A picture is worth a thousand words." Whoever first shared those timeless words of wisdom fell short, because they should have said, "Be sure to label your treasured photos, or they'll go in the trash when you're dead." Call the oldest loved ones you know right now and make a date to visit them as quickly as possible to go through family photos. Photo by photo, we need to ask our elders, "Do you recognize this person?" Or maybe, "This photo is labeled Aunt Faye. Do you know Aunt Faye? Can you tell me why Aunt Faye is in Grandma's photo album?"

In a team effort, we all need to stop what we are doing and get our hands on the family photo albums—pull them from the closets, drawers, and boxes that entomb them, with the purpose of resurrecting the faces found there. It is critical you initiate this effort right now without delay, because the last person to recognize that face in the photo may not be capable of recalling the name tomorrow. When it comes to identifying faces in old photos, time is of the essence!

Unfortunately, there will never be a facial image associated with the names of millions upon millions of people who did have their likeness captured during their lifespan because

- the image was not sufficiently labeled with name(s), date, and place;
- the last person who can identify the image has died or suffered memory loss;
- the image has not been placed in front of the last person capable of identifying the face;
- the last image of a person was destroyed by fire, water, humidity, or other causes; and/or
- the last image of a person was thrown in the trash when cleaning out after a death.

All old photos need to be found, looked at, the faces identified, labeled with correctly spelled full names, digitized, shared with loved ones, and uploaded to the internet for others to find. Digitizing can be completed in several ways, but simply taking a photo of the old picture using your smartphone camera is sufficient. My experience with my iPhone camera has been that less light is better, and avoiding direct light sources from overhead is optimal to eliminate glare. Wherever I'm digitizing old photos, I look for a shaded area in a room where light is being cast upon the photo from only one direction. I back away from that one light source far enough to where a glare is not reflecting as a bright spot on the old photo when viewed on my iPhone screen.

I take most of my photos while down on my knees, crouched over the old photo, using my forearms and wrists as tripods to hold my smartphone steady above the old photo. All the while, the single light source is directly high, well out in front of me, typically a ceiling light. Two or more light sources will cast shadows across the old photo, resulting in a poor quality digitized reproduction of the original old photo. My mindset is, "If you're going through the effort, you may as well capture the best duplicate image possible."

Wanting the best duplicate images possible, I remind myself to focus, focus, focus! Once I have the photo in the optimal place to avoid glare and shadows, and I'm crouched down over the photo with my forearms and wrists touching the ground to steady my iPhone camera, I touch the screen to autofocus. I do this at various incremental height positions above the old photo so that I can get as close to the original physical photo and still obtain a sharp focus. I'm talking about maybe a quarter-inch incrementally up or down to find the optimal height where I can fit the entire image within the confines of my viewing screen and achieve sharp focus. Keep in mind digital cameras have the ability to zoom in, enabling the subject to fit exactly to the maximum dimensions of a camera viewing screen.

While I'm zooming in, sometimes I'll want to zoom in to a face, creating a portrait, seeing details as if I were a forensic photographer. Another key factor is to make sure my smart phone is flat level in relation to the surface holding the old photo, whether that's a counter top, table, or the floor. Otherwise, the image is skewed somewhat, or stretched, or fish-eyed.

Once I have my smartphone camera positioned exactly where I want it above the old photo, and the focus is sharp, I hold the image on my screen as steady as possible while moving my finger slowly to touch the camera button. I then compare my new digital photo with the original to confirm I have a quality duplicate.

Don't just look at the face. See the entire story going on in the photo. Better yet, get hold of a quality lighted magnifying glass to reveal details not achievable with the naked eye, regardless of 20/20 vision. The better the focus, the more fine details you can decipher.

As you travel back in time by way of old black and white images of ancestors, ask yourself the following questions:

- What is the setting? Studio, farm, pioneer homestead, outdoor activity?
- What is the occasion? Family portrait, birthday, Easter, Christmas, homecoming?
- Based on the person's age and known birth year, what year might this photo have been taken?
- What type of clothes are they wearing, and what might that tell you about this person?
- Challenge what you observe. Why is there no grass? Why is that ladder so tall? Is that a church building in the background? Why is he standing in what appears to be a machine shop?
- That necklace she's wearing. Was it her mother's? Where is that necklace now?

Once digitized, I share photos with others in several ways.

1. I text the photo to people I think might enjoy seeing it.

2. I email the photo to people who don't text.

3. I upload the photo to my family tree on Ancestry.com
   a. I click on the person's name in my family tree.
   b. I click on "Gallery" in the navigation bar below their name and relationship.
   c. On the right side of the Gallery page, I click on the "Add Media" button.
   d. In the drop-down menu, I click on "Upload Photos"

e. On the Upload Photos page, I click on the "Choose Files" button.

f. It can get a little tricky here, because you have to know where your photo files are located, but once you can see your photos, click on the photo, and then click on the "Upload" button. Or *drag and drop* the photo onto the Upload Photos page.

g. Once the photo uploads to Ancestry.com, you can give the photo a Title, Date, Place, and Description. This adds credibility to the photo.

h. Click the "Done" button.

i. The photo will now be displayed in the Gallery of photos.

j. Click on the photo to view it.

k. On the right side, there is an "Add" button. Using this Add button, you can link this photo to other people in your tree who are also in the photo. This is a great feature, because it displays the same photo for multiple people in your tree.

4. I upload the photo to Findagrave.com

a. Search for and select the Memorial for the person associated with the photo.

b. Click on "Add Photos" button.

c. Click on "Select Photos" button.

d. It can get a little tricky here, because you have to know where your photo files are located, but once you can see your photos, click on the photo, and then click on the "Upload" button. Or double click the photo.

e. Once the photo is uploaded, you can add a caption, then select a photo type.

I didn't immediately begin collecting family photos in earnest. The photo obsession sort of steadily grew on me, slowly gained momentum, picked up steam as my interest gained strength, but mostly because over time I was getting to know the deceased ancestors in my tree and becoming curious to know what they looked like. Seeing one ancestor for the first time was a thrill, seeing another was exhilarating, then another. Sometimes I would see a photo during my travels, sometimes I would find a photo in my own collections, sometimes I would find a photo on Ancestry.com, and sometimes a memorial on Findagrave.com would have a photo attached. Discovering the joy of finding a photo of an ancestor online, I decided to give back by participating in uploading photos to the internet, specifically to Ancestry.com and Findagrave.com.

Looking through my own cache of family photos, I came to the realization I hadn't really cared much about the posterity of any of my ancestors beyond my grandparents. The oldest photos I found within my own home were those in my parents' wedding album. Turning the pages, I recognized profile views of my great-grandparents signing the guest book in one photo, and a very young version of my paternal grandmother with some guy I didn't recognize. That young guy would later be determined to be her brother, my Great-uncle James Haynes, who looked then absolutely nothing like he looked when I had seen him maybe three random times during my teens, twenties, and thirties.

In addition to the one aging wedding album, I did have some digital photos I had taken of old photos I had found in my maternal grandmother's photo albums while searching for photos of her at various ages for her funeral collage.

I got my first true taste of old photos of ancestors during my first road trip to honor my DNA. Toward the end of the first day, my great-aunt gave me a small framed photo of my paternal grandfather, her brother, in which he appeared to be maybe thirteen years old wearing a dress shirt and tie. The old frame was really cool! His mother, my great-grandmother, had kept this photo on a table in her bedroom until she died at ninety-nine years old. My great-aunt had taken it from her mother's bedroom and felt I should have it considering my interest in the family tree.

Circa 1935:
My grandfather as a boy.

A few weeks later, at my maternal grandfather's house, he showed me photos framed on his living room wall and said they were his maternal grandparents. On my second major ancestry road trip adventure, I happened to meet a man related to one of my great-great-grandmothers. That man shared with me a photo of his grandfather, who was the brother of my great-great-grandmother. To me, the seemingly irrelevant man in the old photo was now my 3rd great-uncle.

Traveling by way of a quick flight to Atlanta and a rental car to the assisted living facility where she lived near Athens, GA, I made an effort to visit my paternal grandmother as often as possible. Spending time with her was important to me, because I loved her deeply and knew she felt the same toward me. The excuse "I don't have time" falls on deaf ears with me, because a single day can be carved out of anyone's busy schedule. A 6 a.m. flight in the morning, drive time between the Atlanta airport and Athens, and a 7 p.m. flight that same evening afforded me five priceless hours and lunch with my grandmother. At ninety-five years old, painfully, I was aware my days of opportunity were dwindling.

Visiting with Nanny in Athens, GA to label old family photos.

On one such trip, after having built out my family tree fairly well, we were sitting together talking, and I asked my grandmother if she had any photo albums here in her apartment. She said she had a few, but she wasn't sure what happened to all her photos. When she and my grandfather left their home to move into assisted living, they only took what could fit in the trunk of a car, not fully comprehending they would never return to their home filled with seventy years of marriage accumulation. Pointing toward the TV stand, she said the albums she had were there.

I got up and took the three steps to the TV stand, knelt, and carefully removed a few old binders stacked beneath movie CD cases and knickknacks. I had always enjoyed looking at photo albums, but this time was different, because I had acquired an appreciation for and familiarity with the names previously discussed around me. I had heard the names, but sadly those names at those times were not significant enough to me to be worthy of sincerely paying attention. Without an organized documented family tree, I couldn't see, and didn't care to see, where each name fit within the order of things. When you one day see a written report scoring the DNA you share in common with these once insignificant people, they and their stories quickly become important.

Opening the first of four photo albums, I was thrilled to see old black and white photos.

Trae: Who are these people, Nanny?

Nanny: Those are my grandparents. Charles Branson Self and Eleanor Eliza Jarratt. They were my mama's parents. She was a Self. That's where I got my middle name. He and my daddy ran a boiler shop business together in Samoset. She was a bit uppity and better than other people, because she was a Jarratt, and they came from big money, once owning large plantations here in Georgia.

The photo looked like it was taken in the 1940s based on my great-great-grandparents appearing to be in their seven-

2nd greats Eleanor Eliza Jarratt Self and Charles Branson Self.

ties. It was a quality picture, in excellent condition, providing me with clear images to attach to their online memorials as primary headshots. Next there were pictures of me being held by my parents when they were twenty to twenty-two years old.

Trae: Who are these two guys?

Nanny: Oh, that's Papa's Uncle Jimmy and Uncle Johnny, Grandma's brothers. They ran a tile business in Houston, and Papa went to work for them when he was about seventeen years old in the late 1930s. Uncle Jimmy died a young man, but Grandma always said she thought his wife killed him and covered it up. That woman was nuts. They put her in an asylum. They had a boy. We visited him, but I'm not sure whatever happened to him. Uncle Johnny was a really nice man. Oh, that picture there is Uncle Johnny and his wife Gladys. They couldn't have children, so they adopted two girls and then Gladys got pregnant with a third daughter. That's a picture of Grandma Smith with Johnny and Gladys' two daughters."

Trae: Who are these people?

Nanny: That's my mom and dad when they came out to California to visit us when Papa was still in the Navy and your daddy was a baby.

Trae: Is that you, Nanny?

Nanny: Yeah, that's me.

Trae: Nanny, you're taking a selfie there. You may have invented the selfie back in 1940. Who is this girl?

Nanny: That's Papa's mama.

Trae: That's Grandma McKamey?

Nanny: Yeah, that's her.

Flipping the photo over, written on the back in my grandmother's handwriting was a detailed description of my great-grandmother, including her name, birthday, the names of her children, etc. She was born in 1907, and the girl appeared to be about twelve years old, so the photo was taken around 1919. Two

My great-grandmother, Lydia Louvinnie Anderson, at twelve years old.

years later, the girl would be married, and a year after that, she would give birth to my grandfather. I knew her as my great-grandmother in her eighties and nineties, but here she was at twelve years old. Un-freaking-believable.

For an hour or two, my grandmother and I talked about old photos and reminisced about her life from childhood to mother-hood, the photos serving as a reason to recall the past and share stories. It was then I realized I was here for a higher purpose. I was guided here to honor my DNA, to become the next protector, the next ambassador, of these family images, memories, and stories, just as my grandmother had been given the same task many years before this day. Somehow, these very old photos had been transferred to her care, and without speaking of it, she and I both knew my turn to take the baton was near.

Then I got an idea. I thought to myself, I need to purposefully seek out old family photos and label them while there are still people alive who can tell me the names and stories of the people captured long ago in black and white. Thinking about where I might find old family photos of my ancestors and who was still alive to possibly recognize faces, I came up with three places. First, my ninety-two-year-old maternal grandfather had photos at his house. Second, his mother, my great-grandmother, had lived with his sister, so any old photos in my great-grandmother's possession when she died would have been found by her daughter, my Great-aunt Caroline. Aunt Caroline had passed away a few years prior, so maybe Great-grandma's final belongings would still be there at Aunt Caroline's house. If I could find any old photos, I could get them in front of my grandfather, and maybe he would recognize the faces. Third, my paternal grandfather still had one living sister and one living half-sister. Between the two of them, maybe they had their mother's photo albums, and maybe they could identify the faces in those photos.

My spiritual journey continued, guided along by unexplainable circumstances and sequences of events, as unlikely as the path of a solar eclipse casting its shadow upon the United States from coast to coast. It had been more than ninety-nine years since a solar eclipse had traveled across the contiguous states beginning in Oregon and exiting across Florida. It had been more than thirty-eight years since the last time the sun was blotted out by the moon visible anywhere within the continental United States. As someone drawn to all things unique and interesting, such as astronomy and Einstein's Theory of Relativity, I was willing to travel wherever necessary to view this once in a lifetime opportunity.

Pulling up on my computer screen via the internet a map of the solar eclipse shadow band, my eyes were drawn due north from Florida to where the eclipse would cross the United States nearest to my home. Anderson, SC was near dead center of the eclipse, and I thought if you're going to travel to see an eclipse, why not position yourself right smack dab in the middle of it? And there was zero doubt I was going. As I zoomed-in to Anderson, SC on the Google map, a familiar name, just to the east, stood out to me. It was the town of Belton, SC, the hometown of my Great-aunt Caroline and the location of her home where my maternal grandfather's mother's final belongings might be found. None of what was happening to me was coincidence.

On our way driving north to Belton, SC, we detoured west at Atlanta to visit two ancestor cemeteries; then east to spend a few hours with our Nanny; then NE to Abbeville, SC to visit two of Nanny's ancestors' gravesites, one of which was Revolutionary War Patriot Samuel Cross; then to Belton. Aunt Caroline's husband and one of her daughters met us in the front yard as we rolled to a stop, eager to fix our eyes upon whatever they were able to find for us to peruse. Her daughter led us to a closet shelf area at the center of the home and retrieved a plastic bin while explaining she was not able to find any family Bible. I had hoped maybe my great-grandmother had had possession of the Helms and/or Bass family Bibles, possibly containing a handwritten family tree including the names of 2nd Great-grandpa J. Cyrus Helms' parents and 2nd Great-grandma Amanda Louise Bass Helms' parents.

My daughter hollered from across the room at the front door, "Come look at this praying mantis! It's eating a live wasp!" Although totally unrelated to the ancestry adventure we were on, I have to admit the praying mantis eating the wasp was pretty cool.

Moving to a large table, I opened the bin and inside were my great-grandmother's final possessions. Photo albums, scrapbooks, handkerchiefs, and my great-grandfather's driver's license. I carefully went through each and every item of significance to her, searching for clues that might help me learn more about her family, my family. I took digital photos of everything I had found with the intent of delivering the images to my grandfather hoping maybe he could identify the young faces in the old photographs. Hugging and thanking, we left the home in Belton to drive the couple of miles north to the open field of a church where the center line of the solar eclipse ran through it. The eclipse, the plastic bin containing my great-grandmother's keepsakes, the four cemeteries, a visit with our Nanny, just one of many trips of a lifetime during the first months of my quest to honor my DNA.

As I mentioned earlier, my grandfather, Gigi, was dying, so I literally had no time to waste. I enlarged each photo of his mother's final possessions, printed them on 8.5" x 11" paper, inserted them into a three-ring binder, and drove seven-and-a-half hours to present them to my grandfather. He was there, as always, in his electric-powered reclining chair, but his condition had worsened. His legs were now dark and swollen, his left hand and fingers enlarged like an inflated balloon, his breathing labored. Handing him the binder of large photos, I explained to him how I had obtained them and asked if he could recognize any of the people. Turning to the first photo, he adjusted the page while tilting his head up slightly to bring the image into focus with his eyeglasses. His brain engaged, and he began to talk.

Aunt Janie Helms Smith and Uncle Norman Smith

"That's Aunt Janie and Uncle Norman. And that's Uncle Norman in front of that tractor. He had a big heavy equipment operation around Lake Okeechobee during the Depression."

Some faces he recognized. Others he thought "might" be a certain person. Unfortunately, he stared at some faces trying to recall, but just didn't know who they were. For those people, I was too late. At ninety-two, Gigi was the last person alive who could recognize the faces. His mom knew who they were, or they wouldn't have been in her photo albums and scrapbooks, but she had died fifteen years ago in 2002.

I was a grown man in 2002, but it never crossed my mind to go visit my great-grandmother in South Carolina to go through her photos with her. And what about all the other adults descended from her? Not one of us took an interest in her photos while she was alive, to the point where we cared to ask her who the people were, or why they were important to her. I'm sure she would have loved for that to have happened, for someone to have labeled the photos with her. I guess we all just took it for granted that someone else would do it, or someone else would remember.

I had been through my Muffy and Gigi's photo albums over the years, but this visit took on a whole new level of urgency, aware that this may be my last opportunity to ask my grandfather to identify the photos, so I could put names, places, and dates with the faces. My grandmother, Muffy, had done a great job labeling photos, but there were still some without helpful identifications attached. Muffy had died two years ago, so it was just me and Gigi sitting on the couch turning pages and talking about each unlabeled photo.

Gigi had been an Army soldier on the front lines of Europe during World War II, so I paid close attention to his words when he shared the names of fellow soldiers like Lt. Homer E. Burgraff and Lloyd E. Burr. I haven't been able to find these two men from the 79th Infantry Division, so if their names ring a bell with you, please let me know because I have a photo of them in uniform in Europe.

Lloyd E. Burr, Lt. Homer E. Burgraff, Esly Paul Surgnier

One photo stood out among the rest, because it was a young man in a Navy uniform.

Trae: Who is this guy, Gigi?

Gigi: Oh, that's Robert Kline. When I was wounded in the shoulder at Cherbourg, France, I sat on the beach for four days waiting to be seen by a surgeon. There were countless guys worse off than I was, and they just kept bringing an endless stream of more wounded men to the field hospital. My wound got infected, so they put us on boats to transport us across the English Channel back to England. We departed at night, to avoid German planes and subs, but they still sank two ships next to us, and we had to help pull survivors out of the water. They were all covered in oil. Anyway, I was in the chow line on the ship, and I heard a familiar voice. I thought to myself, what in the world? By the time I got close to the serving line, I recognized the voice. When I reached to get my plate, I leaned down to look through the hole where he was serving food and said to him, Boy what are you doin here? It was Robert Kline, a boy I knew from back in Bradenton. He took me back to his room, and we talked, and he gave me some of his candy. I don't know what ever happened to him.

Being a Navy veteran myself, I searched for a Robert Kline, so I could share the photo, but Robert Kline is a popular name with various spellings such as Kline, Klyne, Klein, Clyne, Cline, and so on. About fifteen months after Gigi died, I was watching a videotaped interview he had done for my mom, and in that interview, Gigi told the story about Robert Kline. I listened closely and heard Gigi say Robert was a classmate of his at Bradenton High School. Knowing Robert Kline was in high school with my grandfather, I used his birth year as Robert's birth year to search online for a Robert Kline born in Florida around 1925. I found a good lead for a Robert Kline who was born in Arkansas in 1926 and lived in Bradenton, FL. I knew I had found him when I pulled up a Findagrave.com memorial for a Robert Kline, born 1926, buried at Sarasota National Cemetery, and saw a white marble veteran headstone inscribed ROBERT C. KLINE, CSG2, US NAVY, WWII. The description included the following: He served in the U.S. Navy from December 1942 through September 1949. He was assigned to the LST-288 and was in the invasion of Normandy on D Day. He was a cook on the ship, and it transported troops from England to France and then the wounded back to England.

Having finally found the Robert Kline who was the Navy cook in my grandfather's story and his WWII photo album, I uploaded the photo of Robert Kline in his Navy uniform to his Memorial on Findagrave.com to share with his family.

Robert Kline in Navy uniform

I don't remember if it was Gigi or my mom, but someone suggested I call my grandmother Muffy's brother, Uncle Billy. So, I called him, and we talked all about his family, including his dad, who was my great-grandfather. I few days later, a yellow manila envelope arrived in my mailbox addressed from Uncle Billy. Inside, I found copies of family tree documents my grandmother Muffy had given to him years ago, and photos of his dad, my great-grandfather, in a World War II flight jacket. *Oh, my goodness!* I thought to myself. *He really did Fly the Hump in World War II.* It was while looking at those photos I realized I had not two, but three grandfathers who fought in World War II. How many people can say that?

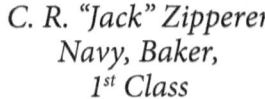

C. R. "Jack" Zipperer
Navy, Baker,
1ˢᵗ Class

W. Raymond
"Ray" Mathis
Army, Pilot, Flying Sgt.

E. Paul "Gigi" Surgnier
Army, Infantry,
Platoon Sgt.

I called Uncle Billy to thank him, and he invited me to come visit him any time. That was a mistake on his part, because I hopped in my truck a few days later and away I went to go through my great-uncle Billy's photo albums and hear his family stories.

I called the daughter of my paternal grandfather's sister and asked if she and her mother would be willing to allow me to come visit with them to look through any old family photos they may have in their possession. She asked her mom, and both agreed. Another cousin interested in family history said he would like to join in, so I picked him up along my route to central Florida. He and I shared genealogy research experiences as the miles faded behind us. Pulling into the sandy driveway shaded by 100-year-old oaks, we walked toward the wood-frame house and entered to the warmth of welcoming greetings, smiles, hugs, and smells of good Southern cooking emanating from the kitchen. On the dining table were stacked numerous photo albums. Some were my great-aunt's, some were my great-grandmother's, and some were my great-great-grandmother's. All had been passed down by successive generations to assemble for this gathering of four people sitting around a dining room table, four people who shared a large percentage of DNA as measured by recent test results. For the next several hours, well beyond sunset, we viewed photos, listened to stories, discussed situations, and digitized dozens of priceless notes and images. And, we texted a few of the best photos to Aunt Cordia. Within a few minutes, a text came back from Aunt Cordia containing a 106-year-old family photo from 1911. That photo blew my mind.

Elijah Newton "Lige" Anderson Family

The entire photo blew my mind, but there was one person out of the six looking back at me who I never expected to see. While studying census records, I had discovered my great-grandmother had an older sister, Alcy, and Alcy had died at seven years old in 1912 when my great-grandmother was five. I found her burial site near Brooker, FL. I added her to the family tree. I linked her Findagrave. com Memorial to her mom and dad. And, I took over as manager for her Memorial. My paternal grandfather, my great-grandmother, nobody had ever mentioned my grandfather having an aunt who died at seven. Alcy was my 2nd great-aunt, and she was alive and well on the left side of that photo taken in 1911.

Trae: Where did you get that photo, Aunt Cordia?

Cordia: I took it off Mama's dresser when I came to attend her funeral. It's hanging on the wall in my dining room.

Trae: Do you have any more old family photos?

Cordia: I have some you may be interested in seeing.

Trae: Can I come to your house in Georgia?

Cordia: Sure. When do you want to come up here?

Then my uncle texted me an old, blurry grainy photo of four generations of Zipperers including my dad, my grandfather, my great-grandfather, and my great-great-grandfather.

Trae: Okay, dude, where did you find that!?

Uncle: I was looking through some paperwork in Nanny's filing cabinet and found an envelope with a few old photos in it. Want to see some more?

Trae: Heck yes, I want to see more.

In addition to the envelope containing old photos, my uncle had found the boxes labeled "family photos" at the rented storage unit. He had packed some photos from Nanny and Papa's house when he brought them from Texas to live at the assisted living facility in Georgia. He wasn't sure what all he grabbed as far as pictures were concerned, but I was welcome to come up to his house near

Nanny to go through them. With two newly discovered caches of old family photos east of Atlanta, within 20 miles of one another, I had found another good excuse for an ancestry adventure road trip.

By now, you may be wondering how I found the time and money to partake in such adventures. In summary, if something is important to you, and you sense the urgency, adventures will move up your list of priorities to where you'll make time and find the money to travel. And isn't life about seeking out adventures and experiencing them? Isn't life about choosing to maximize the value of your limited presence on Earth to create lifelong memories? Isn't each day precious and perishable? Will you wait until your grandmother dies to get around to it? Will you wait until the old family photo treasures have already been thrown away, or destroyed by a leaky roof, or consumed by a natural disaster? There is no guarantee of tomorrow, so if not now, then when?

The more time and effort I invested into honoring my DNA, the more I appreciated new discoveries. The puzzle picture of my life's history began to take shape and continued to become clearer with each piece I put my hands on and inserted into its proper place. Like working a puzzle on a table, the farther along I got, the more familiar I became with the pieces, the easier it was to recognize where pieces fit.

Aunt Cordia's house was closest to the Atlanta airport as compared to my uncle's house, so she was my first stop. She was actually my great-aunt, my half great-aunt, my grandfather's youngest sister, a product of his mother's second marriage. I had heard her name my entire life, but as important a piece in my life's puzzle as she was, until this point, I had not yet recognized where she fit. It was the 1911 Anderson family photo she had shared that brought her puzzle piece to the forefront. Until that instant, it had not clicked with me that Aunt Cordia was my great-grandmother's daughter, that my great-grandmother was her mama. As my great-grandmother's daughter, Aunt Cordia had every right to take that Anderson family photo from atop her mama's bedroom dresser after her mother had passed away. Just like I know my mama well, Aunt Cordia knew her mama well, which meant she could tell me with first-hand knowledge all about my great-grandmother.

My great-grandmother had sisters and brothers, who from my perspective were distant, but for Aunt Cordia, those people were her aunts and uncles. My great-grandmother would have spoken of her siblings around Cordia, and Aunt Cordia would have taken notice during conversations, interactions, and recollections.

You have to seek out the Aunt Cordias in your family tree. They are out there, but they aren't pinging a signal alerting you to their presence. Seek and ye shall find. Unbeknownst to me, Aunt Cordia had become interested in genealogy many years before my interest awoke. Which was fortuitous for me, because she had way more to offer than an old photo in an album or frame. She had a family tree. She had photos. She had documents. She had stories. She had the knowledge and capabilities to interact with me while working on family tree mysteries as a team effort. We could look at an old photo together with a better chance of identifying faces, using process of elimination to conclude the only plausible identity for the one face not known.

Hugging Aunt Cordia's neck, it was getting late in the day and my Nanny was waiting for me at my uncle's house. With my new discoveries from Aunt Cordia's house dancing in my head, I covered the 20 miles in what seemed like a blink of an eye. Arriving at my uncle's house, there were boxes next to the breakfast room table in the well-lit alcove. In the boxes were a few familiar photo albums, but most of what was there was new to me. Having traveled here for this purpose, I sat down at the table with Nanny and reached for the first of many albums, envelopes, binders, and boxes holding pictures she had come into possession of over the course of her ninety-six years.

Much of what was there were images taken during my lifetime, but what I was in search of were the faces only Nanny could identify. As the oldest surviving member of her clan, having been born in 1922, she was the last person living who actually knew my great-great-grandparents, could recognize them, and tell stories about them. Amazingly, she even told me about my 3rd great-grandfather, Joseph Wheeler Dansby, who was born in 1852 and died when my Nanny was twelve years old. You can imagine what it was like to hear my grandmother tell me first-hand recollections about a man born 166 years ago whose DNA lives within me today.

The old photos were important to identify, but something less tangible and much more significant was taking place. I didn't know it at the time, but my Nanny was making herself available to me this day, for this project, because she knew from experience what I was about to go through when she left for Heaven. Turning over hundreds of photos, one at a time she told me the names of every face, shared the stories behind each photo, and provided clues that would help me fit together the pieces of my puzzle. At one point, while listening to one of her stories, I opened the Voice Memos app on my phone and tapped the record button. She talked and I encouraged her along. From another room in the house my uncle tuned into what was happening and without knowing I was recording her, he brought his phone to the table and began recording. Some of the stories I'd heard before, while others were new to me.

Nanny shared her stories about the following:

- Spending summers with her grandparents.
- Walking the bull to the dipping vat.
- The first time she saw Papa in the school yard when they were fourteen years old.

- Peddling a bike to town for their date with Papa riding on the handlebars.
- Working the drugstore counter as a soda jerk.
- Being a welder during World War II.
- The day her brother was killed during World War II.
- Not seeing Papa for four years while he served in the Navy throughout the Pacific.
- Catching grunions on the beach in Oceanside, CA.
- Papa accepting Jesus during a men's group meeting at church.
- Getting married to Papa.
- How children in California thought Papa was Roy Rogers.

As we went along, during short breaks in the action, I would take several old photos to the spot I had found in the room on the floor where only a single, indirect light source dimly lit the photo. Crouching down into my smartphone tripod stance, hovering the camera level just above the old photo to achieve sharp focus, I touched the red button, snapping a digitized duplicate image. Accessing the name in my Ancestry.com family tree matching the person in each photo, I added the images to each person's Gallery, making my contribution to the giant team effort photo album accessible to everyone via the internet cloud. Knowing how excited I was on the receiving end to see photos others had uploaded, I found even greater happiness to be on the giving end. Envisioning how excited someone would be to see this image for the first time, it felt good to share with all those distant relatives I'd never met who cared about this same ancestor, but who would never have been able to peek inside my grandmother's photo albums.

And like with so many other things in life, the more I gave, the more I got. When I posted photos, or stories, or notes, or documents to my ancestors in my family tree on Ancestry.com, other people found them, and linked them to the same person in their respective family trees. One step further, Ancestry.com enabled me to communicate with other members via messaging. I just clicked on the other member's username, and a message screen popped up where I could send them a note.

One such note popped up on my screen one day from a Tim Parramore thanking me for a story I had written and shared via Ancestry.com pertaining to a grandfather from the 1800s we shared in common. Turned out he knew my mother during their childhoods and had some photos his father had taken back in the 1950s. He sent me a link containing the most amazing, candid, incredible color photos of my mom's family we had ever seen. What made them so special, so candid, was that they were taken by a trusted third party who captured them as they were in relaxed everyday settings distinct from the common snapshots staged with forced smiles at a Thanksgiving dinner table. The amateur photographer was my grandmother Muffy's cousin. The two of them had grown up together, essentially raised as siblings.

He took that film roll home, had it processed, had prints made, and stuck them in a family album never viewed by the four members of my mother's immediate family. That was until sixty years later when Tim read my story, figured out who my mother was, recalled his childhood visits to Florida, remembered the color photos, and initiated contact with me. My mom said viewing the photos changed her life.

Among the photos Tim shared with me were several featuring members of my grandmother Muffy's mother (my great-grandmother), Pearl, and Pearl's siblings who would have been my Muffy's aunts and uncles. I had never heard of these relatives, except for Pearl's sister, Carrie, but I did have them listed in the family tree I was building. I had been working with Y-DNA and had reached a dead end with my 3rd great-grandfather, James I. Mims, so I got the idea to seek out a male descended from James I. Mims to obtain a Y-DNA sample. Using Y-DNA matches, it would be possible for me to find a living Mims male with a better Mims family tree than I had put together, where maybe they had documented the parents of ancestor James I. Mims.

My Great-grandmother Pearl had one brother, William Mims, and I now had a photo of him with his three sisters, including Pearl. In another photo, I saw William Mims standing with a woman and a young boy maybe fourteen years old. In the photo, William Mims and the woman appeared older. With a little bit of research, I was able to determine William Mims and his wife did have a son together when he was thirty-nine and she was thirty-two, making them fifty-three and forty-six in the photo, where the boy appeared to be fourteen. Actually, I initially thought the boy looked like maybe nine years old, making his parents in the photo look more like his grandparents.

2nd Great-uncle Willie Mims and his son. Both carried Y-DNA passed down by James I. Mims.

Eventually I found the name of the fourteen-year-old Mims boy. I hoped maybe he was still alive. If so, I could contact him, and maybe he would agree to do a Y-DNA test for me, so I could research the Mims paternal line. Unfortunately, I discovered he had passed away several years ago. However, I did locate his obituary, which listed the names of two sons and the cities where they lived. Searching their names in their local county's property appraiser's office, I found a homesteaded property in one of the son's names, which signified the address was his primary residence. So, I wrote him a letter explaining why I was reaching out to him, how we were related, and inserted a copy of the story I wrote about our common ancestor James I. Mims. Then, I waited.

I had written the letter to Larry Mims, but when the call came in a few days later, it was Barry Mims on the line. Barry told me his brother Larry had received my letter, but he wasn't much interested in family tree stuff, so his brother gave the letter to him. Barry was intrigued by what I had put together about the Mims family and wanted to know more about the Y-DNA testing I was seeking to do. Barry had a very strong Southern accent and joked about how Siri on an iPhone was useless for him, because she couldn't understand a thing he said. Then he said something in that familiar-to-me Southern accent dialect that twisted my mind.

Barry: So, Aint Pearl was your great-gramaw?

Trae: Did you just refer to my great-grandmother as Aunt Pearl?

Barry: Sure. Why wouldn't I?

Trae: Barry, did you know my great-grandmother?

Barry: Why sure I knew Aint Pearl. Her and Uncle Sandy. She was a sweet old lady. Took me shoppin' and always kept me real close to her like someone was gonna steal me. And, she would always slip money to me.

A few days later, I met Barry at a local Cracker Barrel for lunch, as he was driving through my area on business. Watching him step out of his truck and walk toward me, it was surreal to see this tall stranger smiling at me with body language of unconditional family. Technically, we were 2nd cousins 1x removed, but we may as well have been brothers based on his sincerity. I had the sampler with Diet Coke, and he had the catfish with iced tea. He told me about his dad, his business, his memories of Aint Pearl, and his Granddad Willie. Finishing lunch, I broached the subject of DNA testing and why his Y-DNA as a male Mims served a valuable purpose. Agreeing to help me with DNA testing, Barry said, "What do I need to do?" Just like that, never met him in my life, but he could sense it was important to me and stepped up without expectations of anything in return. It was easy to sense Barry was a genuinely good person, the kind who would give the shirt off his back, some spit in a tube, or a swab from the inside of his cheek. By the time his test results came back, I had already found the parents of James I. Mims, but it was really cool to see Barry pop up in my DNA matches on Ancestry. com. I'm proud to share DNA in common with him.

Then one night, I received a text from Barry with an old photo of my great-grandmother attached, and then another.

Trae: Barry, where did you find these photos?

Barry: I've got a whole bag of 'em.

On the back of one of the photos, I recognized my great-grandmother Pearl's handwriting from photos she had mailed to her daughter, my grandmother, Muffy. Somehow Barry had inherited my great-grandmother's family photos. Without hesitation, I made time in my schedule and drove the five hours to Barry's office. We went through the photos together, and it was Barry who introduced me to the idea of using a magnifying glass to see the finer details of each old black and white photo. Mel Fisher couldn't have been more excited diving on the Atocha compared to me sifting through these heirlooms that had been sealed up in a clear plastic Ziploc bag for thirty years. The old photos had been patiently waiting for me to

1. write that story about James I. Mims,

2. receive the message from Tim Parramore,

3. receive the color photos from Tim Parramore,

4. get the idea to seek Y-DNA from a living Mims male,

5. identify a fourteen-year-old boy from a photo taken in 1957,

6. find an obituary containing names: Larry and Barry Mims,

7. find Larry Mims in his local county appraiser's records,

8. write Larry Mims a letter,

9. receive a call from Barry Mims after his brother Larry Mims gave him my letter,

10. meet Barry Mims at Cracker Barrel,

11. receive a texted photo from Barry Mims,

12. recognize my great-grandmother's handwriting,

13. realize Barry had my great-grandmother's photo collection, and

14. be willing to drive five hours to see the photos for myself.

The images were incredible, but three stood out as truly great finds. One was a profile of my 2nd great-grandmother apparently staring out a hospital room window just days before she died. Another was of my 2nd great-grandmother in a group photo with her Tomberlin brothers. The other was determined to be the only known photo in existence of my 2nd great-grandfather, Norman M. Mims, who died in 1935.

2nd Great Lee Annie Tomberlin
Mims days before her death.

Priceless photos hidden away in closed, dust-covered albums, faded manila envelopes, taped-up cardboard boxes, or even in a sealed Ziploc plastic bag should be a thing of the past. Join the movement to find, identify, label, and digitize these troves of our interconnected human stories. The photo hanging on the wall in your dining room just might be an image of my 2nd great-grandmother.

Tell your oldest family members about this photo-sharing movement, and mark your calendar right now for the day you will set aside in the very near future to put your eyes and hands on the stashes of old photos that most likely contain irreplaceable images of your ancestors. Make it a group effort by inviting other family members to join you where the photos are housed. Look at the photos together. See if all agree, or one knows for sure, just who that is standing next to the 1924 Ford Model T. Listen to comments from around the table. Challenge one another. Use other photos known to be a specific person and compare them to group photos to possibly reveal an identity. Use process of elimination to narrow the list of suspects. And most importantly, have fun along this rewarding journey to see for the first time the faces of those who contributed to your DNA.

Lydia "Linnie" Louvinnie "Vinnie"
Anderson. Photo taken 1908.

Chapter 17

LOSING MY HERO

Uncle Major called with the news. My seven-and-a-half-month marathon effort to learn, discover, document, and share had reached its finish line. The old photos were labeled. The stories had been told. And the DNA test results were posted. Having fulfilled God's plan, Gigi had gone, gone to where heroes go, after having served as an example to the next generation. Men like Gigi who stepped into the breach between good and evil sometimes came out of the bloodletting alive, but they hadn't survived. Their bodies came home breathing, walking, talking, but who they were before entering the outskirts of hell's abyss had been sacrificed upon liberty's alter, irrecoverable, gone.

Humble, mild mannered, and never one to draw attention to what he had done, in 1994 I secretly communicated my intentions to my grandmother. It would soon be Gigi's seventieth birthday, and I wanted to honor him as my hero. As I had requested, she mailed to me a copy of Gigi's Form DD-214 military discharge papers and his vehicle registration. I carried the proof to my local county tax collector's office and bought him a Purple Heart vanity license plate issued by the State of Florida to put on his station wagon. For the next twenty-two years, patriotic people would pass him on the highway, honk their horns, smile, wave, and salute him. The honor plate displayed a single image of a Purple Heart medal awarded to United States military members who were wounded or killed during actions against enemy forces. It was the best I could do, but it only told half his story of combat wounds. My Gigi had earned two. He was a legend.

My grandfather, Esly Paul Surgnier, was born May 7, 1925 in Sulphur Springs, FL. His mama called him Esly. His daddy called him Sonny. As a young man, until his early forties, he was Paul. Around 1967, he became Gigi, because his first grandchild simply couldn't say Gampy. So, the name stuck, and for the rest of his life, he was Gigi.

Gigi was a storyteller. His mind was fantastic to the point where he could recall names like you couldn't believe. For example, if he told you the story about the man who drowned in Lake Okeechobee, he would include the man's name, the clothes he was wearing, his occupation, and the name of the company where he worked.

Two World Events Defined His Life:
The Great Depression and World War II

Today, we literally have no idea how bad it was during the Great Depression. We cannot begin to comprehend the hardships, but Gigi was our window into the past, and he could tell it so we could see it. One possession at a time, each item of value was sold, anticipating a financial rebound that unknowingly was not just over the horizon. First the car, then the bird dog, then the shotgun. At one point, the family of five with no car, no horse, no wagon, physically dragged everything they owned on top of a mattress more than a mile through the woods to reach the home of Aunt Thelma seeking shelter from the relentless poverty storm. Homeless and starving, his mother received a Penny Postcard from her sister, Janie Lee Helms Smith "Aunt Janie." The postcard read, "Tot (that's what her family called her), get your family ready, we're coming to get you." And they did. Aunt Janie and her husband had found work in the Everglades south of Lake Okeechobee. Gigi said it was like *Grapes of Wrath* with nine people piled in and on that old car, their prized mattress tied on top.

They lived in conditions unimaginable, worse than your wildest dreams. During the night, they would wake for mosquito killins. Wet rags were used to swat the bloodsuckers off the walls and ceilings. Above the family at night, while parents slept on the only mattress and children on the floor, rats scurried across the exposed wood trusses. A long yellow rat snake, to a Floridian a chicken snake, waited patiently in ambush, striking and quickly coiling round its rodent prey. Gravity, flopping, thud, the mortal throws of constricting asphyxiation fell onto the feet of Esly's mother below.

Transportation was by foot unless his daddy happened to drive home a company truck. No electricity. No running water. They had a shallow well that produced a colored smelly liquid not fit for drinking. His dad would carry jugs to the "fillin" station, that's what they called the gas station, and fill them with their drinking water. To scrape out a meager wage, his dad found work building the Herbert Hoover Dike around the lake and with the sugar company.

Possibly his fondest memory as a boy was awakening on Christmas morning to find the only substantial gift he recalls ever receiving. It was a 22-caliber rifle. He doesn't know how his daddy pulled it off, but it's possible he traded a few otter skins or softshell cooters with the merchant at the fillin station. Or maybe Gigi's prized calf intended for a 4-H project, but instead slaughtered to pay the family's grocery tab, had generated a sufficient surplus. Ammunition was cheap in those days. A young boy could walk into a store, pull a dime from his pocket, and walk away with a box of lethal rounds in either shorts or long rifle.

Gigi taught himself to shoot, becoming an expert marksman by lining up along the top of a wooden rail, small marbles the size of the tip of your finger. One by one, each glass sphere disintegrated in successive pulls of the trigger. He discovered how to align his rifle sights for elevation based on distance to his target and how to aim slightly to the right or left to compensate for windage. Soon he began putting meat on the table by substituting duck heads far in the distance and rabbit eyes glowing red in his light at night, for those marbles on the rail.

Life in the Everglades began at age seven and lasted nine years until age sixteen, when Gigi's daddy was able to get in front of the telephone company president in Tampa. Of course, Gigi would have included the company president's name in his version of the story. This life-changing opportunity arose because the sugar company allowed his dad to borrow a company truck to drive to Tampa for a "visit family" vacation, most likely to visit Uncle Henry Surgnier. The job created by the company president for Gigi's dad was in Bradenton. He said his dad felt guilty about accepting another job while using the company truck, but it was something he had to do for the family.

In the Everglades, and Bradenton, Gigi was an outdoorsman. He would pull a wagon for miles into the wilderness, or paddle a canoe he had made by hand well beyond the boundaries of civilization. He and his buddies would camp out, catch fish, shoot game, build shelters, and live off the land. Those were the olden days, when it was free range in Florida. There were no fences and a boy could explore as far as his legs and curiosity would take him in any direction. He depended on his rifle for what little spending money he knew during those hard times. Gigi rented a bean box at the local icehouse where he would store the wild rabbits he hunted at night, sometimes bagging twenty-six in a single outing. A buyer would stop by the icehouse, gather the cold rabbits, and leave ten cents a piece with the manager.

God has a plan for each of us. It was not happenstance a 22-rifle arrived on Christmas morning in the depths of the Great Depression to hone his self-taught rifleman skills to perfection on marbles, wild rabbits, and ducks. It was not by accident Gigi learned to survive in the woods. In hindsight, it is relatively clear, but he couldn't have known during those seemingly mundane outings how his life would soon depend on those specific skillsets.

Gigi began his senior year of high school in Bradenton, but it lasted only a few days. A letter arrived containing draft papers stating his country needed him more on the battlefield than in a classroom. He was just a boy of eighteen years. His dad met with the recruiting official and begged him to allow Esly to complete high school, but his request fell on deaf ears. His high school diploma would one day arrive, seventy years later, at age eighty-eight, direct from the State of Florida, in response to my personal request. What they did pulling those boys out of school, they should have sought him out. They should have sought them all out. But that's another story.

On August 25, 1943, Gigi was inducted into the United States Army at Camp Blanding just west of Jacksonville, FL. Watching him tell it through tears, of his attachment to his little sister Caroline and baby brother Perry, the pain of leaving them to go off to war, was heart-wrenching. Before he left home for the war, Gigi's grandmother, Amanda Louise Bass Helms, gave him a little Bible and told him if he went to church every chance he got, and read the Bible daily, God would bring him home safely. Army camps in Oklahoma and Kansas would provide him with basic military training, but nothing could prepare him for what lay ahead.

On April 7, 1944, Gigi boarded a ship in Boston, MA with the entire fighting force of the 79th Infantry Division, and others. He said it was one of the largest armadas ever to take to the seas. As far as the eye could see, countless numbers of ships filled with tens of thousands of men, war fighting equipment, and unimaginable quantities of supplies were sailing as one massive convoy, eastward, toward England. And my grandfather, Gigi, was among them.

He arrived in England on April 16, 1944. Like hundreds of thousands of other fighting men staging in the British Isles, the 79th began preparing for the imminent invasion of Europe. Within three weeks, Gigi's beloved grandmother would pass away on his nineteenth birthday: May 7, 1944. There was little time to mourn.

On June 6, 1944, Gigi would have received a copy of the following letter from General Dwight D. Eisenhower:

Soldiers, Sailors and Airmen of the Allied Expeditionary Force!

You are about to embark upon the Great Crusade, toward which we have striven these many months. The eyes of the world are upon you. The hopes and prayers of liberty loving people everywhere march with you.

Your task will not be an easy one. Your enemy is well trained, well equipped and battle-hardened. He will fight savagely.

The free men of the world are marching together to Victory! I have full confidence in your courage, devotion to duty and skill in battle. We will accept nothing less than full Victory!

Signed: Dwight D. Eisenhower

If you want to catch a glimpse of what it must have been like for Gigi, just watch the series *Band of Brothers*. I see so many of his stories play out on the screen in vivid detail just as he described to me in those few times he was willing to provide snippets of what he endured. Digging foxholes, potato mashers, bazookas, tank killers, mortars, artillery tree bursts, house-to-house combat, foraging for food, looting, reconnaissance patrols, and frozen ground. Gigi never once mentioned to me shooting a German soldier. Only once did he describe battle wounds, death, the dying, or the dead. But we knew the sharpness of his brain and his uncanny ability to recall even the finest of details. An enemy soldier's helmeted head at 300 yards, a duck's head on Lake Okeechobee. A lit cigarette in the distance at night, a rabbit's eye glowing bright. I'm certain he remembered every pull of the trigger, every traumatic instance, in vivid clarity.

The 79th Infantry Division crossed the English Channel and landed at Utah Beach on the Normandy coast of France on D-Day +6 (June 12-14, 1944). Remnants of the first five days of establishing a beachhead must have overwhelmed the senses of the now nineteen-year-old young man from the Everglades of Florida when Gigi stepped off the landing craft. As he looked around at his 219 brothers-in-arms of Company I, of the 3rd Battalion, of the 314th Regiment, he couldn't have known that only one of those 218 other men would be returning home with him when the carnage was over.

Within ten days, on June 23, 1944, he was in the thick of it, pinned down in front of a German re-enforced concrete defensive bunker known as a pillbox on the outskirts of Cherbourg, France. As the mortars and artillery shells rained down on Company I, the only cover Gigi found was a rock about the size of a loaf of bread. Lying prone, he took aim at the small open slits of the pillbox and fired round after round until his rifle burned red hot. He couldn't see any German soldiers, but he thought maybe his bullets would ricochet around in there and do some good. Then, an enemy mortar round landed and exploded just to his left. As he turned toward the blast, he saw his sergeant next to him killed by the explosion—guttural sounds, involuntary muscle contractions, reflexes. It was then he noticed the blood trickling, realizing shrapnel had entered his left shoulder.

Word was passed that it was every man for himself. Gigi recalled thinking behind that little rock in the open field, *How am I going to survive when I stand up?* In front of him were the German machine gunners. Behind him was a long, upward-sloping, wide-open field with a hedgerow at the top. He got rid of all his gear except for his rifle, his canteen, and a few rounds of ammunition in case he would happen to run into a sniper on the way back to base. He said an NFL running back had nothing on him when he took off up that hill crouched and zig-zagging, basic training technique, toward that hedgerow. He said, "Buddy, I could flat run!"

As he reached the hedgerow, maybe it was his grandmother's voice, but something drew his attention to a small hole at the base of the hedge. Instead of jumping the hedge, he dove for the gap. At that very instant, the top of the hedgerow was raked by machinegun fire as the German gunner had anticipated his leap. He covered the next 2 miles alone, walking the hedgerows, not knowing if an enemy rifleman had him in his sights.

Gigi was an outstanding soldier, as evidenced by his promotion up the ranks from Private to Technical Sergeant (or Platoon Sergeant), the top-ranking enlisted soldier (E-7) of 3rd Platoon, Company I, consisting of thirty-nine men. Keep in mind he was only nineteen years old and responsible for leading thirty-nine men into frontline combat on a daily basis. Gigi advanced through the ranks to E-7 at an astounding speed, achieving in seventeen months what takes on average seven to fifteen years. And, he was my grandfather.

What he saw, the life and death decisions he had to make, what he had to do. It's no wonder he couldn't sleep after the war. Not one, but two Purple Hearts, a Bronze Star, and a wallet that still has a piece of shrapnel lodged in it from an artillery shell that exploded in the trees above him, cutting his jacket to shreds. And yet, he still played army men with me on his back porch when I was a boy. That must have been so hard for him, but I had no idea.

Gigi Uniform Portrait

Gigi's Two Best Decisions: Accepting Jesus and Marrying Myrtle Ellen Mathis

I was fortunate enough to spend three days with Gigi a few weeks before he went to Heaven. I took him to his favorite barber shop for his last haircut, and it was wonderful to see him in that chair feeling like a man again, if only for a few minutes. But the trip to get his hair cut had a higher purpose. It was an opportunity for me to talk with my grandfather about Jesus. I asked him if he believed in Jesus. He responded, "Yes." He shared with me his story of accepting Jesus

Christ as his Lord and Savior when he was seventeen. He and his dad would go to church together on Sunday evenings. They were both Baptized together on the same night at Southside Baptist Church in Bradenton, FL. I wish my dad had taken me to church.

Joshua 24:15 *And if it seems evil to you to serve the Lord, choose for yourselves this day whom you will serve.*

One of my favorite questions to ask Gigi was, "Hey, Gigi, what outfit was Muffy wearing on your first date?" Man, I tell you his face would light up! He would tell you all about that red and white horizontal striped shirt, and those shorts, and on and on. Muffy was Myrtle Ellen Mathis. Like Gigi, she got her name from her first grandchild. The preferred grandmother name was "Mumsy," but all the cute little girl could say was "Muffy," and it stuck. His love was so great for her that he had his knee replaced in his late eighties just so he could care for her at home. On their headstone, it reads, "Muffy I love you, Gigi."

Gigi was a plastering contractor. Today, they use drywall, but back then, they built interior walls by hand, known as plastering. The name of his company was E.P. Surgnier Plastering Company. And he was highly skilled at his trade. His company thrived, and it provided well for his family. However, the trade was literally backbreaking, and many died from asbestos inhalation, so he retired from it around the age of fifty and lived a relatively quiet life on his signature five-acre ranch with a comfortable two-bedroom, two-bath house and barn. He built the same house on four different five-acre parcels in four different Florida towns.

At ninety-two and a half years old, he was proud of becoming the oldest living male in the known history of his family. He went for walks daily until his body just couldn't handle it any longer. He ate oatmeal for breakfast every day. He made the best ham, tomato, pickle, and Everglades Seasoning sandwiches. He could grill and smoke the best meat you've ever tasted. He battled skin cancers for many years, so he always wore a wide-brimmed postal worker hat. And he drove a station wagon until 2004, when he purchased his last vehicle, a Chevy Tahoe SUV.

I couldn't have asked for a better grandfather. Was he perfect? No. Did he do some things I didn't understand? Yes. Was he an exceptional grandfather? Absolutely. He attended every birthday, every Christmas, every Easter, every Thanksgiving, every graduation. What I'm going to miss most are his birthday calls. He always remembered my birthday, even my wife's birthday. When the phone rang, I would answer to the sound of him singing happy birthday to me.

During my last visit with him, I drove him to his local grocery store deli, because he raved about their catfish dinners. The ladies behind the counter recognized him and were sweet to him. As he walked away from the counter using his walker, and out of hearing distance, in a hushed voice I told them, "That man is a war hero. He landed at Normandy. He has two Purple Hearts and a Bronze Star." I lost my hero a couple weeks later on November 20, 2017.

Goodbye, Gigi. God speed. You are with God and Jesus now. The war will no longer keep you up at night. As a fellow believer, I am confident and without doubt that you made it to Heaven and have a brand new tent.

Love, Your grandson

Chapter 18

IS MY LAST NAME REALLY ZIPPERER?

Another day was thirty-three years later in 2017 when I pulled out that old spiral-bound Zipperer family tree on my quest to find a Civil War soldier grandfather who was at the Battle of Gettysburg. Resurrecting my ten-year-old internet-based family tree on Ancestry. com, I first made sure I had my parents, grandparents, and great-grandparents entered accurately. Having been to the Zipperer Cemetery in Lake Park, GA when I was a teenager, having my dad's list of Zipperer generations, and having the old Zipperer family tree book, my level of confidence about my Zipperer surname lineage was unquestionably solid. Each wife of a Zipperer grandfather was of course a grandmother, so I followed each of their maiden names back in time to their parents, and their parents, and so on, because each of those people were my direct lineage blood ancestors.

I clearly remember sitting in my family room, talking to my Uncle James on the phone about some aspect of the ancestry adventure I was on, and seeing something pop up on my laptop computer screen that shook my personal identity foundation to the core. I said into the phone, "Dude, you are not gonna believe this." I must have been searching on Google for photos or anything of interest pertaining to Grandpa Tony, my 2nd great-grandfather, Charles Robert Lovett Zipperer, but what I saw on the screen hit me like a ton of bricks. Someone had posted online the name of Grandpa Tony's mother as being a Catherine Lovett. I had always known from the time I was fifteen years old standing in the Zipperer Cemetery in Lake Park, GA that Grandpa Tony's mother was Eliza Ann Corbett. But that woman's last name of Lovett commanded tremendous credibility considering Grandpa Tony had four names, one of which was Lovett.

When I began my quest to find my roots, my brother-in-law had warned me, tongue in cheek, about finding something I wouldn't want to know. And there it was, in the 1880 census, a Catherine Lovett, age thirty-five, Cousin, living in the household of Charles Robert Zipperer along with his wife and children. Just below her entry was C.R. Lovett, age five, Cousin, my 2nd great-grandfather. Five years after his birth, his name was Charles Robert Lovett. The surname, the last name, Zipperer, was not affixed to his name, and therefore, not affixed to my name. Two things were certain. First, some never before mentioned woman named Catherine Lovett was the mother of Grandpa Tony, making her my newfound 3rd great-grandmother. Second, the woman I had known to be my 3rd great-grandmother since I was fifteen years old, Eliza Ann Corbett Zipperer, was of no relation to me. Using a genealogical set of pruning shears, I trimmed the Corbett branch from my tree. In its place, I grafted a Lovett shoot to grow.

An even bigger shock to my system came next. I thought to myself, *Is my last name really Zipperer?* Grandpa Tony was named Charles Robert Lovett, having been given his mama's last name at birth, and was still known as a Lovett five years later. Who was his father? What was that man's last name? Knowing I was a Lovett, but no longer certain I was a Zipperer, I began referring to myself among close family as Tripp Lovett, because Uncle James was calling himself Jimmy Lovett. It was fun to make light of our doubt, but an identity crisis had taken place. The aliases were no more than temporary dressings on our newly inflicted "who's your great-great-granddaddy" wounds.

A last name is important to boys and men, because we are the next generation implicitly burdened with the responsibility of carrying on the family name. Without producing a son of our own, the last name ceases to exist. It's heavy, really heavy, a serious source of worry. A surname that has continued uninterrupted down through the ages for what seems like a billion years depends on us to reproduce until we father a male child bearing our last name. Among other inexplicable God inserted enablers of survival, like the fourth generation of Monarch butterflies migrating to the same spot in Mexico where they've never been, it's instinctive.

My instincts kicking in, I went after the Catherine Lovett story with vigor. Listed as thirty-five years old in the 1880 census, her birth year was 1845. She was listed as a "Cousin," but I would later learn that was just a fictitious form of relationship the head of household declared to the Census taker while standing at the front door extemporaneously deflecting further curiosity. Clearly marked by dark slashes in each column, she is described as not being able to read and not being able to write. She was born in Georgia. Her father was born in Georgia. And her mother was born in Georgia.

Someone else online had concluded the mother of Grandpa Tony was a Catherine "Kate" Lovett Stallings, born 1842. Unable to find any other Catherine Lovett myself, I followed that person's conclusion all the way down a rabbit hole, all the way to Mrs. Stallings' gravesite at a remote cemetery in Pavo, GA, but the puzzle piece just would not fit into place. The birth year was wrong. The married last name was wrong. The residence location was wrong. Unable to find another Catherine Lovett suspect, I called the Lowndes County Library in Valdosta, GA.

A nice man asked what he could do to help me. I shared the Grandpa Tony situation with him and asked if the library would have any information about the Catherine Lovett living in the Charles Robert Zipperer household, because I couldn't find any information or documentation pertaining to a Catherine Lovett in Lowndes County during the time period of 1880, other than the 1880 census. He said he would look into it during lulls in his work action.

The next day, the librarian called and said, "I think her name was Isabel." Leading me to the 1870 census for Lowndes County, GA taken 29 Jul 1870, he pointed out an Isibel Lovett, age twenty-five, Seamstress, living in the household of Charles Robert Zipperer. The birth year for the female Lovett remained constant at 1845 based on her age of twenty-five in 1870 and thirty-five in 1880. I searched the census records in Georgia looking for an "Isabel Lovett" born around 1845. And there she was in the 1850 census, in Lowndes County, GA, Isabella Lovett, five years old, born in 1845, daughter of Joshua Lovett and Elizabeth Lovett. There were five children, including Isabella, living in the household. A sixth child would be born in 1851. The oldest child, Merzelle, and the youngest child, Mary Angeline, would prove to play key roles 167 years later in confirming the identity of Grandpa Tony's mother.

Grandpa Tony died in 1960, so I ordered a death certificate from the State of Florida to see what light it might shine on the identities of his father and mother. A few days later, an envelope appeared in my mailbox containing Grandpa Tony's death certificate. There's something about holding an ancestor's death certificate. Not many handwritten words are scratched onto the limited number of blank entry lines, but each word is special, meaningful, and insightful with the potential to blast through brick walls that have denied you access to the previous generation.

The informant was his granddaughter, Myrtie Zipperer Cummins. All five of Grandpa Tony's children were alive, so I'm not sure why his then thirty-year-old granddaughter was tasked with being the informant, but she obviously had plenty of knowledgeable living resources to consult with for relevant answers. In the father field, Myrtie provided the name Charles R. Zipperer. In the mother field, she stated, "Unknown."

How was it possible a granddaughter selected as the informant for her grandfather's death certificate wouldn't know the name of the deceased's mother? In 1960, wouldn't she have made a phone call, or three, to find the answer to such an important piece of information for such an historical document? Or, did Grandpa Tony not know the name of his mother? The last known record of his mother Catherine Lovett was the 1880 census when he was just five years old. The 1890 census for the United States burned in Washington D.C. and by the 1900 census, Grandpa Tony was married with children living next door to Charles Robert Zipperer and his wife Eliza Ann Corbett. What happened to Ms. Isabel or Catherine Lovett? Did she die soon after the 1880 census while Grandpa Tony was near five years old and nobody in the Zipperer household had reason to speak her name again? Did Grandpa Tony forget her name? Or, was she simply "Mama?" Wouldn't you think he would ask someone about his mother's name at some point beyond his childhood?

When my grandfather "Papa" was a boy, he lived with his grandfather, Grandpa Tony. Papa's parents had some little ones at home, and his mother was sick, so Papa went to stay with his grandparents. By the time his parents were ready for him to come home, Papa had become comfortable sleeping at his grandparents', so from then on, he would go to his grandparents' before dark to sleep at their house. I called my Uncle James.

Trae: I sure wish Papa was still alive, so I could ask him what he knew about his grandfather, Grandpa Tony.

James: Yeah, he lived with his grandparents out on Zipperer Road.

Trae: It sure would be nice to have Papa's DNA right now.

James: Why's that?

Trae: Because he had twice as much of Grandpa Tony's DNA than you do and four times as much as I do.

James: Why don't you get Aunt Leona's DNA?

Great-aunt Leona was my grandfather's last surviving full sibling and would carry the same quantity of DNA passed down from their parents. As a granddaughter of Grandpa Tony, Great-aunt Leona would carry approximately 25% of his DNA in her body, as compared to 12.5% in my uncle and only 6.25% in me. With her DNA, we would have the potential to reach at least two generations further away in the family tree, matching DNA with people who were simply out of our genetic reach. I called my ninety-five-year-old grandmother and said, "Hi, Nanny, do you have Aunt Leona's daughter's phone number?"

I called Cathy Jo, reminded her I was Robert's son, caught up a little bit, and asked her, "Do you think your mom would be willing to spit in a tube for me?" I explained what I was doing and how her mother had the best genealogical DNA in our family. She said she didn't know why her mama wouldn't, but she would ask her and get back to me.

Great-aunt Leona appreciated what I was doing and agreed to provide her DNA sample for me to manage. Within a few days, I was driving the three-hour route up I-75 with an Ancestry.com DNA kit to Cathy Jo's house to visit with her and Great-aunt Leona to literally honor our DNA.

With anticipation, it seemed longer than it really was, I finally received an email notification that Great-aunt Leona's DNA test results were ready to view. Logging into my Ancestry.com account, clicking on DNA, and clicking on View Another Test, I accessed Great-aunt Leona's DNA test results. My name was high on the list, so as my Nanny had assured me, there was no Milk Man involved in my father's conception. Some matches had public family trees associated, some had private trees, while some had no tree. If a DNA match did have a tree, I could click to see the names entered into that person's list of ancestors.

As I worked my way down the list from closest genetic match to fewer centimorgans in common, I could see where our family tree crossed with other DNA matches at a common ancestor. I recognized many of the surnames in the matches' trees. Now to see if Great-aunt Leona's DNA could identify the "Unknown" mother of my great-great-grandfather, Grandpa Tony. With more than 1,000 DNA matches, I narrowed the results to only those matching on the surname "Lovett."

Starting with the closest match and working my way down the list, I looked at each match's Lovett surname family line. The two strongest DNA connections between Great-aunt Leona and other Lovett family descendants were considered "Extremely High" by Ancestry.com DNA at 153 and 127 centimorgans, respectively. A third match at 53 centimorgans left no doubt I had found Grandpa Tony's mother.

The 153 centimorgans match was with Ancestry.com DNA participant "#1." DNA Participant #1's great-grandmother was Merzelle Lovett. I contacted the manager for #1, and she confirmed with her reply, "I'm certain Merzelle was my great-great-grandmother, because my mom was born in 1904 and knew her grandmother Merzelle very well." The name "Merzelle" is obviously an extremely uncommon name, and clearly establishes father Joshua Lovett as the common link between Merzelle and her siblings, including one sister named Isabella.

The 127 centimorgans match was with Ancestry.com DNA participant "#2." #2's great-grandmother was Mary Angeline Lovett. I contacted the manager for #2, and he shared with me the identity of #2 was his wife. He said his wife recognized the names of her ancestors in the family tree linked to her DNA results, including her Great-grandmother Mary Angeline Lovett. Accessing #2's family tree, I could see it contained documentation connecting #2's grandfather to a Mary Angeline Lovett. Supporting documentation included the 1880 census and the marriage record for Mary Angeline Lovett. Two of Angeline's sisters were named Merzelle and Isabella.

A 53 centimorgan DNA match existed between my Great-aunt Leona and Ancestry.com DNA participant "#3," who descended from Mary Angeline Lovett. I communicated with #3 to confirm they added Angeline to their family tree with a high level of confidence. Several more DNA test participants matched my Great-aunt Leona via the "Lovett" surname, all having trees descending from siblings of Isabella Lovett, daughter of Joshua Lovett and his wife Ann Elizabeth Ihly Keebler Lovett. *Pioneers of Wiregrass Georgia*, Vol. 4, pages 186 and 187, provides a sketch for Joshua Lovett b. 1795 d. 1865. Six children are listed including 1. Murzelle, 3. Isabelle, and 5. Mary Angeline. Four of the children were daughters. Three of the four daughters have their husband's names listed. The married column for daughter Isabelle is stated as (unknown).

Based on all of the supporting documentation, DNA evidence, and analysis, I was able to conclude that the mother of Grandpa Tony, my 3rd great-grandmother, was Isabella Lovett, born 1845. Her full name was probably Isabella Catherine Lovett. Had my great-aunt not provided her DNA for me to manage and use for our family research, the identity of Isabella Lovett most likely would have been lost forever.

I don't yet have any information about Isabella Lovett's life between five years old in the 1850 census living with her parents and twenty-five years old living in the household of Charles Robert Zipperer in the 1870 census. She would have been sixteen years old when the Civil War began in 1861. Many of the young men of marrying age would have been off to war as Confederate soldiers. Maybe her sweetheart was killed or died from disease during the war. Her mother died in 1862, when Isabel was seventeen. Maybe Isabel felt obligated to stay at home to care for her father until he died three years later in 1865 when Isabella was twenty.

Georgia was devastated at the end of the Civil War in 1865. Times were hard, beyond difficult, to say the least. Her name remained Lovett, so she must not have ever married during the five-year period between the end of the war and showing up as living in the Zipperer household in the 1870 census. As of 1865, she had no husband, her mother and father had died, Georgia was a disaster, carpetbaggers were everywhere, the economy was in shambles, and federal troops occupied the South under martial law. Ownership of the Joshua Lovett homestead was lost for one reason or another. It probably wasn't safe for a twenty-year-old young woman to be alone, and she may have just needed a roof over her head. Sometime between 1865 and 1870, she moved into the home of Charles Robert Zipperer, his wife, and his children.

Charles Robert "Tony" Lovett Zipperer was born on 30 Aug 1874. Therefore, he would have been conceived in late November 1873 when Isabel Lovett would have been twenty-eight years old. Within our family, it had been assumed Charles Robert Zipperer, born 11 Jun 1830, was Tony's father. Personally, I couldn't escape the cloud of uncertainty swirling around the accuracy of my last name. I had to know. Was Charles Robert Zipperer really my 3rd great-grandfather? Or was my last name something other than that of Zipperer, which I had identified with my entire life? But, how could I determine, 145 years later, whether or not Charles Robert Zipperer was actually the biological father of Charles Robert "Tony" Lovett Zipperer? For that answer, I turned to Y-DNA.

As mentioned earlier, Y-DNA passes unchanged from father to son. Therefore, as a male descendant of Charles Robert "Tony"

Lovett Zipperer, I inherited his Y-DNA. In order to find out if Charles Robert Zipperer was the father of Grandpa Tony, I needed to find a Y-DNA match between myself and a Zipperer male not descended from Grandpa Tony. The earliest known Zipperer in North America was Christian Zipperer from the mid-1700s. If a Zipperer male today was known to descend from Christian Zipperer via one of his two sons, Christian Jonathan Zipperer born 1757 or Samuel Zipperer born 1759, then their Y-DNA should be an identical match with my Y-DNA.

As of the writing of this book, Ancestry.com only offered atDNA tests. FamilyTreeDNA.com (FTDNA), however, offered all three types of DNA tests, including atDNA, Y-DNA, and mtDNA. So, I ordered a 67-marker Y-DNA test kit from FTDNA. With Ancestry.com, I spat in a tube. With FTDNA, I swabbed the inside of my mouth cheeks. So, I swabbed the inside of my right cheek with the first swab, then the inside of my left cheek with the second swab, sealed up the envelope, and dropped the completed test kit in the mail.

Wanting to confirm my real last name, I patiently, but eagerly, waited with anticipation. I envisioned a cluster of several matches, all with the last name of Zipperer. Or, I knew there was a possibility a cluster of several matches may all have a same last name other than Zipperer. I had been to dozens of old cemeteries in South Georgia and North Florida, so I had become aware of several common names. Maybe I would see a cluster of matches all with the name Strickland, or Moody, or Touchton.

Checking my email, the results were in! All I had to do was enter my kit number, enter my password, and click sign in. The suspense building, I reached the results pages listing all my Y-DNA matches. In the left side column containing the names of men who had submitted their Y-DNA for analysis, I saw Pettigrew, Shadd, Jansen, and fifteen other surnames. There was no cluster of Y-DNA matches with multiple males having the same last name. Not only was a cluster of names not visible, not a single male with my exact Y-DNA had submitted a test kit. The matches displayed were only close matches, not identical matches.

I thought to myself, *Some man out there in the world descends from the same family surname as the man who fathered my Great-great-grandfather Tony.* I could have sat around and waited indefinitely for a man carrying my Y-DNA to submit a test kit to FTDNA, or I could handle the situation proactively with the God-given initiative instilled inside my DNA. The prime suspect was Charles Robert Zipperer, so rather than looking for a needle in a haystack, it made logical sense to seek out a Zipperer male who was willing to take a Y-DNA test. Any Zipperer male might work, as long as they weren't also descended from Grandpa Tony.

I called some of my newfound cousins in Valdosta asking if they personally knew any Zipperers. I searched the Lowndes County property tax records for Zipperers and mailed a letter. My cousins were helpful, the Zipperer man responded to my letter, and I was eventually referred to a lady who was organizing the 72nd Annual Zipperer Family Reunion. I ordered four 37-marker Y-DNA kits from FTDNA, so in the event I found a Zipperer male willing to participate, I would have a kit ready to go. I also thought it would be a good idea to have at least four different Zipperers take a Y-DNA test to create the cluster of matches I had originally envisioned and sought.

Then I remembered my son had met a young woman with the last name of Zipperer while attending college in Florida. I called my son and asked if he still had contact with that young Zipperer woman. My son said they texted from time to time, so I asked him to ask her if she would ask her dad if he would be okay with her giving me his cell phone number. My son sent the girl a text, she asked her dad, and her dad gave her permission to provide me with his cell number. I sent her dad the following introductory text message.

Hello fellow Zipperer. My name is Trae Zipperer. My son, Leroy, met your daughter at college. I'm working on our family tree and trying to fill some gaps. Our Zipperers were part of the Salzburgers from Austria who pioneered Ebenezer, GA. We descend from a Theophilus Zipperer from Lake Park near Valdosta. I'd love to speak with you when you have a few minutes. Sincerely, Trae Zipperer.

It wasn't too long before he gave me a call. We talked about how unlikely it was that our children with such an uncommon last name would run across each other at a Florida college campus. He and I were both military veterans, my son was a veteran, and his dad was a veteran. He said, "You should talk with my dad, because he knows more about our family tree than I do." I asked if he or anyone in his family had taken a DNA test, and he said he wasn't aware of anyone. He did share his grandfather Zipperer's name and his great-grandfather Zipperer's name.

When we ended our call, I went straight into Ancestry.com to see what I could learn about the names he had given me and where our family trees might intersect. The father of the man's great-grandfather was Benjamin Franklin Zipperer. His father was Joseph Alexander Zipperer. His daddy's name was John Martin Zipperer. His daddy was Christian Jonathan Zipperer. And, his dad was Christian Zipperer. I, too, descend from Christian Zipperer, so the Zipperer man I had just hung up the phone with should have the exact same Y-DNA as mine, if Charles Robert Zipperer was in fact the biological father of Grandpa Tony. I looked forward to speaking with his father, optimistic I wouldn't have to wait long.

A couple days later, the phone rang, and it was the grandfather Zipperer of the young woman my son had randomly met at college. We talked for more than an hour and shared what we knew about our Zipperer family trees. I shared with him my quest to resolve the paternity question of my great-great-grandfather. He enthusiastically shared with me that he had just received his Ancestry.com DNA test results the day before yesterday and was over-the-moon excited about his discoveries. I thought to myself, *What are the odds this Zipperer man just received his DNA test results two days ago?* Turns out he had a brother who had also taken a DNA test, so I had just found not one, but two Zipperer men who had already embraced DNA testing.

Looking through my great-aunt's atDNA matches on Ancestry. com, I searched for any matches where the surname Zipperer was included in the match's family tree. Match #14 was 49 centimorgans across three segments. I scrolled down through the family tree for #14 and noticed the surname Zipperer. But it wasn't just any Zipperer, it was Benjamin Franklin Zipperer, and his daddy was Joseph Alexander Zipperer, and his daddy was John Martin Zipperer. Scanning this family tree, I recognized no other matching surname other than Zipperer. My great aunt's DNA was matching with someone known to be descended from Christian Zipperer. It wasn't the strongest DNA match as measured by centimorgans, but it was significant and there was no other surname by which the two DNA results could have matched.

I called the young-woman-from-college's grandfather Zipperer and asked him if he would do me a favor. He said, "Sure, what can I do for you?" I asked him if he would check in his DNA matches to see if he matched with #14. He called me back the next day and confirmed that yes, he did have #14 in his list of matches. He didn't match with my great aunt, but he and my great aunt both matched with #14. This was the first solid atDNA match connecting a Grandpa Tony descendant to a Zipperer NOT descended from Grandpa Tony. With atDNA evidence pointing toward Charles Robert Zipperer as Grandpa Tony's father, my determination to verify paternity via Y-DNA matches only heightened.

I would be traveling to Valdosta on Labor Day weekend to attend the 72nd Annual Zipperer Family Reunion, so I made arrangements to meet with the two brothers during my drive northward. With the same Zipperer father, their Y-DNA would certainly match. In addition, not being descendants of Grandpa Tony, but known to descend from the original Zipperer in America, Christian Zipperer, their Y-DNA should match my Y-DNA if Charles Robert Zipperer was in fact the father of Grandpa Tony. Both brothers had already taken atDNA tests with Ancestry.com. Both understood the power of DNA testing. And, both were open-minded to learning more about DNA testing, specifically Y-DNA testing.

I had spoken with both of these Zipperer men on the phone and each had been a joy to converse with about family, religious beliefs, life stories, DNA, and the multiple unexplainable recent coincidences that had brought the three of us together. Each felt strongly about there being a higher purpose behind our coming together, so I really wasn't surprised at their response when I posed the question about whether they would be willing to participate in my quest to confirm the paternity of Charles Robert "Tony" Lovett Zipperer. They knew it was important to me to know whether or not my last name I had known all my life was really my last name. Without hesitation they asked only what they needed to do in order to participate. We followed the easy instructions enclosed in the test kits, registered the kits online at FamilyTreeDNA.com, sealed the envelopes, and dropped off the completed kits at the nearest post office.

The common ancestor between myself and these two Zipperer brothers was none other than the very first known Zipperer in North America: Christian Zipperer b. unknown d. 15 Feb 1781. The distance between test subjects was fifteen degrees of separation, with me being a 6th great-grandson and the two brothers being 5th great-grandsons. The results of this Y-DNA test initiative would push the limits of genealogical genetic investigations reaching back nearly 270 years and relying on the legitimacy of fifteen conceptions.

The first of the Zipperer brother's 37-marker Y-DNA test results came back as a perfect match with my Y-DNA on 26 Sep 2018. atDNA had already confirmed the two Zipperers as brothers, so the second brother's matching Y-DNA results five days later was of no surprise, but still nice to see in the cluster of Zipperer matches I had created from my own initiative. No longer with any doubt, Charles Robert Zipperer was the biological father of Charles Robert "Tony" Lovett Zipperer as proven by Y-DNA test results.

Are you a biological blood Zipperer male? The only way to be sure is to take a 37-marker or 67-marker Y-DNA test with FamilyTreeDNA.com and join the Zipperer Project to see if your Y-DNA matches that of the four Zipperers now known to be descended from Christian Zipperer.

I would like to find out what happened to Isabella "Catherine" Lovett, mother of Charles Robert "Tony" Lovett Zipperer. I am grateful for her as my grandmother, and she needs to be found. The last known record of her was the 1880 census, where she was thirty-five years old living with five-year-old C.R. Lovett in the Lake Park, GA household of Charles Robert Zipperer near Valdosta. She was the daughter of Joshua Lovett b. 6 May 1795 d. 1865 and Ann Elizabeth Ihly Keebler Lovett b. 1815 d. 1862 as per the 1850 census and *Pioneers of Wiregrass Georgia*.

A Zipperer man I spoke with near the old Zipperer homestead in Lake Park recalled his grandfather showing him a single grave in the woods surrounded by a metal fence. His recollection was the grave was that of a woman, but it had been so long since he saw it, he doubted the metal fence was still there and couldn't remember exactly where the grave was located. If found, that grave may have been Grandpa Tony's mama.

Chapter 19

SEARCHING FOR CIVIL WAR SOLDIERS

My catalyst to discover my roots was at Gettysburg resulting in a personal goal of discovering any grandfathers who were Civil War soldiers. Specifically, I was determined to find out if any of those men participated in the Battle of Gettysburg. A more accurate assessment was that I very much wanted to find a grandfather who fought in that battle. It didn't matter to me if they were North or South, Blue or Gray, Union or Confederate, Yank or Reb, Billy or Johnny. I knew it was possible, because I did have one known Confederate soldier grandfather, but I had no inkling as to my other grandfathers' identities, or where they were living on planet Earth during that time period. I didn't know their races, their religious beliefs, or their loyalties.

Jimpsey Giddens had been a Confederate soldier, but he was just one out of a total of forty-eight 3rd great-grandfathers and 4th great-grandfathers who would potentially have been of military age during the Civil War. For me, my eight great-great-grandfathers were born between 1862 and 1877, so they were all born during or after the Civil War. My sixteen great-great-great-grandfathers were born between 1816 and 1868, so some were of military age during the period 1861-1865, while some were too young or not yet born. Of my thirty-two great-great-great-great-grandfathers, five were born in the late 1700s, with the other twenty-seven having been born between 1802 and 1835. All forty-eight of my 3rd and 4th great-grandfathers were living in the United States during the period 1861-1865. Before I even determined whether or not each was a soldier during the Civil War, I found it quite remarkable that ALL of my ancestors back to the Civil War period were already living here in America. Not a single one of my ancestors was a recent immigrant to the United States within the past 157 years. How many people, I wondered, could state that claim?

So, on I went with my task of researching each found ancestor of military age during the Civil War. I relied on six source references to confirm whether or not each grandfather was a Civil War soldier.

First, I Googled Civil War soldiers and found the National Park Service website link to nps.gov/civilwar/soldiers-and-sailors-database.htm. This site enabled me to search by name, state, Union, Confederate, and branch of service. I was sure to use variations of spelling, including only initials for first and middle names.

Second, I viewed HINTS for the ancestor in my family tree within Ancestry.com. Some HINTS were specifically labeled "Civil War," while some HINTS led me to other Ancestry.com member family trees. Within other members' trees, I could see whether or not that person had identified my ancestor as having been a Civil War soldier. Sometimes their Civil War service was noted in writing while other times an American flag or Confederate flag was displayed.

Third, I read sketches written about some of my ancestors within the volumes of *Pioneers of Wiregrass Georgia*. Some sketches mentioned military service.

Fourth, if I had found information suggesting an ancestor had been a member of a certain military regiment, I would Google that regiment and click on the www.familysearch.org link. This link would sometimes provide a list of companies within the regiment and a link to a Roster for that company. If the regiment was from Georgia, the source of the Roster would be from *Roster of the Confederate Soldiers of Georgia* made available by Hathi Trust Digital Library.

Fifth, I entered my ancestor's name into the Search bar at FOLD3.com, as I had witnessed the volunteer do at the Gettysburg Visitors Center. A soldier's muster rolls and other interesting documents were found and viewed at FOLD3.com.

Sixth, I Googled pension records both for the soldier and their widows. Union soldier pensions were paid by the federal government whereas Confederate soldier pensions were paid directly by the state government of former Confederate states. Pension records for Confederate soldiers in Florida can be found at floridamemory.com.

Simply finding my ancestor's name noted as a Civil War soldier did not mean he was actually a soldier, because often there was more than one person with the same name. Therefore, it was necessary to cross-reference as many sources and records as could be found to conclude my ancestor was the person whose name was listed as a Civil War soldier. An example from my tree was Zeno Worth Whitney born 1816, or forty-seven years old in 1863. He was shown as a "Watchman" at the Macon Arsenal, GA during July 1863. I knew this was my ancestor because he was listed in the 1870 census in Macon, GA within a household of known family members with his occupation written as "Watchman."

I entered this journey of ancestral discovery with an open mind, not knowing who or what I might find. Turns out all of my ancestors during the period 1861 to 1865 lived in the South. Each time I found a grandfather of military age during 1861 to 1865 and plugged his name into FOLD3.com, I found a Confederate soldier. With a high level of confidence, seventeen of my grandfathers were Confederate soldiers and two of my 3rd great-grandmothers' first husbands were Confederate soldiers. I was unable to discover two of my 4th great-grandfathers whose probable birth years and Southern residences in North Carolina and Georgia made them prime candidates to have been Confederate soldiers. Of the seventeen who were confirmed soldiers, eight were determined to have been in combat, and a ninth, John Matthew Allen, died within two months of arriving at Camp Davis for military training. He had quickly contracted a disease described as brain fever.

Death caused by disease during the Civil War was referenced in most all written accounts of the conflict. The significance was typically emphasized as something similar to "twice as many Civil War soldiers died of disease as those who died of wounds from combat." Reading these phrases throughout my lifelong interest in the Civil War led me to assume soldiers randomly became sick throughout the forty-eight-month period of April 1861 to April 1865, with deaths caused by disease evenly distributed from month one to month forty-eight. However, while researching Company I of the 12th Georgia Infantry Regiment, I discovered my assumption that soldiers died randomly from disease was inaccurate.

Using a spreadsheet and the roster of Company I of the 12th Georgia as detailed in *Roster of the Confederate Soldiers of Georgia*, I charted all casualties by type, date, and location. This personal effort to dig a little deeper brought forth a new level of understanding and appreciation for what men endured, specifically when it came to bacterial, viral, and parasitic diseases of which rarely result in death during our time. Clusters of deaths from disease began to take shape as time and again I transcribed the words died, disease, camp, Bartow, and Allegheny from the published roster to my little spreadsheet, telling a certain story long forgotten and uncovering a major Civil War detail missed or overlooked by historians. A total of thirty-six men of Company I would die from disease: twenty-five within the first three months compared to eleven over the next forty-five months. Even more shocking than half of deaths during the Civil War being caused by disease, 69% of those deaths caused by disease occurred within three months of healthy men joining the army.

From personal experience, it was quite sobering to see a written description of my young, vibrant, twenty-seven-year-old grandfather, a man who contributed to my DNA, suffering and dying from an incurable brain fever. As a Jr. 2nd Lieutenant commissioned army officer, his peers in Company A of the 50th Georgia Infantry Regiment perceived John Matthew Allen as being a man possessing significant leadership qualities. The command sent him home from Camp Davis near Rincon, GA, which was essentially what we refer to today as a military boot camp, on sick furlough. I envisioned him in his bed at home, sweating profusely, his body writhing, moaning in delirium, as his thirty-year-old wife (my 4th great-grandmother) and five children ages two months to seven years, watched helplessly, praying for a recovery that wouldn't come. They buried him somewhere at Shiloh Primitive Baptist Church Cemetery in Blackshear, GA, but his grave was no longer marked when I walked the cemetery.

Discovering one of my grandfathers had died in the Civil War certainly had an impact on me, but that realization pales in comparison to the moment it became clear to me my 3rd great-grandmother's first husband, Coleman Groover, had died on a Civil War battlefield, directly leading to my eventual birth. In order for me to have been born, the Civil War had to happen, and Coleman Groover had to die as a result of that war. That was some heavy history to reconcile! But for me, it happened twice, first on my dad's side with Coleman Groover, and then on my mom's side with a man named John T. McElhany.

John T. McElhany was married to my 3rd great-grandmother, Mary Ann Allen. In December 1861 they had a son, William McElhany. Less than three months later, on March 4, 1862, John enlisted as a Private in Company A of the 50th Georgia Infantry Regiment. Does that unit sound familiar? It should, because that was the exact same unit in which my grandfather John Matthew Allen served! Scrolling through the roster of Company A, I saw my 3rd great-grandfather, Jr. 2nd Lt. John M. Allen, and a little further down the list of names, Private John T. McElhany.

Six months after enlisting, John T. McElhany would find himself pinned down at Fox's Gap during the Battle of South Mountain, where the 50th Georgia was tasked by General Robert E. Lee with preventing Union troops from flooding through the mountain pass from the east to attack Lee's army on the west side of the mountains where Lee's forces were amassed near Antietam Creek. John T. McElhany's muster rolls stated "missing in action Sep 14" for the period August through December 1862. The 50th Georgia was cut to shreds at Fox Gap on 14 Sep 1862. There are no records of him being captured, and he never came home to his wife and baby. Had John T. McElhany not been killed at Fox Gap during the Battle of South Mountain in Maryland three days prior to the Battle of Antietam, his wife Mary Ann Allen would never have married my 3rd great-grandfather, James I. Mims.

As I searched for grandfathers who were of military age during the Civil War, I noticed their older and younger brothers. Sometimes the entire family would be listed in *Pioneers of Wiregrass Georgia,* and a death date of 1861, 1862, 1863, 1864, or 1865 for a young man stood out as an obvious candidate as a deceased Confederate soldier. Other times the sketch would include mention of a certain son having died in service to his country.

Curious, I began researching each uncle's name. Again, and again, over and over, Confederate soldier muster rolls matched the names of my uncles born between 1825 and 1845. About every third uncle had a death date sometime between 1861 and 1865. One, two, three, four. Sixteen, seventeen, eighteen. Thirty-three, thirty-four, thirty-five. Fifty-eight, fifty-nine, sixty. Eighty-one, eighty-two, eighty-three uncles. Eighty-three of my uncles were Confederate soldiers.

Of those eighty-three uncles, twenty-six of them died Confederate soldiers during the Civil War. These figures are based on the 75% of ancestor families I have been able to identify so far. Statistics suggest I will find another twenty-eight Confederate soldier uncles, and nine of those will have died during the war, bringing my personal totals to 111 uncles who served, and thirty-five who died as young men wearing gray and butternut uniforms. Most were infantry. Some were cavalry. And a few were artillery.

My parents had three brothers in total, and no sisters, making me the fortunate nephew of three fine uncles. These three men have been outstanding examples throughout my lifetime, each providing invaluable lessons, regarding both what to do and things to avoid. All three graduated from college, all three pursued successful careers, and all three produced cousins I adore as siblings. Using the level of love I felt toward my three uncles as a baseline for comprehension, those 111 uncles who fought and thirty-five who died in the Civil War are no less significant to me. When I saw their names and envisioned them as they were in 1860, before events transpired steering the course of history toward those dreadful four years of unimaginable suffering and sacrifice, I saw my three uncles.

Civil War Deaths of Grandfathers and Uncles

First	Middle	Last	Age	Co.	Unit	Death	Cause of Death
Moses		Tomberlin	20	I	27th Georgia Infantry	25 Nov 1861	Disease: Typhoid
Thomas		Giddens	28	K	29th Georgia Infantry	26 Mar 1862	Disease: Camp Fever
Albert		Blair	19	K	41st Georgia Infantry	6 May 1862	Disease: probably
John	Matthew	Allen	27	A	50th Georgia Infantry	20 May 1862	Disease: Brain Fever
John	Robert	Lovett	22	K	50th Georgia Infantry	29 May 1862	Disease: unknown
William	Garrett	Jarratt	20	G	45th Georgia Infantry	10 Jul 1862	Disease: probably
Isaiah	A.	Self	30	H	7th Georgia Infantry	12 Aug 1862	Continuous Fever
John	T.	McElhaney	24	A	50th Georgia Infantry	14 Sep 1862	Killed in Action
Francis	Marion	James	26		4th Georgia Cav. (Clinch's)	27 Nov 1862	Disease: probably
John	Edmondson	Mathis	38	I	50th Georgia Infantry	11 Dec 1862	Disease: Typhoid
Lloyd		Blair	28	K	41st Georgia Infantry	20 Dec 1862	Killed in Action
Redden	B. maybe	Holland	21	G	50th Georgia Infantry	1863	Disease: probably
Willett	F. M.	Kirkland	32	K	50th Georgia Infantry	27 Jan 1863	Disease: Pneumonia
Henry	M.	Mathis	29	I	50th Georgia Infantry	8 Feb 1863	Disease: Typhoid
James	Andrew	Thomas	30	B	2nd Battalion FL Infantry	15 Apr 1863	Disease: Pneumonia
Reuben		Rountree	30	A	61st Georgia Infantry	1 Jul 1863	Killed in Action
Reuben		Register	32	E	54th Georgia Infantry	14 Sep 1863	Disease: Typhoid
Coleman		Groover	28	B	5th Florida Infantry	6 May 1864	Killed in Action
Joseph	Howard	Evans	31	A	53rd Georgia Infantry	27 Jun 1864	Killed in Action
Martin	M.	Deen	25	F	47th Georgia Infantry	6-9 Jul 1864	Killed in Action
Samuel		Deen	40	F	47th Georgia Infantry	6-9 Jul 1864	Killed in Action
Ezekiel	P.	Buford	55	C	2nd GA Sharpshooters Batt.	25 Aug 1864	POW Rock Island, IL
James		Douglass	44	E	9th Florida Infantry	12 Sep 1864	Killed in Action
William		Thomas	39	B	2nd Battalion FL Infantry	30 Sep 1864	Killed in Action
Riley	L.	Mathis	47	H	12th GA Cav. State Guards	15 Oct 1864	Unknown
Benjamin	Franklin	Evans	33	A	53rd Georgia Infantry	19 Oct 1864	Killed in Action
Samuel	S.	Moody	39	G	7th Georgia Cavalry	29 Oct 1864	POW Point Lookout, MD
James	Anderson	Self	33	B	55th Georgia Infantry	9 Dec 1864	POW Camp Douglas, IL
Edmond	W.	Mathis	34	K	29th Georgia Infantry	11 Feb 1865	POW Camp Chase, OH

Taking the analysis a step further, I acknowledge the husbands of approximately 111 aunts, as well as the hundreds of 1st cousins 4x or 5x removed who were most likely Confederate soldiers. Name any battle fought during the Civil War in any theater of war and somewhere on those hallowed fields stood a man from the South who shared my DNA. They were there at those places everyone knows like Gettysburg, Antietam, Vicksburg, Manassas, Shiloh, and Fredericksburg. They were there at a hundred more battles you've never heard of like Chickamauga, GA; Olustee, FL; Ox Hill, VA; Jonesboro, GA; McDowell, WV; Champion Hill, MS; Perryville, KY; Franklin, TN; and Fort McAllister, GA. They even participated in the attack on Washington, D.C. at the Battle of Fort Stevens.

I have been to these sacred places. I have stood upon the very ground in which they fought, killed, and died. Famous engagements like Pickett's Charge at Gettysburg, the Dead Angle at Kennesaw Mountain, the Mule Shoe at Spotsylvania, the Stone Wall at Fredericksburg, and Stonewall Jackson's flanking forced march at Chancellorsville. I've visited exact locations where my ancestors actually witnessed their own brothers and cousins being mortally wounded.

Confederate front line at Vicksburg
National Battlefield, MS

As I stood there on Cemetery Ridge at the Battle of Gettysburg, at the catalytic moment of this genealogical odyssey, I sensed a pull,

calling out to me, drawing me toward the past, a subtle but determined desire to be remembered. At that time, I assumed it was a
grandfather in either blue or gray communicating with me via that
sixth sense some of us know is there but can't explain to those who
don't possess it.

The source of the genetic homing beacon would not be revealed
for twenty months, not until after I had returned to Gettysburg,
walked the entire battlefield, and painstakingly researched each
and every grandfather and uncle I could find of military age during
1861-1865. I kid you not; I reached the very last uncle in my tree
and still had not found the source of what had driven me so deep
into a second year of family discovery. I stared at my computer
screen wondering, thinking, pondering, looking at the last set of
grandparents who were within the age range to have had a son born
of military age for the Civil War. Not one to ever give up, there,
just above the last uncle, in the column of 5th great-grandparents,
was Grandma Celite McCall, born 1795. At twenty-three years old,
Celite had given birth to my 4th great-grandmother, Mary Rountree,
in 1818. Assuming she had given birth to a son when she was around
thirty-five years of age, he would have been born in 1830, or thirty-
one years old in 1861. Maybe some of Celite's children would be
named in the first detailed census of 1850.

Clicking on her name in my Ancestry.com family tree, I found
a HINT for the 1850 census. Scanning the highlighted names, I
saw fifty-six-year-old Seletha (Celite) Roundtree, her sixty-seven-
year-old husband Moses Roundtree above, and seventeen-year-old
Ruben Roundtree below. Born in 1833, Celite was thirty-eight years
old when she gave birth to my 5th great-uncle Reuben. In 1853, at
the age of twenty, Reuben married twenty-year-old Martha Ann
Jane Fletcher. The 1860 census showed twenty-six-year-old Ruben
and Martha Rountree had migrated to Lafayette County, FL. When
the Civil War erupted in 1861, Reuben Rountree was twenty-eight

years old. South Carolina seceded 20 Dec 1860, Mississippi seceded 9 Jan 1861, Florida seceded 10 Jan 1861, Alabama seceded 11 Jan 1861, and Georgia seceded 19 Jan 1861 followed by LA, TX, VA, AR, NC, and TN. Within a month after Florida and Georgia seceded, Martha became pregnant with their first child.

On 27 Aug 1861, with Martha six-months pregnant, Reuben Rountree enlisted as a Private in Company A of the 26th Georgia Infantry Regiment. The 26th Georgia would be reorganized into the 61st Georgia sometime during 1862 and assigned to General Thomas Jonathan "Stonewall" Jackson's command for the Seven Days Battles in Virginia. Reuben proved to be a fine soldier in combat, as evidenced by his promotion to 1st Corporal on 17 Aug 1862 following the Battle of Cedar Run. He survived the Second Battle of Manassas and then the bloodiest day in American history at Antietam on 17 Sep 1862. Reuben was wounded at the knee on 13 Dec 1862 during the Battle of Fredericksburg and later promoted to Sergeant on 31 Mar 1863 just in time to lead troops into the exposed right flank of the Union Army during Stonewall Jackson's famous forced march surprise attack at the Battle of Chancellorsville. Sixty thousand Southerners defeated 134,000 Yankees at Chancellorsville, but the victory came at a price too high to pay for the Confederacy with the loss of Stonewall Jackson.

Immediately following his victory, Confederate General Robert E. Lee ordered his Army of Northern Virginia northward in a second attempt to force a peace settlement with the North. As the Confederate Army marched northward from Virginia into Maryland and then Pennsylvania, the Union Army shadowed them to the east, keeping themselves between the Southerners and Washington, D.C. The two armies locked horns at a town called Gettysburg in a "victory or die trying" attempt by Robert E. Lee to destroy the Union Army of the Potomac and therefore the only resistance between Lee and Washington D.C., the literal path to independence for the Confederate States of America.

All those hours, all that research, thousands of names, 102 Confederate soldiers, all the analysis, all those miles traveled, and historical markers read in a relentless determination to discover the source of the gnawing burden inside of me would be resolved in one turn of the muster roll card for my 5th great-uncle, Sgt. Reuben Rountree. The card dated July 1, 1863 read, "Gettysburg Killed in Battle." It was Uncle Reuben whom I had been aware of with a persistent extrasensory perception for so very long. If you've ever experienced what I'm describing, you just feel it, you know it, their presence is real. It cannot be explained.

My sister said to me many, many years ago when I was a young man, "You are a reincarnated Civil War soldier." As a Christian, I do not believe in reincarnation, and neither does my sister, but she made the comment attempting to articulate and emphasize the intensity of my interest in the subject. I share the story as evidence supporting just how long this deeply emotional surreal connection had been in place.

My maternal grandmother told me of one Confederate soldier ancestor, Jimpsey Giddens. From her research notes discovered after her death and during my adventure to honor my DNA, I knew she was aware of 2nd Lt. John Matthew Allen. I interviewed my ninety-two-year-old maternal grandfather, and he knew nothing about Civil War ancestors. I interviewed my ninety-six-year-old paternal grandmother, and she knew nothing about Civil War ancestors. I knew my ninety-four-year-old paternal grandfather extremely well, and my grandmother confirmed he knew nothing about Civil War ancestors. Yet, I had this magnetic passionate innate connection to the Civil War pulling at me from Gettysburg and anything Civil War related. By honoring my DNA, building my family tree, and visiting the graves of my ancestors, it turns out approximately 132 of my grandfathers and uncles were Confederate Civil War soldiers, with approximately thirty-nine of them making the ultimate sacrifice during the war, including Uncle Reuben Rountree killed at the Battle of Gettysburg.

158 years later I marked his resting place in Savannah, GA!

Chapter 20

THEY CALLED HIM LIGE

My Uncle James is known to have paid attention to family history throughout his life and always seemed to know a little something about the people, places, and stories of our past. He was not old, but he was old enough to have known firsthand, as a boy, some of the people who expired prior to my birth and whose facial expressions stared back at me from the slightly out of focus black and white family reunion group photos from the 1950s.

Trae: What do you know about Grandpa Anderson?

James: You mean Grandma's daddy, Elijah Newton Anderson?

Trae: Yeah, Elijah Newton Anderson.

James: Meanest man ever lived.

He expanded on the family story by recalling a trip home from the Marine Corps stopping in to visit his grandma in central Florida. He had grown a mustache, and when he walked through her front door, Grandma confronted him.

Grandma: James, is that you?

James: Yes, Grandma, it's me, James.

Grandma: Get in there and shave that mustache off your face, you look just like my daddy.

There were multiple family recollections about my Great-great-grandpa Anderson, all referencing his meanness. My great-great-grandmother, his second wife, supposedly divorced him because he was so mean. When asked by James to tell him about her husband, Elijah Newton Anderson, her response was, "There ain't nothin' you want to know about that man." My grandmother told me my grandfather (Elijah's daughter's son) disliked his Grandfather Anderson because he whipped him when he was a boy. The story goes that my grandfather went to stay with his grandfather for a week or so, but his grandfather was mean to him, so he decided he would leave and walk the 120 miles home. His grandpa caught up with him and tore his butt up for running away. I guess the whippin' reinforced my grandfather's perception of his grandfather being a mean man. Another account was that he regularly beat on his two sons.

The reason I'm sharing this personal family story with you is because it's vitally important to our personal legacies within our families to be keenly aware of our interactions with others. Our behavior, our personality, our demeanor, is witnessed and retained by our family members, because they are the people with which we spend the majority of our very limited number of days between birth and death. We've all heard the saying, life is too short—well it's true, and if you aren't kind, caring, and loving, you just might end up being referred to by all of your descendants as the meanest person who ever walked the planet, or worse.

Relying on extemporaneous oral recollections as a definitive life story for ancestors is deficient and unfortunate for three main reasons. First, as humans we tend to spend an inordinate amount of conversation time focused on the salacious, failures, mistakes, and shortcomings of others, especially when the topic of discussion is a fellow family member. Second, people lead busy lives, so it's not too often the topic of discussion happens to migrate to the life and times of great-grandfather Elijah Newton Anderson born in 1869. Sufficient quantities of time and effort are rarely allocated by grateful descendants to justly analyze, interpret, comprehend, and articulate those who contributed to our DNA. Third, once three generations have expired, firsthand interaction, observation, and knowledge of living, breathing Grandpa Anderson ceases to exist.

Along my journey of ancestral discovery, I came across a few stories and written accounts of certain people who contributed to my DNA. Anything was insightful when I had nothing more than a name. A data point, a sentence, a paragraph, please. But sadly, descriptions of ancestors' lives written by people who actually knew the deceased beyond simply their name were rare instances, which left me empty knowing nothing more than "He was mean." Tired of hearing the "mean" story multiple times for several grandfathers, I decided to do my own work, so I started with my Great-great-grandfather Elijah Newton Anderson.

Maybe he was just a mean-spirited hateful person deserving of nothing more than to be erased from the memories of all who descend from him, but I've uncovered some old photos where he appeared to be a happy person with a friendly, smiling face. In one family group photo, he was the tallest standing in the back. In another, side by side with his brother, the top of his head was even with his brother's shoulder. In a separate photo of his brother's family, his brother appeared to be of normal height. Glancing back to the family group photo where he was in the back, if you look closely, he was standing atop a set of front porch steps. Turns out, Grandpa Anderson was extremely short in stature! Did he have a bit of a Napoleon complex, escaping his insecurities among men via his power of authority over children?

Elijah Newton Anderson
and Lem Anderson

Adding more to the story, my great-great-grandfather was actually Reverend Elijah Newton Anderson of the Primitive Baptist faith. As a product of the Primitive Baptist Church, I have taken time to study and learn about their ways, beliefs, and practices, even attending a Sunday service with dinner on the grounds. Their numbers have dwindled since the 1800s, but there are still those who hold fast to this Christian protestant denomination. Known as Hard Shell Baptists or Old School Baptists, members and leaders believed strongly in following the words of the Bible. From an outsider's perspective, Primitive Baptists may have appeared too strict, too unbending, too firm in their layman's reading of scripture.

However, if I truly believed the Bible was the word of God, then it was hard to criticize Primitive Baptists for following God's clearly written guidance. Opening a King James Version of the Bible and turning to 1 Timothy 3:4-5, Reverend Anderson may have been something other than "mean."

1 Timothy 3:4 says, "One that ruleth well his own house, having his children in subjection with all gravity; 5 (For if a man know not how to rule his own house, how shall he take care of the church of God?)."

One of my favorite words is "context." The first Google search result for context definition is, "the circumstances that form the setting for an event, statement, or idea, and in terms of which it can be fully understood and assessed." As you discover and get to know your ancestors, be mindful of the context in which they lived—not only of the historical time period in general, but also their personal context. Our ancestors were human beings, no different from ourselves, but the contexts they experienced during their lives must be taken into account as we try to understand their opportunities, challenges, choices, decisions, and actions.

I take you back to Grandpa Elijah Newton Anderson and provide his life story of my own research in my own words as an effort to demonstrate what's possible if you desire to know your ancestor when no one else remembers. The story is there, if you take the time to look, pay attention, and piece together their puzzle with limited but insightful information from various sources. A large part of the adventure, in getting to know your ancestors, is doing your own work. Reference the work of others but reach your own understanding and your own conclusions only after completing an independent investigation, meeting your personal standards of what constitutes a sufficient comprehensive study.

Elijah Newton Anderson was born February 16, 1869, but his life and the lives of his numerous descendants actually began sometime prior to the 1860 census when his grandfather, George Anderson, moved his family to the Lake Butler area of then New River County, FL. Elijah's daddy, Leonard Anderson, was fourteen years old in 1859, and like most every fourteen-year-old boy, he had an eye for pretty girls. But testosterone and time had not yet chiseled him into the man he would become. Working as a farm laborer, Leonard tried to stay focused on furrowing the fields of his family's farm, guiding the mule-pulled plow, but his fourteen-year-old mind couldn't avoid the constant distractions of daydreaming about the beautiful sixteen-year-old Lydia Douglass just across the fence on the neighboring homestead.

Sundays made matters worse, because back in 1859 the Sabbath was sacred and all in the area attended church services at Mt. Zion Primitive Baptist Church just north of downtown Lake Butler. Spotting Lydia Douglass next door on a daily basis was certainly a distraction, but entering the church building on Sundays and seeing her in her Sunday's best scrambled his brain. Dinner on the grounds exaggerated his queasiness, because he had to pass by her in the serving line. Lydia had the same swooning feelings, but not for the boy next door, Leonard Anderson. She waited with anticipation all week for Sunday sunrise to begin her "Sunday best" preparations, hoping to turn the head of twenty-three-year-old Coleman Groover.

Coleman Groover couldn't help but take notice, and sometime prior to 1860, Coleman asked Lydia's father for her hand in marriage. The date was set, the wedding bells rang, and their first child, John C. Groover, was born around 1860. Leonard could only watch, helpless, trapped inside the body of a boy, not able to compete romantically with a strapping young man of twenty-three.

Happily married, madly in love, and totally unaware of Leonard Anderson, Lydia Douglass Groover gave birth to Coleman's second son, James Rhoyand Groover, on March 1, 1861. Three days later, Abraham Lincoln was inaugurated into office as the 16th President of the United States.

Talk of war around Lake Butler, FL dominated all forms of communication. Florida had just two months prior been the third of eventually eleven states to secede from the United States of America to establish the Confederate States of America. All eyes were on Fort Sumter at Charleston, SC.

For four long months, the South had been in negotiations with Major Robert Anderson (no known relation) to vacate Fort Sumter without hostilities. Major Anderson, without orders, had secretly moved his small force from indefensible Fort Moultrie accessible by land to Fort Sumter located smack in the middle of Charleston Harbor. The situation finally came to a head on April 11, 1861, when navy ships arrived intent on re-supplying the fort with arms, food, and fresh troops. If the supplies and troops reached the fort, the vital port would be closed for maritime commerce indefinitely. Unable to extricate United States forces via four months of negotiations, and resupply ships rendezvousing just offshore, Confederate guns opened up on Fort Sumter early the next morning on April 12, 1861.

Fort Sumter surrendered the next day on April 13, 1861. Within two days, on April 15, 1861, President Lincoln called out for 75,000 volunteers to invade the Southern states under rebellion, which included Florida. Patriotism abounded both North and South, each man having his own personal reasons for stepping forward to enlist. On July 21, 1861, Lincoln's volunteer army marched southward from Washington D.C. as an offensive invasion force confident an easy capture of Richmond, VA was imminent.

Greeting the 51,000 invaders at a town called Manassas along Bull Run Creek were 33,000 Southern men determined to defend their states, families, farms, and country. Among the Southern leaders on the field was Thomas Jonathan Jackson. The Union forces appeared headed to victory, pushing Confederate forces back in disarray when Confederate General Bee, in an effort to rally his troops, pointed to Jackson and hollered to his men, "There stands Jackson like a stone wall! Rally behind the Virginians." An avid Bible reader, Jackson believed Christ's promise of eternal life with God awaited him after death. Faith enabled Jackson to stand firm in battle, fearlessly unrattled despite overwhelming peril.

Along with 115 of his neighbors, seventeen-year-old Leonard Anderson answered the call to arms on March 8, 1862 at Lake Butler, FL enlisting as a Private in Company A of the 7th Florida Infantry Regiment. The State of Florida would contribute approximately 15,000 soldiers to the Confederate States army, which as a percentage of the white male population was the highest among all Confederate states. While the 7th Florida assembled at effectively a boot camp near Gainesville, FL, a shipment of almost 10,000 Enfield rifles smuggled from England sat on railroad cars nearby en route to a battle brewing near a place in Tennessee known as Shiloh. More than 500 of those Enfield rifles somehow disappeared from those rail cars and ended up in the hands of 7th Florida recruits. Upon entering a hospital sometime during the war, a receipt shows that Lenard Anderson, Co A, checked in 1 Enfield Rifle, 1 Cartridge Box, 1 Cap Box, and other equipment.

The 7th Florida would travel north to the theater of war via the Chattahoochee River to Columbus, GA and then by rail to Chattanooga, TN. Joining forces that would eventually be known throughout the remainder of the conflict as the Army of Tennessee, they marched northward to Knoxville, TN and eventually deep into Kentucky. Following Confederate General Braxton Bragg's victory at Perryville, KY, the combined forces retreated back to Chattanooga, TN. Union General Rosecrans would dislodge the

Army of Tennessee from Chattanooga and push them southward into Georgia to a small creek named Chickamauga.

On September 18, 1863, the Battle of Chickamauga would tangle 125,000 soldiers (60,000 Union against 65,000 Confederates) in a quest of mortal combat, resulting in casualties inflicted on North American soil second in quantity only to the Battle of Gettysburg. At the end of three days fighting, almost 35,000 men would be dead on the field, wounded, or prisoners of war. Chickamauga would become the first National Military Park in the United States twenty-seven years later in 1890.

The last shots in the battle were fired into the 7th Florida Infantry Regiment whizzing and zipping past Leonard Anderson as the 7th, part of Trigg's Brigade, encircled and captured three entire Union regiments. With this action, the Battle of Chickamauga concluded. Trigg's Brigade suffered staggering casualties, near 26% over the course of the epic three-day battle.

Studying casualty reports for the 7th Florida, the Battle of Missionary Ridge just two months following Chickamauga stands out as having been a very bad day for Leonard Anderson and the men from Lake Butler, FL. To find out why, you must travel to Chattanooga, TN and drive the two-lane road atop Missionary Ridge, stopping along the way to read the red lettered metal historical markers. One such marker is labeled "Finley's (Florida) Brigade." In part, the sign reads, "This brigade was brought up from the trenches early the night of Nov. 24th and formed on the left of Bate's (Tyler's) Brigade. Subsequently, the 7th Florida, Lieut. Col. Ingram was sent back to the trenches with orders to hold them at all hazards."

Metal tablet atop Missionary Ridge: 7th Florida in battle.

Given the order, Leonard Anderson, Company A, and the rest of the 7th Florida headed back down the ridge to man the rifle pits. With the ridge to their backs, and the Union Army in their front positioned behind defensive works on the outskirts of Chattanooga, Leonard waited. He watched and waited all morning on the 25th of November. It was a Wednesday. There were 9,000 Southern men in the rifle trenches stretched thin, nearly 6 miles long. At 3:40 p.m., Union cannons roared, signaling their planned assault of the Confederate lines. More than 23,000 Union soldiers came over their works, advancing toward the Confederate rifle pits. On they came, like an unstoppable blue wave.

As the blue uniforms reached the gray rifle trenches, those rebels not already killed, wounded, or captured ran for their lives to the perceived safety of the top of Missionary Ridge. Uphill for nearly a quarter mile they ran, climbed, and dodged, bullets whizzing, rico-cheting, or finding their mark of thwapping flesh, then shattering bone. Leonard made it to the ridge top only to look back at enemy warriors in hot pursuit. Soon the Yankees would breach the works and begin raining enfilading rifle fire into gray flanks. The route was on! How they were able to escape to Dalton, GA to fight another day is anyone's guess. And fight they did. Buzzard Roost, Resaca, Kennesaw Mountain, Jonesboro, Atlanta, Murfreesboro, Franklin, Nashville, Bentonville, and a dozen more battles along the way.

On April 19, 1862, Coleman Groover, like most every other Southern man between the ages of sixteen and sixty-one, enlisted in the Confederate States Army. He joined family members and neighbors as a Private in Company B, 5th Florida Infantry Regiment, at Lake City, FL. They all went.

I'm sure you can envision what it must have been like for Coleman and Lydia on the night before he picked up his rifle and walked steadily towards the horizon. John was two, James was one, and nineteen-year-old Lydia Ann Douglass Groover was most likely pregnant with baby Lydia Groover. He had no choice but to go. As an honorable man, when your home and family are threatened, you don't back down from a fight.

The 5th Florida Infantry Regiment would eventually combine with the 2nd and the 8th Regiments to create what is known as the Florida Brigade, or Perry's Brigade. To pinpoint Coleman Groover's whereabouts during the Civil War, just follow the exploits of the Florida Brigade, because his muster roll entries state "Present" for most time periods. The Florida Brigade was assigned to General Robert E. Lee's Army of Northern Virginia and took part in all of those famous battles of 1862 and 1863, including 2nd Manassas, Antietam, Fredericksburg, and Chancellorsville. Sometime during the period of June 30 through October 31, 1862, Coleman Groover was captured near Leesburg, VA and later returned to his Company.

At 2:30 p.m. on the afternoon of July 3, 1863, Coleman Groover stood in formation shoulder-to-shoulder with his fellow Floridians just behind the Emmitsburg Road looking out across a mile and a half of open field. His brother, Rowan Groover, also a member of the 5th Florida and present for the period July and August 1863, was most likely standing beside him. As he looked to his left, he could see a line of Southern men 12,500 strong and extending a full mile to the north toward the town of Gettysburg, PA. All faced east waiting for the command to advance toward their objective of breaking the Union center on Cemetery Ridge.

William Faulkner describes it best in his *Intruders in the Dust*: "For every Southern boy fourteen years old, not once but whenever he wants it, there is the instant when it's still not yet two o'clock on that July afternoon in 1863."

The command came with a nod from General Longstreet, and Coleman stepped forward, most likely on bare feet. The Florida Brigade was the extreme right flank of what would go down in history as "Pickett's Charge." In Ken Burns' *The Civil War*, a federal officer recalled, "We could not help hitting them at every shot."

The men from Florida had already been at this same point of the Union line the previous day during brutal fighting. Today they would step over the bloated corpses of their fallen cousins and neighbors as they charged into immortality at the high-water mark of the Confederacy. Unknown by most, the Florida Brigade suffered the highest casualty rate at Gettysburg at a staggering 65% killed, wounded, missing, or captured.

Both Coleman and Rowan would live to fight another day. The specific day was most likely ten months later on May 6, 1864 at the Battle of the Wilderness. The muster roll for Rowan Groover states he was captured at the Battle of the Wilderness on May 6, 1864. Brigadier General Edward A. Perry (Perry's Brigade) was severely wounded on May 6, 1864 at The Wilderness. Coleman Groover's muster roll for the period February 29 to June 30, 1864 simply states "Kiled" (not a typo). If not May 6, 1864 at The Wilderness, then it was somewhere along that rolling battlefront of Lee checking Grant's every flanking movement southward from Spotsylvania Court House, to North Anna, to Cold Harbor, to Petersburg. Either heaved into a hastily dug mass grave trench or left to decompose where he crumpled from the thwap of a Minie ball entry and exit, his body was never returned home to his Lydia in Lake Butler, Florida.

Assumed place where Coleman Groover
died: Wilderness Battlefield

The war ended for Leonard Anderson in April 1865 with General Joseph E. Johnston's surrender to General William Tecumseh Sherman following the Battle of Bentonville, NC. Paroled at Greensboro, NC on May 1, 1865, the now twenty-year-old, battle-hardened Private Leonard Anderson, Company A of the 7th Florida

Infantry Regiment would have walked home barefoot the 500 miles from Greensboro, NC to Lake Butler, FL. Like "The Burning" of the Shenandoah Valley by Union General Phillip Sheridan bringing total war to the civilian population of the South, General William Tecumseh Sherman had brought his scorched earth policy to Georgia, burning and laying waste to a path 50 miles wide, from torched Atlanta to Savannah. Therefore, all modes of transportation were literally non-existent between North Carolina and Lake Butler, FL.

It's unknown the circumstances that brought them together a year after the war. But, on 11 Nov 1866, Leonard Anderson would court and marry his former teen crush girl-next-door neighbor, Lydia Ann Douglass Groover, widow of Private Coleman Groover. Leonard would help raise Coleman's three young children as his own, along with the six children he and Lydia would conceive together.

The second oldest of those six Anderson children, Elijah Newton Anderson, took his first breath as a child on February 16, 1869, but his real birthday, likely May 6, 1864, was the moment Coleman Groover breathed his last. Had it not been for the Civil War, Coleman and Lydia would have remained happily married, head over heels in love, and had many more children together, none of which would have been Elijah Anderson. Therefore, for the descendants of Leonard Anderson to exist, the American Civil War literally had to happen, and Coleman Groover had to die during the conflict.

The 1870 census, Charlton County, GA, July 28, 1870, shows twenty-five-year-old Leonard Anderson, twenty-six-year-old Lydia, two-year-old Lemuel, one-year-old Elijah, three-month-old Lucretia, ten-year-old farm hand, John C. Groover, nine-year-old James R. Groover, and seven-year-old Lydia Groover living on a 400-acre farm they owned just north of the Florida Georgia state line. Charlton County was that area of land dipping down into Florida following the St. Marys River just west of Jacksonville. Their post office was located at Sanderson, FL, which was located about midway between their farm and their hometown of Lake Butler about 20 miles away.

The oldest son of Coleman Groover, working as a farm hand at age ten, was an interesting point to contemplate. Scraping out a living in rural north Florida/south Georgia in post-war Southern Reconstruction was a hard row to hoe, especially with eight mouths to feed.

There would be three more mouths to feed with the births of Amanda in 1872, Leonard in 1874, and George in 1876, bringing the total to eleven. For reasons yet unknown, according to Lydia's Widow's Pension Application dated July 27, 1909, the family moved back across the St. Marys River into Florida around 1876 when Elijah Newton Anderson was seven years old. The location where they settled was Brooker, FL located in Bradford County, because that's where the family was living on July 7 in the 1880 census, and that was Lydia's statement in her Widow's Pension Application dated July 18, 1907.

Three years after moving back to Florida, in August 1879, Lydia received devastating news that her husband Leonard Anderson had died somewhere in Ware County, GA. Or, maybe it was Clinch County, GA. Two witnesses, Joseph C. Harrell and Thomas W. Sweat, both confirmed members of Company A of the 7th Florida Infantry Regiment, stated, "Did not see him but have good reasons to believe he died in August 1879," and "I have good reasons to believe he is dead," respectively. Elijah Newton Anderson was just ten years old, fatherless, living on a farm in sparsely populated Brooker, FL with his mom and eight siblings. Fortunately, his two Groover half-brothers were now able-bodied young men of nineteen and eighteen.

Recalling that nineteen-year-old John Groover was a "farm hand" at age ten back in 1870, it can be assumed ten-year-old Elijah Newton Anderson had to do the same in 1879 when his father died.

For the next six years, the physical work responsibilities of farming never abated for young Elijah. By the Florida census of 1885, his two older Groover bothers had left the nest and his older eighteen-year-old brother Lem was noted as suffering from some sort of disability. This would have left sixteen-year-old Elijah as the lead farm hand for his mother.

Elijah Newton Anderson's first love was Lou Anna Thomas. Elijah was seventeen, and Lou Anna was nineteen in 1886. They probably met at church, a Primitive Baptist Church. Church records from in and around Brooker, FL may reference membership of these two, or Elijah's mom Lydia, or Lou Anna's parents. We know they were crazy about each other because Lou Anna became pregnant with their first daughter, Leona, in December 1886 two months prior to Elijah's eighteenth birthday. We can only assume they were married prior to December 1886, but not too soon before December, because of Elijah's young age. Leona A. Anderson was born 9 Sep 1887.

During their first thirteen years together, Lou Anna would give birth to six children, all daughters. You can envision proud Elijah holding the reigns to his team of horses, pulling his wagon to the front of New Hope Primitive Baptist Church near La Crosse, FL on Sunday mornings with Lou Anna by his side and six beautiful daughters all dressed up behind them. We know this was their church in June of 1899, because that's where thirty-year-old Elijah buried the love of his life just before her thirty-second birthday. Her cause of death is unknown, probably childbirth, but the effect on Elijah must have been beyond devastating, his grief unbearable. At age ten he lost his dad. At age thirty, he lost his wife. The 1900 census shows him a widower with all six girls ages twelve, eleven, nine, six, four, and two living on the farm he owned in Bradford County, FL adjacent to his mother Lydia's farm.

For five years, from 1899 to 1904, Elijah raised those six girls alone with the help of mother Lydia and I'm sure other family and church members residing in the community. After five years of mourning, at age thirty-five, it was time for Elijah to love again, and he found his new life partner in seventeen-year-old Linnie Obedience Smith from 45 miles away in Green Cove Springs, FL. She was only eight months older than Elijah's daughter Leona, so the family dynamics must have been awkward to say the least. They were married October 10, 1904, and Linnie was soon pregnant with Elijah's seventh daughter, Alcy.

His eighth daughter in a row, Lydia Louvinnie Anderson, was born on March 15, 1907. For almost 100 years she would be known as Vinnie. Then, on April 9, 1909 at age forty, and twenty-two years since he heard his first baby cry, Linnie produced a boy for Elijah, and they named him John Elijah Newton Anderson after her daddy, John Smith, and of course Elijah. A second son, James Leonard Anderson, was born August 7, 1911, and life was good, very good. He had ten children born, ten children alive, eight girls, and now two boys, Johnny and Jimmy, to carry on the Anderson name. Elijah and Linnie sat for a family portrait in late 1911 with Alcy, Jimmy, Vinnie, and Johnny all dressed sharp thanks to Linnie's skills as a seamstress. Elijah had his dapper hat cocked back. In hindsight, the photo captured Elijah Newton Anderson's high-water mark.

The headstone at Rock Primitive Baptist Church just east of Brooker, FL in Bradford County reads: Alcy M. Anderson 1905-1912. She was six or seven years old depending on her unknown date of birth and unknown date of death. There's a good chance she died in late September, because Elijah's brother Lemuel also lost his seven-year-old, Henry, in 1912 on September 20. Family members recall Vinnie mentioning a sister dying from an illness described as "bloody diarrhea" and that little brother Johnny had also been sick and almost died. The culprit has the tell-tale signs of dysentery, an infectious disease caused by consumption of food or water contaminated by certain bacteria, viruses, and parasites resulting in severe abdominal pain, cramping, fever, and extreme diarrhea. Alcy most likely suffered an agonizing week to ten days of dehydration, chills, fever, and gut-wrenching stomach cramps. All Elijah and Linnie could do was watch, pray, try to get fluids into her, and wait. It was 1912 in isolated rural north central Florida.

Great-great-aunt Alcy M.
Anderson, age six or seven

I've not lost a child, so I cannot speak from experience, nor can I begin to imagine or explain what it must be like to be in the presence of a lifeless child. I have had to hold beloved family pets when the time came to put them down, and while the emotions associated with those events are exaggeratedly painful, they pale in comparison to the death of a child, your own child. The loss of Alcy had to have been staggering for Elijah and Linnie, probably lost their minds. For twenty-five years her grave would be the lone burial at Rock Cemetery until unrelated fifty-year-old Joseph Frank Brown joined her in 1937.

By the 1920 census taken on 7 Jan 1920, the Anderson family had migrated 200 miles south to the town of Bradenton located in Manatee County, FL. Why did they move to Manatee County? When did they move to Bradenton? Were they distraught from Alcy's death? Did they want to escape the illness that plagued Alcy, Johnny, and Henry in Bradford County? Or, was the death of Elijah's mother, Lydia, in 1919 the catalyst for the change of scenery? Maybe financial opportunities were calling from Manatee County.

On 18 Mar 1920, eleven months to the day following the death of Elijah's mother, Lydia, a dust-covered horseman rode into Lake Butler, FL from a point unknown. With a city population of only 756, everyone knew every familiar face in town, but no one recognized the old man who seemed oddly enough to be rather comfortable in his new surroundings. A week passed by, then two. The old man appeared in his mid-seventies but carried himself with a posture of strength. Conversation among neighbors often transitioned to the newest visitor who acted more like a resident fixture.

About six weeks after the old man's unexpected arrival, on 26 Apr 1920, hundreds of people from many miles around Lake Butler began their annual pilgrimage toward downtown. It was Confederate Memorial Day, a time set aside to remember and honor fathers, sons, husbands, brothers, uncles, cousins, grandfathers, sweethearts, friends, and neighbors who as Southern patriots had paid the ultimate sacrifice for their definition of freedom, just as their grandfathers before them had done against England in the Revolutionary War, the War of 1812, and Indian Wars. The somber occasion was celebrated all across the Southern states, with Florida specifically setting aside the 26th of April on each year's calendar, because on that day in 1865 the largest remaining Confederate Army was surrendered at Durham, NC following the last major battle of the Civil War at Bentonville.

Among those troops at Bentonville and Durham was Company A of the 7th Florida Infantry Regiment comprised of brave men raised as a volunteer fighting force at Lake Butler, FL. Out front of the General Store on Main Street was ole mister one-legger John Craft leaning slightly leftward as countless steps had worn off the first inch or so of his wooden left leg. Back in 1862 to 1864, Sergeant John Craft had been a highly revered, battle tested Florida warrior fearlessly fighting across Kentucky, Tennessee, and Georgia. The war ended for John on 5 Apr 1864 at Dallas, GA when a Minie ball fired from a Union Springfield rifle ripped through his left leg, shattering the bone. The field surgeon had no choice. He sliced round through good flesh above the wound down to the bone and quickly traded his sharp knife for a well-worn hand saw.

Watching the gathering crowd with their Army of Tennessee battle flags in hand and other grave decorations, John Craft's slouch hat slipped from his grasp, ending top down against his right and only leather boot. As he repositioned his wooden leg to attempt a retrieval, the old man with the new face in town standing beside him reached for the hat. Both old men clutching the same butternut hat and raising back up at the waist found themselves looking directly into each other's eyes, face-to-face.

John: Leonard? (In an astonished tone.) There was a long pause. Leonard Anderson, is it really you?

Leonard: Yes, John, it's me all right. Been a long while, hasn't it.

Nobody knows where Leonard Anderson had been for all those forty-two years after walking out on his wife and nine children. The timing of his return not long after Lydia's death and Elijah's move leaves little doubt he had maintained communications with

someone in Bradford County. Possible motives for his disappearance stoke imaginative thought, but none are good enough to excuse
the easily predictable anguish and hardships the act of his leaving
inflicted upon those he was assigned by God to protect and nurture.
But Leonard had his reasons. He didn't just wake up one morning
and brainlessly ride off into the sunset. Something triggered his
decision to plan and fake his own death. Plotting and implementing
his plan took significant time and effort, yet during that period of
preparation, nothing occurred that altered his course.

Elijah's daddy, Leonard Anderson, appeared before the Clerk of
Circuit Court for Union County, FL at Lake Butler on 24 May 1922
and made application for a Confederate soldier's Pension Claim.
With him appeared two fellow members of Company A, being duly
sworn according to law, did declare that the man making application for a pension was in fact Leonard Anderson. The witnesses
were John Craft and Mathew L. McKenny, and both attested they
had honorably served alongside Leonard Anderson: John until
wounded and carried to a hospital and Mathew until surrendered
with Leonard 13 Apr 1865 at Bentonville, NC.

On 5 Jun 1922, a total of five Union County Commissioners
and the Clerk of Circuit Court signed a "Report of County
Commissioners" stating they were satisfied Leonard Anderson's
application was in fact true and a pension should be granted.
However, Leonard Anderson received a letter dated 29 Jul 1922
from the State Board of Pensions denying his pension claim due to
not being a Florida resident for the required minimum of the prior
eight-year period.

News of Leonard Anderson back from the dead would have
spread rapidly through the close-knit community between 1920 and
1922. Elijah would have been fifty-one years old living in Bradenton
when he received word of his father's return to the area north of
Gainesville. One can only imagine how Elijah and his siblings must

have reacted when blindsided by such a deplorable scenario. The emotional toll exacted on Leonard's children must have been mortifying. I asked Aunt Leona if she had ever heard anything about her Great-grandfather Leonard Anderson having faked his own death and abandoning his family. She recalled there having been something like that happen, but all she could remember was a vague recollection about one of Leonard's children, maybe her Grandpa Elijah Newton Anderson, having confronted him at a hotel in Tampa about what he had done.

Elijah Anderson elevated on steps. My grandfather in overalls.

In 1921, Elijah and Linnie's fourteen-year-old daughter, Vinnie, married Frank Robert Zipperer. A family photo taken about 1926 showed Elijah, Linnie, Vinnie, Frank, Johnny, Jimmy, and Vinnie's oldest three children. The photo date was estimated based on the age of Vinnie's third child who was born in 1926 and was a baby in the photo. This was the last confirmed year prior to Elijah and Linnie ending their marriage. The reasons behind their divorce were unknown, but by age thirty-nine in 1926, with her three surviving children at or nearing adulthood, Linnie was no longer a child bride bound to her now fifty-seven-year-old husband Elijah. Sometime between 1926 and 1930, Elijah and Linnie went their separate ways.

The 1930 census shows E N Anderson age sixty-one residing back in his hometown of Brooker, FL labeled as a widower rooming in the household of fifty-four-year-old widow Sarah A. Conerly and her sixteen-year-old son, Wilson Conerly. I'm adding these next few lines to this paragraph to share that I didn't know who Sarah A. Conerly was in this story until editing my final draft of this book. Between the time I wrote the first sentence of this paragraph and now, reading my work, I had visited with my distant cousin, Bob Holder, the man I had met in that Brooker, FL cemetery at the grave of Lydia Anderson on that Memorial Day of my first road trip to honor my DNA. His cancer was advanced. At his home, in his living room, he had an old family photo hanging above his fireplace mantle. I asked Bob who the people were in the photo. He said, "That's my great-grandmother, Sarah Amanda Conerly, Lydia Anderson's daughter, sister to your Elijah Anderson." As I silently read my own writing, hearing the words in my head, reaching the name Sarah A. Conerly, I heard Bob Holder's voice from the grave plain as day, "Sarah Amanda Conerly." In the 1930 census, my Great-great-grandfather Elijah Newton Anderson was living with his sister and nephew!

The widower marital status in the 1930 census wasn't 100% untruthful, because his first wife had passed away, but it certainly wasn't accurate considering Linnie was alive and well. At sixty-one, he was earning his wage as a farm laborer. Divorce was frowned upon in 1930's society and even more so within the Primitive Baptist Church where a member could be asked to leave under certain circumstances. Apparently, Linnie O. Anderson had also chosen to label herself as a widow, but she was 250 miles south in Punta Gorda, FL working on her own account as a Dress Maker.

In 1933, Elijah Anderson, then sixty-four, married the sixty-seven-year-old widow Kizzie E. Parmenter, making her his third bride. Kizzie was born Keziah E. Norman to parents Isaac and Margaret Norman in Clay County, FL adjacent to the east of Bradford, County. At age twenty-four, she married James L. Parmenter and gave birth to nine children, eight of which survived as per the 1910 census. James died in 1927, leaving Kizzie a widow for six years before her second marriage. A unique connection shared by Elijah and Kizzie was that both of their fathers, Leonard Anderson and Isaac Norman, fought together as Confederate soldiers in Company A of the 7th Florida Infantry Regiment, with Isaac being wounded at Marietta, GA on 2 Jul 1864 and again at Murfreesboro, TN on 6 Dec 1864.

Two years later in 1935, Elijah and Kizzie made their home in Starke, FL, moving to Lake Geneva, FL by 1940. The 1940 census listed Elijah as "Clyde Anderson" age seventy-one owning a home valued at $500 and unable to work, but it also mentioned he had a source of income. We know.this Clyde Anderson was in fact Elijah Newton Anderson, because his seventy-three-year-old wife, Kizzie Anderson, was noted living in the household. Most would move right on past the name Clyde, but I paused to consider why my grandfather would intentionally try to hide his identity using an alias. Providing his wife's name to the census taker completely blew his cover, so he wasn't trying to hide his name on purpose. And then it hit me. My great-great-grandfather went by the nickname Lige. In his Deep South, Florida accent, he told the census taker his name was Lige, but the census taker interpreted him to have said Clyde. How do I know? Because his grandson, my great-uncle, was named Elijah after his grandfather, and we all called him either Uncle Burr, or Uncle Lige, short for Elijah.

Elijah Newton Anderson passed away into Heaven on 12 Sep 1943 at the age of seventy-four. It was a Sunday, which was fitting considering the importance of the Lord's Day in his life as a Reverend in the Primitive Baptist Church. His wife, Kizzie, and his children, chose to inter him next to his first wife, and most likely the true love of his life, Lou Anna Thomas Anderson. Elijah and Lou Anna are buried under the shade of a magnificent live oak tree in

New Hope Primitive Baptist Church Cemetery near La Crosse, FL just north of Gainesville. The same oak stands watch over the grave of Elijah's mother, Lydia.

Grave of Elijah Anderson and first wife,
Lou Anna Thomas Anderson

Accept a succinct description of an ancestor at face value and go on about your mundane, or choose to step inside an hours long historical records time machine, where Grandpa Anderson comes to life in your mind's eye. Organized in chronological order and enhanced by context, the name, dates, and circumstances become a person, and your DNA contributor becomes a remembered loved one. Were they extraordinary, complex, and worthy of analysis? Or is the memory of their traversing upon this earth best summarized by a single word of degradation or admiration? Do your own work, reach your own conclusions, and leave your best effort in writing for those beyond you as a foundation of remembrance.

I never personally knew my 2nd Great-grandfather Elijah Newton Anderson, but I was blessed to have visited his second wife, my 2nd great-grandmother, Linnie Obedience Smith, in her nursing home room. I have one recollection of a great-grandfather before I was six years old, I met two of my great-grandmothers, I knew very well my other two great-grandmothers, and I spent almost fifty years with all four of my grandparents. To help my ancestors to be remembered, I will write their stories to the best of my ability, so hopefully 100 years from now, their future descendants may have an opportunity to know something about these amazing people who gave them life. I hope the following example will encourage you to write the stories of your ancestors from a position of integrity and objectivity, all the while striving for accuracy.

Chapter 21

MY VALIANT VALDOSTAN

Afternoon storm clouds were rolling in from the south as I stood on the front porch of a stranger's home. Having rang the doorbell, I backed off two paces and removed my sweat-soaked ball cap so as not to appear threatening. The door opened, and a man asked what he could do for me. I apologized for imposing before sharing I was looking for a cemetery and wondered if he might know of one nearby. He hesitated for a moment before saying, "There is a small, old, abandoned cemetery back behind my house, but it's in really bad shape. An older couple used to come here and maintain it, but they eventually quit coming. I took over mowing and cleaning up debris as best I could, but some vandals got in there, broke some things, and made a mess. Then a giant dead tree crashed down on top of the graves, and it's been like that ever since." He kindly offered his driveway for access, and I let him know how much I appreciated his past efforts.

As I stepped out of my blue Ford pickup, a cold wind began to blow, and large raindrops plunked down. The dark thunderstorm squall line was upon the cemetery as the depth of what the man

263

had shared appeared before me. Massive and complete describes the size and coverage of the fallen tree. The St. Augustine grass was knee deep, and shards of white marble peeked up, entangled in vines. Somewhere amongst this chaos of once a graveyard rests a Southern patriot, a veteran of more than thirty-eight battles, a member of General Thomas Jonathan "Stonewall" Jackson's Foot Cavalry, and a warrior wounded in action against future President of the United States Rutherford B. Hayes. Of the once formidable 12th Georgia Infantry Regiment, more than 1,200 men strong, he was one of only sixty survivors still in the fight at Appomattox, VA when Lee surrendered to Grant on April 9, 1865.

Wisenbaker Cemetery in Valdosta, GA

Walking atop the now horizontal trunk and sturdy limbs of the once proud sentinel tree, looking down into the twisted heap, evidence of broken burial sites did exist. The rain was beginning to fall more rapidly when appeared the name "James Wisenbaker" on a damaged stone resting flat on top of a crushed, red brick, above-ground grave structure. Hopping down into the grass, and feeling around with my feet, I found five historic marble puzzle pieces that eventually read "Sarah Dasher." Like most of us after death, forgotten in three generations. Somewhere in the ground beneath those damaged grave markers was physically the source of 3.125% of me.

Marble Puzzle: SARAH DASHER
WIFE OF JAMES WISENBAKER

Crushed graves: James A. Wisenbaker
and Sarah Ann Dasher Wisenbaker

James A. Wisenbaker was one of my 4th great-grandfathers. He was born in 1810 and lived in the area of Valdosta, GA. At age twenty-seven, on October 16, James made the best decision of his life and married the mesmerizingly attractive eighteen-year-old Sarah Ann Catherine Dasher. Every woman fits this description in the eyes of the one man who asks her father for her hand in marriage. Over the next twenty-two years, they would produce at least twelve offspring in Lowndes County, GA including five girls and seven boys, one of whom would be my 3rd great-grandfather, Adriel Herman Wisenbaker, born in 1844. They farmed land located between, and contiguous to, lands owned by James' brothers William and John.

In 1859, there was no such place as Valdosta, GA. An east to west railroad track was being planned, and leaders within Lowndes County, like everyone else living at that time, knew the importance and value of proximity to railways for trade, travel, commerce, and communications. The county seat at that time was Troupville, but plans revealed the new rail line would bypass the town just a few miles to the south. For the benefit of the county for future generations, the decision was made to select a location along the planned rail route for a new county seat. The optimal location was determined to be situated at the home of James Wisenbaker's brother, William Wisenbaker. In December 1859, Lowndes County purchased 140 acres of land from Mr. Wisenbaker to set out from scratch a new city.

Think of any city in America, and at one time, nothing existed there—no town square, no residents, no stores, no streets, no courthouse. Planners laid out the new city's vision and design, complete with city blocks enclosed by streets now named after area pioneers, such as Patterson and Ashely. Built entirely upon Wisenbaker land, they named the new city Valdosta.

Now, put yourself into the mind and context of James A. Wisenbaker at the beginning of 1861. Your Salzburger ancestors from Austria landed upon the shores of Georgia with literally nothing in the 1740s. Your grandfather, born in Georgia, was a Patriot in the American Revolution fighting for independence against England and the Loyalists. You, your ancestors, your family members, and your neighbors have been members of local militias for at least 120 years, literally carving out and sustaining a way of life against overwhelming odds. You own a fair amount of land and personal property. You have a wife, sons, daughters, and grandchildren. Your home state of Georgia has seceded. Abraham Lincoln has amassed a horde of 75,000 armed men with the intent to invade, defeat, conquer, occupy, and subjugate. You are a farmer. You have been a member of your church for forty-one years. Your Christian faith is that of a Protestant who strongly disagrees with a central episcopal polity hierarchy of governance. You have seven children in your home. You are fifty-one years old. What do you do?

The call went out in Lowndes County, GA for volunteers to meet the imminent invasion from Lincoln's legions. On June 14, 1861, 118 men boldly stepped forward and signed up to form the "Lowndes Volunteers," which would be known as Company "I" of the 12th Georgia Infantry Regiment. Among those men were James A. Wisenbaker, George Henry Wisenbaker, and John Flerl Wisenbaker. Like others soon heading off to war, James and his wife Sarah sat down in front of a relatively new invention known as a camera to have their images captured. Some of the motivation was surely pride of a new gray uniform. There was also the real possibility of never coming home, so this may have been the last and only opportunity to record one's self for posterity.

You will find these historic photos of James A. Wisenbaker and his wife, Sarah Ann Dasher Wisenbaker, among a collection of Civil War photos housed at the United States Library of Congress in Washington, D.C. One photo is of Sarah A. Dasher and a second photo is of both Sarah A. Dasher and her husband James A.

Wisenbaker sitting together as a couple. James is dressed in what appears to be a gray Confederate soldier uniform. With his hairline receding to the top of his head, his age is obviously advanced beyond what you might expect for an infantry soldier.

The photo of the couple seated together, along with a photo of Sarah A. Dasher sitting alone, was purchased by Tom Liljenquist on July 2, 2012 at a Gettysburg Civil War Show, from Richard Ferry of Macclenny, FL, on consign-

Sarah Dasher Wisenbaker and James A. Wisenbaker: Library of Congress

ment from a Tim Tyler. The photos were donated to the United States Library of Congress. "Mrs. Sarah A Dasher" and "GA" was written on the back of the frame. I know this to be true, because I contacted the Library of Congress myself, requested that a staff member retrieve the photos, take digital photos of the backs of the photos and frame, and email them to me. The handwritten name and state on the photo frame were used by a Laura Elliott to identify the Wisenbaker couple. The identification and authenticity were confirmed and accepted by the Library of Congress and expert Civil War photo collector Tom Liljenquist.

From just north of the Florida border at Valdosta, GA, the Lowndes Volunteers formed ranks and headed north. Company I soon arrived at Camp Bartow located in present day West Virginia, which at that time was the western side of Virginia. Most of the men lived and worked on isolated farms, so this was their first time to congregate in close quarters in large numbers. It didn't take long for disease to rapidly spread throughout camp. Within two months of enlisting, typhoid pneumonia claimed its first victim, Private Hardy H. Jordan, on August 18, 1861. Within the next forty days, by the end of September, only three months after Company I was formed, twenty-five men, or 21% of the Lowndes Volunteers, were dead from sickness and disease. A muster roll for James A. Wisenbaker lists him as "Sick" during the period June 27, 1861 through August 31, 1861. Fortunately, he survived the camp sickness.

The boys from South Georgia would soon get their first taste of battle on October 3, 1861 when Union forces attacked Camp Bartow. The next engagement occurred on December 13, 1861 when Union forces attacked Camp Allegheny. Using football as an analogy, these two engagements were pre-season or scrimmage games. These two skirmishes would prove to be only the tip of the iceberg, as the 12th Georgia would soon join other units under command of legendary Major General Thomas Jonathan "Stonewall" Jackson. Known to history as one of the greatest infantry field commanders of all time, his men nicknamed themselves "Stonewall's Foot Cavalry" for good reason. Jackson could mobilize his army, march them beyond expectations of opposing Union generals, and successfully attack the enemy where least expected.

Keep in mind, James A. Wisenbaker was fifty-two years old when Stonewall Jackson began to push men beyond the physical limits of whatever an able-bodied man was capable of withstanding. Infantry soldiers travelled mostly by foot and carried their gear along the way, covering vast distances during forced marches. At the end of these treacherous journeys was not a soft, comfy bed at a Fairfield Inn. Instead, it was immediate charges into battle under a hail of concentrated enemy rifle fire and essentially gigantic shotgun blasts of canister rounds discharged from cannon barrels. Double canister was used if the enemy got too close. James Wisenbaker did his job as a soldier, and did it well, being promoted from Private to Corporal.

Follow the 12th Georgia's movements, and you're following the movements of James Wisenbaker. Follow the movements of Stonewall Jackson up until his untimely death at the Battle of Chancellorsville, and you're following the movements of James Wisenbaker. The Southern man from Valdosta was a beast of a soldier. Study the Civil War, and you probably won't find a fighting man who experienced more of the war than James. It was absolutely awe inspiring to ponder his strength, wits, discipline, stamina, and resolve.

The list of battles mounted—some famous and many you've never heard of. Each claimed men from the Lowndes Volunteers' ranks. The muster rolls were heartbreaking to read. Casualties reported included died of disease, died from wounds, amputation, captured, killed, missing, wounded in eye, disabled, and worse. James A. Wisenbaker continued fighting.

He was among the Confederate troops that captured Union General Pope's supply depot at Manassas Junction, which initiated the battle of 2nd Manassas. The men stuffed their bellies full of Union rations, looted what they could carry, and set fire to the remaining cache. He was there with Stonewall Jackson behind the unfinished railroad bed where Jackson initiated a fight with passing Union forces and held on for Lee and Longstreet to arrive.

Until further research is completed, it must be assumed James A. Wisenbaker did not participate in the battles of Harper's Ferry and Antietam. Among his file at FOLD3.com, his name, J. A. Wessenbaker, appeared on a list of absentees, without proper authority, from the 12th Ga. Vol., during the battles of Sept. 15-20, 1862. Immediately following the Battle of 2nd Manassas, Stonewall Jackson marched his army to Ox Hill in an attempt to cut off the Union's avenue of retreat from Manassas to Washington D.C. At the Battle of Ox Hill, the 12th Georgia was engaged in severe combat, resulting in the death of their Captain William F. Brown. Was James Wisenbaker wounded at Ox Hill? Was James Wisenbaker tending to members of the Lowndes Volunteers killed and wounded at Ox Hill? If James did not travel with the 12th Georgia to Lee's first Maryland Campaign, it was most likely related to what transpired at the Battle of Ox Hill. At fifty-two years old, maybe he was just flat worn out from 2nd Manassas and Ox Hill. Or, maybe he actually was at Harper's Ferry and Antietam.

12th Georgia Infantry Regiment Battles

Battle	Date	Battle	Date
Camp Bartow	Oct 3, 1861	Spotsylvania	May 12-19, 1864
Camp Allegheny	Dec 13, 1861	North Anna	May 23-26, 1864
McDowell	May 8, 1862	Bethesda Church	May 31, 1864
Front Royal	May 23, 1862	Cold Harbor	Jun 3, 1864
Winchester	May 26, 1862	Valley Campaign	Jun 18 - Sep 1, 1864
Cross Keys	Jun 8, 1862	Lynchburg	Jun 17-18, 1864
Port Republic	Jun 8-9, 1862	Monocacy	July 9, 1864
Seven Days	Jun 25 - Jul 5, 1862	Fort Stevens: Wash DC	Jul 11, 1864
Cedar Run	Aug 8, 1862	Cool Spring	Jul 17-18, 1864
2nd Manassas	Aug 29, 1862	2nd Kernstown	Jul 24, 1864
Ox Hill	Sep 1, 1862	Strasburg, VA	Aug 17, 1864
Harper's Ferry	Sep 14, 1862	Summit Point	Aug 21, 1864
Antietam	Sep 16-17, 1862	Smithfield Crossing	Aug 29, 1864
Fredericksburg	Dec 13-15, 1862	3rd Winchester	Sep 19, 1864
Chancellorsville	May 3, 1863	Fisher's Hill	Sep 21-22, 1864
Gettysburg	Jul 2-4, 1863	Cedar Creek	Oct 19, 1864
Manassas Gap	Jul 23, 1863	Fort Stedman	Mar 25, 1865
Mine Run	Nov 26 - Dec 2, 1863	Appomattox Campaign	Mar 29 - Apr 9, 1865
Valley Duty	Dec 1863 - Apr 1864	George Henry Wisenbaker Surrended by Lee	Apr 9, 1865
Wilderness	May 5-7, 1864	James A. Wisenbaker Surrendered by Lee	probably Apr 9, 1865

At Chancellorsville, James Wisenbaker, among thousands of Stonewall's finest, marched 12 miles around the Union right flank. At 5:30 p.m., Union soldiers relaxing for supper noticed rabbits and foxes bounding out of the woods just before James and 28,000 Confederates charged out of the woods shouting the Rebel Yell. The boys in blue were caught completely by surprise. As night fell, with intentions to launch a night attack, Jackson rode out between the lines to investigate Union defensive positions. The sound of musket fire may have fallen on the ears of James Wisenbaker, as Confederate troops from North Carolina fired a volley into the darkness assuming a Union cavalry attack. Their own beloved Stonewall Jackson was hit by the friendly fire, had his arm amputated, and lost his life to pneumonia eight days later.

At Gettysburg, the beginning of the first day of fighting on July 1, 1863, James was among Dole's Brigade on the north side of the town, pushing Union forces back through downtown to their defensive position on Cemetery Hill. Can you imagine? He was there, aiming his rifle, firing, removing another cartridge from his case, reloading, cocking back the hammer, removing another percussion cap from the leather pouch on his belt, his coolness and dexterity enabling him to carefully grasp between finger and thumb a single tiny metal explosive device, precisely setting it securely atop the tip of the combustion chamber cone while staring into the acrid smoke belching repeatedly from Union guns. Bullets whizzed and zipped so close he could feel the instant change in air pressure very near his earlobe as heated projectiles of conical lead traveling 950 feet per second narrowly missed their mark. An acorn-shaped granite monument was erected to honor Dole's Brigade at the place north of town where James Wisenbaker and four regiments from Georgia stared death in the face—and didn't back down.

*Gettysburg Battlefield monument for DOLES'S
BRIGADE & 12th Georgia Infantry*

James was there among the tattered gray and butternut uniforms, in the thickest throws of mortal combat, against incomprehensible odds, in the killing fields of such epic major battles as follows:

- Wilderness   (65,000 CSA defeated 124,000 Union)
- Spotsylvania   (60,000 CSA defeated 110,000 Union)
- Cold Harbor   (60,000 CSA defeated 115,000 Union)

Despite being outnumbered 2-to-1, with inferior weaponry, with inferior supplies, the Southern men commanded by General Robert E. Lee kept on winning. And fifty-four-year-old James was still in the fight.

Bogged down in trench warfare at Petersburg, VA, Lee ordered General Jubal Early northward on a mission reminiscent of Stonewall Jackson's successful Valley Campaign. Traveling up the Shenandoah Valley, Jubal Early launched a surprise attack against Washington D.C. from the northwest. Part of Lee's bold plan was to free 15,000 Confederate soldier prisoners of war at the Union POW Camp at Point Lookout, MD. General Early's army, which included the 12th Georgia, carried out Lee's orders, reaching Washington on 11 Jul 1864. The attack force was delayed just long enough on 9 Jul 1864 at the Battle of Monocacy to allow Union reinforcements time to arrive at Fort Stevens, one of almost seventy such forts surrounding the capital city. President Lincoln was so close while observing the attack, his doctor was shot while standing beside him.

The Yankee prison at Point Lookout, MD, 95 miles away, was a POW camp too far. The planned Southern cavalry raid to end the misery at Point Lookout and save my 5th great-uncle, thirty-nine-year-old POW Samuel S. Moody, was commendable, but not feasible. Sadly, Sam died there three and a half months later on 29 Oct 1864. A Christian man, my uncle was tossed into a mass grave along with 4,000 other Confederate soldier prisoners who succumbed to exposure and neglect purposely inflicted in a land of plenty. General Grant and President Lincoln had done the math, concluded the drawn-out suffering and wasting away of 50,000 American men, both Northern and Southern, was a sacrifice they were willing to make to achieve their end goal. They refused to resume prisoner exchanges and were steadfast in their resolve as the corpses of POWs at places like Elmira, NY, Point Lookout, MD, Andersonville, GA, Rock Island, IL, Camp Chase, OH, and Camp Douglas, IL piled up by the tens of thousands. When I think about my eighteen uncles and cousins who died as POWs in Yankee prisons, I listen to Lee Ann Womack's song, "The Legend of the Rebel Soldier."

Then came the Battle of Cedar Creek on October 19, 1864. At 8 p.m. on the night of October 18, James Wisenbaker's unit began a seven and a half-hour all-night, single-file down a "pig trail" march in preparation for a surprise attack against far superior numbers of Union troops on the opposite side of Cedar Creek. These Union soldiers had just completed a 75-mile path of total war, known as The Burning, against the civilian population of the Shenandoah Valley. Non-combatant Virginians, farmers, grown men, on their knees, begged for mercy and wept in front of their wives and children, as soldiers in blue uniforms, Yankees, set torches to the barns their grandfathers had built, burned their stores, lit their crop fields ablaze, and shot dead their livestock by the thousands. At 5 a.m., 14,500 Southern troops sprang upon 32,000 of their despised adversaries. The unsuspecting Union encampments were taken completely by surprise, and the rout was on. Unfortunately, the victory was going so well, Confederate soldiers, hungry and tired, began to forage through the abandoned Union camps looking for food.

The Union counterattack came at 4 p.m. Brigadier General George Armstrong Custer's cavalry charged the Confederate left flank, broke through, and raced to the Confederate Army's rear, blocking their escape route. Union Major General Philip Sheridan pressed an attack against Confederate Major General Dodson Ramseur, Division Commander over the 12th Georgia. How fierce was the fighting? It was so bad, even Ramseur was mortally wounded. It can't be known exactly when or where on the battlefield it happened, or where the projectile entered James Wisenbaker's body, but records state he was wounded at Cedar Creek.

*Site where James A. Wisenbaker was most likely
wounded: Cedar Creek National Battlefield*

The Confederate Army had to leave their cannons at the water's edge, because the bridge over Cedar Creek collapsed. The extent of James' wounds was not documented. Muster rolls do not mention him being captured, so that indicates he was most likely wounded in the morning and evacuated to the rear during the lull between 10 a.m. and 4 p.m. Had he been wounded during the Union counterattack in the late afternoon, he most likely would have been captured, because fleeing soldiers being pursued would not have had time to carry him from the field. The remnants of Early's force retreated to the trenches of Petersburg from whence they came.

At the end of March 1865, Lee's withered Army of Northern Virginia was hard-pressed by General Grant's Army at Richmond and Petersburg, VA. Not willing to surrender, and not able to retreat, the outnumbered Confederates chose to attack on the 25th of March. The idea was to break through the Union line at a place where no man's land between opposing trenches was the narrowest and where a concentrated force could inflict the most damage once behind enemy lines. The objective was Fort Stedman. Confederate Major General John B. Gordon would lead the assault comprised of 10,000 men, the 12th Georgia and Wisenbakers among them.

At the front of the attack were axmen. That's right, Southern men wielding axes to literally chop holes in the Union abatis defenses—large, sharpened wooden spikes and dried tree branches pointing toward the Confederate lines to slow advances and prevent cavalry charges. Under direct fire, the axmen made quick work of the formidable obstacles, swinging sharpened steel hard and fast, wood chips flying and determined men in gray filing through every breach. A three-pronged attack, upon penetrating the Union line, one group would pour enfilade fire to the left, a second group would pour enfilade fire to the right, and a third group would advance straight ahead to reach and cut the Union supply railway.

Surprisingly, they actually broke through, captured the fort, and advanced behind enemy lines, but troops became confused in the unfamiliar trenches, hungry Rebels stopped to eat Union rations, and reinforcements assigned to capitalize on any success were not well-coordinated. This allowed Union officers to stage a response, slow the momentum, and mount a counterattack.

Following the attack on Fort Stedman, Lee's plan was to withdraw his army, abandon Richmond and Petersburg, and retreat toward the west to fight another day, possibly by joining his remaining forces with those of General Joseph E. Johnston in North Carolina. As Lee withdrew toward the west, Grant's soldiers remained in contact and pursuit of his forces, engaging in skirmishes and battles while on the move until April 9, 1865 when Lee finally surrendered at Appomattox Court House, VA. Read the events of the Appomattox

Campaign to experience a glimpse of the controlled chaos James Wisenbaker would have fought and survived through until his surrender at Lynchburg, VA on an unspecified date in April 1865. Lynchburg is 20 miles west of Appomattox, so it is unknown how or why James was surrendered at Lynchburg.

Lee's surrender to Grant applied to a 25-mile radius around Appomattox, and Confederate forces were scattered, fighting a rolling fluid battle, so it is assumed James A. Wisenbaker was in Lynchburg, VA when Lee surrendered. Traveling to the Visitor Center at Appomattox Court House National Historic Park, listening to the park rangers, reading the information placards, walking the battlefield, and standing where the remnants of the 12th Georgia prepared for Lee's final order to advance, I envisioned the following account of James A. Wisenbaker's last battle.

General Robert E. Lee's army, what was left of it at Appomattox Court House, VA, was surrounded. Holding a council of war with his generals, it was decided they would make an attempt to breakout toward the west, toward what they believed to be the enemy's weakest point. In what would prove to be General Lee's last offensive battlefield chess move, he amassed 9,000 men, including the only fifty-five remaining officers and men of the once mighty 12th Georgia Infantry Regiment. Remarkably, two Wisenbakers from Valdosta, GA, James A. and George Henry, had beaten the odds of survival and grasped their Enfield rifles under the shade of the trees, concealed behind Tibbs Lane. Many of the Southern men standing in formation awaiting the order to advance had no rifle. From experience, they knew a weapon would soon be available, picked up off the ground from the hands of the soon to be fallen somewhere in the open field to their front. On the Confederate right was the Southern cavalry commanded by General Fitz Lee, Robert E. Lee's nephew.

The objective was a ridge defended by 1,200 Union dismounted cavalry and two cannons. Orchestrating a flawless left wheel maneuver, the right side of their line moved forward at a faster pace than the left. As the Southerners surged toward the ridge, now at the double step, their line all the while wheeling toward the left as if a closing gate, gaps appeared along their line at each pull of the Yankee lanyard. Men beside them eviscerated in stride, they closed ranks and continued toward the rifled barrels spewing death and carnage. Quickening the pace, they reached the ridge, overwhelmed the defenders, and repulsed several Union counterattacks. Losing forward momentum while stopping to defeat the counterattacks, on the opposite side of the elevated objective, before them appeared 25,000 new uniforms, blue.

The breakout was not to be. It was now 28,000 vs. 150,000. As Confederate Major General John B. Gordon ordered a general withdrawal, Captain Wilson Thomas Jenkins, Company A of the 14th North Carolina Regiment, stepped forward with twenty-five volunteers willing to make a rearguard final stand. These twenty-six men would face and hold off 25,000 Yankees long enough for the Confederate forces to leave the field. A placard there on the battlefield today reads, "As the last of Gordon's corps retreated to the Appomattox River valley 25 volunteers of the 4th and 14th North Carolina Infantry under the direction of Captain Wilson Jenkins remained behind, near here, to slow the Federal pursuit. The stalwart band fought until nearly surrounded and forced to surrender."

Seeing surrender of the Confederate Army of Northern Virginia inevitable, Cavalry General Fitz Lee, his situational awareness high on adrenalin, surveyed the horizon for any possible avenue of escape. Never one to give up, James Wisenbaker eyed a riderless warhorse standing over its fallen Virginian horseman, and there was zero hesitation. He could see Fitz's cavalrymen anxiously facing northwest. With a few swift barefoot steps, a reach for the saddle, toes in a stirrup, the creak of leather, and a loud heeyaah! sent James galloping across the field to join the other horse soldiers loosening the reins as hundreds of spurs found their marks and the race to Lynchburg was on. For the first time, if only for a day, James was a cavalryman.

General Fitz Lee did lead his cavalry 20 miles to Lynchburg. It's the only reasonable explanation as to why the location of James Wisenbaker's prisoner of war card is labeled Lynchburg, VA while his brother George Henry Wisenbaker's name is forever inked for posterity in the record books at Appomattox Court House.

As you consider your level of reverence for Cpl. James A. Wisenbaker as a Southern man, you must first understand the context. That he participated in the many battles both described above and well documented down through history is enough to boggle the mind. Now consider the casualties experienced by the Lowndes Volunteers as a whole. Of the 118 men who joined Company I of the 12th Georgia Infantry Regiment on June 14, 1861, only one man made it through to Appomattox without being noted as either died, killed, wounded, or captured. One. That's it. Five were discharged for unknown reasons, but probably due to post-traumatic stress disorder (PTSD). Five deserted near the end of the war, which is understandable considering the condition and situation of the Confederacy by late 1864. And the vast majority, 107 out of 118, or 91%, either died of disease (thirty-six), were killed in action (twenty-two), were wounded in action (twenty-five), or were captured during combat operations (twenty-three). Three of the POW's are known to have died while in Union hands.

Southerners were a proud people. Yes, a people, distinct and differentiated from any other group, complete with their own Southern Accent dialect and Bible Belt conservative Protestant Christian values. Men of the South stood strong, willing to take up arms to defend and protect, no matter the cost, against any foe, regardless of size or strength. Ponder for a moment and consider their motivation to fight so hard, for so long, against all odds, even in the final days to Appomattox. This is important to know as you watch people tear down monuments erected by family members and descendants to honor sons, husbands, fathers, grandfathers, uncles, and cousins who served or died as Confederate soldiers. It's convenient to point to slavery as the cause of the Civil War, and it's impossible to avoid the issue of slavery as an underlying factor, but there were multiple significant points of contrast between North and South which, combined, ultimately resulted in secession.

Robert E. Lee said of surrender, "There is nothing left for me to do but go and see General Grant and I would rather die a thousand deaths." His men, too, possessed that extreme commitment and heart. The 12th Georgia Infantry Regiment, including the Lowndes Volunteers and James A. Wisenbaker, was a true testament to Southern will. Of the original 1,200 who enlisted in the regiment in 1861, only five officers and fifty men (4.6%) surrendered with Lee's Army of Northern Virginia in April 1865.

12th Georgia Infantry Regiment
Company I, Lowndes Volunteers
Formed June 14, 1861, Lowndes County

of men who joined June 14, 1861   118

Fate	# of Men	% of Total
Died of Illness	36	30.5%
Wounded in Action	25	21.2%
Killed in Action	23	19.5%
Captured "POW" (3 died as POWs)	23	19.5%
Discharged	5	4.2%
Deserted or AWOL	5	4.2%
Not noted as a casualty of war	1	0.8%
% Died, Killed, Wounded, or Captured	107	90.7%

James didn't survive to the 1870 census. He died on April 29, 1868, at only fifty-eight years old. We don't know for sure, but it's reasonable to assume his battle wounds along with the wear and tear associated with the extreme level of combat experienced by this man in his fifties contributed to his early demise. Rest in peace, my Confederate grandfather. Your honor and sacrifice as a Southern American man are no longer forgotten.

I nicknamed James A. Wisenbaker born 1810 my "Valiant Valdostan." To do what he did during the Civil War between the age of fifty-one and fifty-five was awe inspiring. As you can tell from the story I wrote and the details inserted, I invested a lot of time and effort into my 4th great-grandfather, James A. Wisenbaker. I can assure you, I documented him thoroughly online in my family tree and Findagrave.com. Everyone I know, and everyone I met on the street, heard the story of James A. Wisenbaker. You'd have thought my last name was Wisenbaker.

I met a man named Wisenbaker, and I kind of overwhelmed him with my James Wisenbaker story. When I finally took a breath and he saw an opportunity to interject, he asked, "How are you a Wisenbaker?" I think he was hoping I was mistaken about my heritage, so he could distance himself from me, because I was way too enthusiastic about James A. Wisenbaker.

Chapter 22

GETTING IT RIGHT

Iknew James A. Wisenbaker would be a focal point of my book. The story about him I had uncovered was legendary. I remember sitting down early one morning with a fresh brewed cup of coffee, firing up my laptop, and pursuing inspiration to write. One of the first things I did was pull up the 1850 census to confirm a specific detail regarding my 4th great-grandfather, James A. Wisenbaker. I'm not sure exactly what I was confirming, or why I was confirming it, but I will never forget what I saw. Scrolling down the census page, I found James Wisenbaker, age thirty-nine. Directly on the line above his name was written "James A. Wisenbaker, age 14." Oh no, there were two James A. Wisenbakers.

The Confederate soldier's name was James A. Wisenbaker. My grandfather's name was James A. Wisenbaker. This fourteen-year-old boy's name was James A. Wisenbaker. My grandfather was fifty-one years old in 1861. This fourteen-year-old boy in 1850 would have been twenty-five years old in 1861, a more likely candidate to have been a Confederate soldier keeping up with Stonewall Jackson. This fourteen-year-old boy could potentially discredit my work, discombobulate the storyline of my book, and take away the Civil War Gettysburg grandfather that was so important to me. Worst of all, I'd have to eat crow and tell everyone I had been wrong and that my grandfather wasn't really the swashbuckling Valiant Valdostan Confederate soldier grandpa I had bragged about so often. I immediately began researching the younger James A. Wisenbaker born in 1836.

The 1850 census showed the household of John Wisenbaker, age forty-one, born 1809, adjacent to the household of my 4th great-grandfather, James Wisenbaker, age thirty-nine, born 1810. John's wife was Salome, and they had three sons: John C., George H., and James A. Further research showed John age forty-one was the brother of my James age thirty-nine, so the three sons of John were my James' nephews, including James A., making brother John my 5th great-uncle, and his three sons my 1st cousins 5x removed.

Nephew George H. Wisenbaker, was George Henry Wisenbaker. I had become familiar with him while visiting the Wisenbaker Cemetery online at Findagrave.com, because it's a small cemetery of only twelve marked graves, seven of which are Wisenbakers. The headstone for George Henry Wisenbaker tells his story.

His grave was adjacent to my 4th great-grandparents, James A. Wisenbaker and Sarah Ann Dasher Wisenbaker. While visiting the cemetery, I found no evidence of Confederate military service at James' grave—not on his headstone, not on his ledger, no Confederate battle flag, no iron Southern Cross of Honor.

Nephew John C. Wisenbaker, was Judge John Charley Wisenbaker. He was buried in the J. C. Wisenbaker section at Sunset Hill Cemetery in Valdosta, GA near Valdosta State University. John Charley, not to be confused with his cousin, James Crews Wisenbaker, both with initials J. C., was included as a 2nd Lieut. in the 663rd District Lowndes Battalion Georgia Militia. In a letter John Charley wrote to Governor Joseph E. Brown on July 15, 1864, it sounded like he was in charge of a militia unit being called into immediate service to defend the State of Georgia.

The only two references online pertaining to nephew James A. Wisenbaker, born 1836, besides the 1850 census when he was fourteen years old, were the 1860 census and a memorial at Findagrave. com. The 1860 census record was not easy to find, because he was listed as *Jas* A. Wisenbaker, and a search for *James* Wisenbaker did not produce the record. After much effort due to his father having died prior to the 1860 census and a woman's age not being clearly legible, I finally determined his mother was living with him. A search for James A. Wisenbaker on Findagrave.com produced a memorial for him, but there were no memorials linking him to a father, mother, wife, or children. Photos attached to his Findagrave. com memorial contained no evidence of military service, nor was there a written description offering any insights about his life.

A third reference found in the Fort Myers, FL library genealogy room, of all places, was a book titled *Survey of Lowndes County Georgia Cemeteries 1825-1987*. In that random find I discovered a few helpful points of reference. First, on page 152, the brother John Charley Wisenbaker buried next to the younger James A. Wisenbaker in Sunset Hill Cemetery was noted (to right C.S. marker), which meant Confederate States marker, probably an iron Southern Cross of Honor. James A. Wisenbaker's name was directly above John Charley in the text, but no mention was made of any C.S. marker.

Back on page 431 of the cemeteries survey, I found another tidbit supporting my personal desire to claim military service for my grandfather. One observation was that George Henry Wisenbaker, known to have been in the 12th Georgia with James A. Wisenbaker, was buried next to his uncle and assumed brother-in-arms. What other explanation could there be as to why uncle and nephew, James A. and George Henry, were buried next to each other? This cemetery survey book documented these two men being buried adjacent to one another, which was relevant, because the headstones for James and his wife Sarah had been disconnected from the grave structure atop their graves. Because the headstones had been removed, broken, and placed on the ground, it was hard to say on which side James and Sarah were buried. The survey book noted James on the north side, adjacent to George Henry, with Sarah on the south side.

I decided to visit the grave of the younger James A. Wisenbaker at Sunset Hill Cemetery to look for evidence or clues pointing toward service as a Confederate soldier. In my heart, I didn't want to find any evidence, because I really wanted my grandfather to have been Corporal James A. Wisenbaker of Company I of the 12th Georgia Infantry Regiment.

As a veteran, a patriotic American, and a Christian—a man who makes an effort to always be truthful, honorable, ethical and fair without consideration for what's in it for me—I find stolen valor to be despicable and stretching the truth to be unacceptable. I also hold myself and others to an extremely high standard of expectations when it comes to effort. In my opinion, a lack of effort is effectively negligence. Both James A. Wisenbakers, uncle and nephew, were counting on me to get their stories right.

Five hours back to Valdosta I drove. Having already been to Sunset Hill Cemetery, I was familiar with the small, crude, concrete block structure at the geographic center where maintenance staff coordinated mowing, trimming, and debris removal while occasionally fielding questions from visitors like myself. They recognized me from my previous inquiries as I stepped in through the door. I explained I was looking for the grave of James A. Wisenbaker. They looked in their records, then walked to a map, then offered to walk me to the spot. Walking in a straight line directly out of the office door, we may have taken forty steps.

The helpful man said, "There he is. Do you need anything else?"

"Nope, I'm good, thank you," I said.

A large azalea bush had enveloped the back and sides of James A. Wisenbaker's headstone, and fallen acorns thickly covered his ground-level ledger, so I walked back to my truck to retrieve my loppers, rake, and broom. Sweeping away the acorns, sand, leaves, and twigs revealed a ledger either originally void of etchings or completely eroded away over the past 114 years. I had worked on ledgers older than 114 years that still had legible etchings, so I felt comfortable there had never been etchings on his ledger. There were no etchings on the face of his stone signifying any military service, so I began pruning back the azalea bush with my loppers to see what might be hidden from sight behind his monument. Specifically, what I was looking for, and hoping not to find, was a Southern Cross of Honor. It would be etched into the back side of his stone or in the form of a large, heavy, solid iron grave ornament in the shape of the Southern Cross of Honor placed at his grave by the Sons of Confederate Veterans. I knew it was possible to find an iron cross behind a headstone hidden within an overgrown azalea, because I had already randomly found one while pruning an azalea bush in this very cemetery during the past year.

Gaining access with my trimming, I could see the smooth, shiny back side of the stone with no etching. I pulled out my iPhone and snapped a photo of the blank back as evidence this younger James A. Wisenbaker was not the Confederate soldier, thereby strengthening the case in favor of my grandfather, this man's uncle. With the thick green foliage removed, and only sparsely arrayed spindly base branches, I clearly saw no iron cross existed, again, more evidence.

The younger James A. Wisenbaker was born on Christmas Day 1836.

I compared the available evidence and points of reference to make a decision and reach a conclusion as to whether the Confederate soldier James A. Wisenbaker was my fifty-one-year-old grandfather or his twenty-five-year-old nephew.

James A. Wisenbaker, born 1810, age fifty-one in 1861.

- Noted by others online as being a Confederate soldier, Company I, 12th Georgia Infantry Regiment.
- No record of military service noted at his gravesite.
- His nephew, George Henry Wisenbaker, was confirmed to be a Confederate soldier in the same Company I, 12th Georgia Infantry Regiment.

- His nephew George Henry was buried next to him in the Wisenbaker Cemetery.
- A photo at the United States Library of Congress shows James A. Wisenbaker in what appears to be a Confederate soldier uniform.
- The soldier James A. Wisenbaker was wounded at the Battle of Cedar Creek, and James A. Wisenbaker died only three years after the war on 29 Apr 1868 at a relatively young age of fifty-eight years old.
- The Lowndes County 1864 census for Re-Organizing the Georgia Militia lists a Wisenbaker, James, 54 yrs, Farmer, b. GA, shot gun, horse, saddle, bridle.

James A. Wisenbaker, born 1836, age twenty-five in 1861.

- Not noted by others online as being a Confederate soldier.
- No record of military service noted at his gravesite.
- No mention of C.S.A. in *Survey of Lowndes County Georgia Cemeteries 1825-1987*.
- His brother, George Henry Wisenbaker, was confirmed to be a Confederate soldier in the same Company I, 12th Georgia Infantry Regiment.
- His brother, George Henry, was buried next to their uncle, James A. Wisenbaker.

Based on the information presented above, I concluded the evidence weighted toward the older James A. Wisenbaker, my 4th great-grandfather. With no sign of Confederate military service associated with the younger man, and only his age and his brother being in the same Company I of the 12th Georgia, I didn't have anything to hang my hat on with the younger man. On the other hand, there were actual facts pointing toward the older man. There was the photo at the Library of Congress. There was the grave of nephew George Henry Wisenbaker of Company I next to his grave. There was the wound received at the Battle of Cedar Creek October 19, 1864, and the older man's death three and a half years later on April 29, 1868 at age fifty-eight. It was the conclusion I was hoping for, but uncertainty continued to nag at me from my conscience. Could a man in his fifties really withstand the physical and emotional punishment inflicted upon Company I of the 12th Georgia in more than thirty-eight battles over a course of three and a half years? How could the fifty-four-year-old man be listed among the members of the local militia in 1864 when at that same time he would have been on the front line with the 12th Georgia somewhere in Virginia? And on which side of the married couple's damaged grave monument was the older James A. Wisenbaker interred? The puzzle pieces at the red brick monument appeared to possibly point toward his wife Sarah being on the north side next to nephew George Henry Wisenbaker.

With the identity mystery resolved to the best of my ability, I began planning a James A. Wisenbaker Civil War battlefield road trip. The trip would begin at his grave in Valdosta, GA and follow the battles fought by the 12th Georgia all the way to, yes, Gettysburg. I didn't have unlimited time to visit each of thirty-eight battles as they happened in succession over a four-year period, because the war in the east moved back and forth across the same geographic landscape from year to year. In other words, there was no reason to visit the 1862 Battle of Fredericksburg, leave, and then come back to nearly the same place for the 1864 Battles of The Wilderness and Spotsylvania Court House. I marked each battle on a map and then attempted to connect the dots to create an efficient route. But again, I didn't have unlimited time, so I selected the seventeen most significant battles for Company I of the 12th Georgia Infantry Regiment where they sustained the most casualties. It was important for me to go there, to stand where they stood, to imagine the scene, contemplate the sounds, internalize the lay of the land, and reflect upon the human cost.

The Wisenbaker Civil War battlefield trip would take place in July. But an even bigger ancestry road trip was scheduled for June when my teenage daughter, out of school for the summer and able to travel with me, could share in some of what I had learned on previous road trips, and participate in my planned new discoveries. When June arrived and the last day of school had ended, we boarded the new Honoring My DNA motorhome and hit the open road. We headed toward cemeteries not yet visited, living ancestors to interview, historical sites for context, and of course, Civil War battlefields where grandfathers, uncles, and cousins had fought and died.

It took a full day just to get out of Florida, so our first stop was Valdosta, GA. There, we visited with both living and deceased Zipperers and Wisenbakers. With a couple of hours unaccounted for one afternoon before supper, an old Carnegie library, now the Lowndes County Historical Society and Museum, was calling out to me from about 10 miles away. I invited my daughter to join me, so we hopped in our truck, which we towed behind the coach, and headed toward the historic Valdosta library.

Arriving at the library, we parked across the street, which afforded us a favorable vantage point to appreciate the building itself. Built in 1913 with a grant from Andrew Carnegie, a steel tycoon and one of the wealthiest Americans of all time, the design was timeless and quality of construction apparent. Hurrying across the street, we paused to read the historical marker. Up the steps, through the front doors, and we entered into a time capsule from the past. Books, endless books, binders, memorabilia, artifacts, stuff, displays, and two men, buried behind desks piled high with research works in progress. To help you envision the scene, my best description of the interior would be that of a book room you might see at Hogwarts in a Harry Potter movie. An interesting observation was that Andrew Carnegie was of Scottish descent, and Hogwarts school of witchcraft and wizardry was set in Scotland, but I digress. Back to the historical library. The men working there offered to be of service, so I told them I was looking for anything they might have that would help me learn about my ancestors from Valdosta. The men asked if I had been to the Lowndes County Public Library, because that library was known to have some genealogy resources pertaining to local pioneer families.

I shared with them my journey to honor my DNA and that I was trying to learn about my Valdosta people from the Civil War time period. One of the men grasped his chin and turned toward one of the shelves holding countless volumes in what appeared to be in no particular order. He was thinking, pondering, trying to remember where he had seen anything that might be helpful to me. Reaching up to the shelf, he pulled down a book—not really a book, but more of a paperback printing resembling what you might see in a spiral-bound college homework paper. Leaning down behind a glass case, he retrieved another book, and from a desk, another. "Try these. I'll keep thinking and let you know if I come up with any other ideas," he said. My daughter had ventured somewhere within the multi-story repository of all things old in Valdosta.

I walked over to an uncluttered countertop at a far side of the room to distance myself from the conversation that was starting between a new visitor seeking her ancestors, with her husband in tow, and the two men at the center of objects existing in controlled chaos. Looking at my phone to check the time, like always, it was 3:16 p.m. My expectations were low, to say the least, but 3:16 always gave me hope. I set two of the books aside and fixed my eyes on the cover of *Wiregrass Obituaries and Death Notices – Vol. I*, by Wayne and Judy Dasher. Turning back the cover to reveal page one, and the very first obituary of a multi-volume set, I saw none other than

the name James Wisenbaker and the date April 29, 1868. It was the obituary for my 4th great-grandfather. I literally stopped and looked around the room to see if someone was pulling a really well-planned Candid Camera prank. Nothing was happening around me, no cameras that I could see, no movements, no snickering, just inanimate objects and the conversation going on about the woman's husband being employed by a NASCAR race team affiliated with Richard Childress Racing.

Turning back toward the first page I had haphazardly viewed among the literally tens of thousands of pages available in this repository of local history, my grandfather's name, James Wisenbaker, was still there, staring back at me. The page read as follows:

James Wisenbaker
The South Georgia Times – Wednesday, April 29, 1868

Death Of a Good Citizen. We are pained to have to announce the death, on Monday morning last, of Mr. James Wisenbaker, one of our best citizens. He died of an affliction of the liver combined with dyspeptic symptoms. He had been quite unwell for a month past, but no one expected that the Fatal Messenger was so near. Thus "in the midst of life we are in death" but few lay to heart the solemn lesson taught.

He was about 59 years old and leaves a numerous family and many friends to mourn his loss. See obituary where just tribute is paid to the departed citizen, friend, and Christian.

The South Georgia Times – Wednesday, April 29, 1868

Obituary. Died, at his residence near Valdosta, Lowndes County, Georgia, on the 28th inst., Mr. James Wisenbaker, aged 59 years. During the seven weeks illness previous to his death, he exhibited that Christian fortitude which ever characterized his life. He had been a member of the Church for 41 years, and never was other than a devoted Christian. Honorable, pious, charitable and just, he had no enemies, but many friends. Truly has he died with the happy reflection consequent upon a well spent life, and may we not hope that he has been translated to a better world, where the spirits of the good dwell.

Deceased has left a large family and many friends who mourned his loss. A Friend.

There was no explanation as to how my 4th great-grandfather's obituary, not digitized and posted anywhere on the internet, would be printed on the first page of the first book I opened at an historical library five hours from my home. Taken out of context, a verse from the song "I'll Go On Loving You" written by Kieran Kane and performed by Alan Jackson comes to mind.

I don't know what brought us together
What strange forces of nature
Conspired, to construct the present, from the past

His obituary mentioned nothing about service as a Confederate soldier. His cause of death was attributed to an affliction of the liver combined with symptoms of indigestion, not anything related to having been wounded in action at the Battle of Cedar Creek. Three separate times the writer noted James Wisenbaker was a Christian, which explained his grave facing east, in a small family cemetery, not located on the grounds of a church. My head still spinning trying to digest what had just happened, and the words I had just read, my attention went back to the wooden countertop where two more books stared back at me.

The next printed reference I reached for was a spiral-bound effort of love entitled *The Confederate Soldiers of Sunset Hill Cemetery*, by Susan Converse McKey Thomas. I had been to Sunset Hill Cemetery on two occasions. First, to visit two of my 5th great-grandparents, and a second time to inspect the grave of the younger James A. Wisenbaker. This volume was hard for me to open because the title promised to provide the information I had been searching for, but not sincerely wanting to know. What I viewed in the next few moments could be the conclusive evidence I had been half-heartedly seeking since discovering the younger James A. Wisenbaker in the 1850 census. In the absence of a concrete clincher, circumstantial evidence had allowed me to cling to the honor of having a valiant larger than life Civil War grandfather, one who had now become a favorite among my personal heroes.

This was the moment of truth. I opened the pages to find a list of names, scanning down through the list, reaching the W's, hoping not to see a James Wisenbaker—the list did not include the name James Wisenbaker. A moment of relief began to overwhelm me until I realized I was only at the beginning and had not yet skimmed through the entire text. Flipping a few more pages, I found obituaries with last names beginning with A's and B's. Confidently, I flipped clumps of pages toward the back to where the W's, Y's, and Z's would be found. At the top right corner of page 179 in bold was **WISENBAKER, JAMES A.**

James A. Wisenbaker
Born Dec. 25, 1836
Died Apr. 25, 1904

THE VALDOSTA TIMES
Tues., April 26, 1904
Page 8, Col. 2

MR. JAMES A. WISENBAKER DEAD
Well Known Citizen Passed Away
Yesterday After a Long Illness

Mr. James A. Wisenbaker died yesterday morning, between eight and nine o'clock, at the home of Mrs. Mack Ulmer where he had been residing for some time.

Mr. Wisenbaker had been suffering with kidney trouble for some time and several months ago he went to Franklin, Ky., and spent some time under treatment. He received little relief and had been gradually growing worse ever since his return.

Yesterday morning his death occurred, and this morning at nine o'clock his funeral was conducted, the services being conducted at the cemetery by Elder L. J. Jackson. The pall bearers were: M. A. Briggs, W. D. Dunaway, J. M. Boston, D. C. Ashley and R. F. Ousley.

Mr. Wisenbaker had never married though he was upward of sixty years of age. He was a brother of Judge J. C. (John Charley) Wisenbaker and leaves a large circle of relatives and friends in this county and section.

During the war he was a gallant Confederate Soldier and since the war he has given his life to farming, having a good place a mile or so below the city and being one of the most progressive farmers of the county.

NOTE: Grave located in old section of cemetery, to the right of the main road leading into Sunset Hill.

There it was in print: "he was a gallant Confederate Soldier." I knew this was the clarity required under the circumstances, because having already studied this particular soldier's war resume, the word "gallant" fit perfectly. I'm sure not all obituary writers bestowed such an adjective to describe just any Confederate soldier. On one hand, there was disappointment, on the other, relief. His obituary also answered for me the question I had wondered about, why nobody had identified the correct James A. Wisenbaker over all these years as being the Corporal in Company I of the 12th Georgia. He had never married. With no children, he had no direct descendants to ever care to look for him. The physical and emotional scars he brought home to Valdosta after more than thirty-eight battles, sixteen of which were so bad they turned them into National Battlefield Parks, were more than enough reasons to empathize about why he never married. He may not have been my grandfather, but he was my Gallant Valdostan 1st cousin five times removed.

Chapter 23

PROOF OF THE AFTERLIFE

I talk with my Uncle James on the phone, a lot. When he married a few years ago, I'm sure he had to sit down with his soon-to-be bride prior to the wedding to explain how their relationship would be interrupted five or six times each week, or per day, by his phone ringing with calls from his nephew. I made a fine first impression when I showed up to their wedding in sandals, shorts, and a Guy Harvey fishing t-shirt. I was in the wedding photos, so the memory will be lasting for her. Anyway, on one such phone call while driving between appointments, I told Uncle James I'd call him back in a few minutes, because I was about to pass by my buddy Calvin's coin shop, and for some reason it sounded like a good idea to stop in and hold a 1 oz. gold coin.

I had no clue why that feeling came over me that particular day at that specific moment. Without skipping a beat or pausing to think about how out of the ordinary it was for someone to just randomly want to stop at a coin shop to hold some gold, Uncle James said, "While you're in there, get a Morgan Dollar for the year Grandma Laura Lee was born." And I didn't even question how or why he knew anything about coins, because this was the guy who knew quite a bit about everything. For example, on one of our countless phone calls, I asked him if he had ever witnessed a flock of crows, a really big flock, like a thousand birds, flying in a tight formation and all of a sudden in unison they tuck their wings just so, enabling them to dive downward into the wind, producing an ominous giant hollow tube sound. His response was, "Yeah, as a matter of fact I just saw that yesterday, but it's a murder, not a flock."

Walking into the small room filled with coins, glass cases filled with coins, binders filled with coins, bins filled with coins, from floor to ceiling, I peeked around through the doorway to my right to see Calvin sitting behind a desk. Lifting only his eyes from whatever it was he was studying, he acknowledged my presence.

Calvin: Hey, Trae, what can I do for you? What brings you in today? How's the real estate market? I saw your big sale in the paper last week. Looks like you're having another good year. Must be nice selling all those million-dollar houses.

Trae: Hey, Calvin. I just came in to hold one of your gold coins if you don't mind. They just feel good in my hand, the weight, so heavy for something of that size, love the color, the intricate markings, and that specific shine no other metal produces. And my uncle said I need to buy a Morgan Dollar for the year one of our grandmother's was born.

Calvin: What year was your grandma born?

Trae: Hang on, let me look up her birth year real quick in my family tree here on my iPhone. Gimme a second, almost there. Okay, here she is, 1873.

Calvin: Well, that's gonna be a hard coin to find, because they didn't start minting Morgan Dollars until 1878.

Trae: Well then, what coins do you have from 1873?

Calvin started thinking. He looked below the counter to his right, beyond me to the shelves at my back, and then he turned around, head up toward the bookshelves high on the wall behind him. Organized from left to right were coin collector binders, the ones you've seen with circles punched into cardboard inside just big enough for a specific coin type to pop in but not easily pop out. Some binders were brown, some blue, others green, some made of cardboard, while others were of plastic holding clear sleeve pages inside. All were filled with coins organized by type and year. He pulled down one binder and flipped pages until he reached the time period 1873.

Calvin: How much you wanna spend?

Trae: Oh, I don't know. I just want something nice, something in decent condition, where I can actually see the details of the coin, but I don't need some super rare perfect coin costing an arm and a leg.

Calvin looked through his 1873 collection and pulled out a 3-cent nickel.

Calvin: That's a really nice coin for your grandma. Not too expensive. Not rare, but unique, and good condition.

Trae: I'll take it.

Trae: You got any Morgan Dollars?

Calvin: Tons of 'em. What year?

Trae: I don't know. Hang on a second while I look up some of my favorite ancestors.

Trae: What years did they make Morgan Dollars?

Calvin: 1878 to 1904.

Trae: Alright, let me look here a minute. How about an 1879 for Grandma Holland?

Calvin: Scanning through his Morgan Dollars, nope, don't have an 1879. What else?

Trae: Hang on let me look. How about an 1887 for Grandma Smith?

Calvin: Got lots of those. Here's three good ones. Which one you want?

They all looked beautiful, 90% silver, shiny, pretty coins. Calvin handed me a magnifying glass and a scope. I stood there for a few minutes studying each coin, like I knew anything about the difference between one coin versus another. One had a tiny scratch that stood out a little more than the other hundred micro scratches. One had a little stain of some sort along the edge between the stars and the bumps. The last one had kind of a little dent in the number seven in the year. I thought to myself, *Decisions, decisions, Trae, make up your mind.* "I'll take this one, Calvin. How much is it?"

I was now a numismatist. Never heard the word in my life, but I bet Uncle James could have pulled that word out from somewhere. Leaving Calvin's coin shop, I climbed into my truck and Googled "coin shop," resulting in a list of three other storefronts in town. Maybe one of the other shops would have an 1879 Morgan Dollar. Choosing one from the list, I drove to the next coin shop. Unlike Calvin's shop, this place had a remote-controlled door lock. I couldn't see through the glass, but they could see me. A door ringer button to my right had a sign on it stating something like, Ring This Buzzer for Entry. Anyway, I heard the door sort of click and hum, so I pulled on the door handle and stepped inside. Bigger than Calvin's shop, this place had glass cases filled with jewelry, antiques, collectibles, and coins. Wondering why this place had a remote-controlled door lock and Calvin's did not, it dawned on me, Calvin's shop was inside a U.S. Post Office, so someone would have to be really stupid to break into a post office.

I found the glass case where the Morgan Dollars were displayed. While looking down at them, searching for one with 1879 minted at the bottom, an employee walked up behind the case.

Employee: May I help you find something?

Trae: Hi, I'm looking for an 1879 Morgan Dollar, but I don't see one here in the case.

Employee: Looks like we don't have an 1879, but here's a really nice 1880.

Trae: An 1880 won't work. I need an 1879.

Employee: Why do you need an 1879?

Trae: Well, I came up with an idea. Well actually my uncle gave me the idea. But anyway, I'm honoring my DNA by purchasing a coin to commemorate the year one of my favorite ancestors was born.

The man behind the counter gave me a puzzled, perplexed facial response, like, "Why in the world would you be in here looking for a coin minted in 1879 just because one of your ancestors was born that year?" I gave him a brief summary of the ancestry adventure I was on, some of the interesting facts I had uncovered, and some of the things I had done. For example, visiting ancestor gravesites. Like everyone else I shared my adventure with, he got it, he respected what I was doing, and the coin connection to genealogy became clear in his understanding.

Employee: What else you lookin for?

Trae: I don't know. I just started collecting coins about ninety minutes ago. I guess I need to think about making a list of ancestors sorted by their birth years and then buy a coin to honor each one of them.

The man picked up a paperback book from below the counter.

Employee: Do you have one of these?

Trae: Nope. What is it?

He explained it was a coin collector's guide containing descriptions of each coin minted in the United States with information about market values. These types of books were printed each year and sold for $19, but he'd let me have this one for $14, because it was five years old. The coins described inside were no different from year to year. The only thing that changed were the market values for each coin.

Trae: Sure. I'll buy it.

He rang up my purchase, I tucked my new old book under my arm, and walked out to my truck. Not wanting my newfound hobby to end, I looked back at my Google search results to see if another coin shop might be close enough to reach before the end of this business day. A new coin shop had just opened up near the inter-state, so I called ahead to make sure they were open before I made the drive out of my way.

The only parking space in front of the new coin shop was occu-pied by the shop owner's small SUV, wrapped in printed marketing plastic film advertising the coin business, like a mobile billboard. At the door was the now familiar buzzer button.

Owner: What brings you in today?

Trae: I'm looking for old coins to honor my ancestors. I plan to put together a list of different types of coins organized by year, with each one assigned to the name of a specific grandparent in my family tree. The names will be irrelevant to you, but they mean something to me.

Owner: That sounds like a really cool idea.

His response let me know he had never heard of anyone doing what I was doing. Being as this was a new business, he didn't have nearly the inventory or selection as the other two coin shops I had visited, but he seemed like a knowledgeable guy and his store was well-lit, sort of like a jewelry shop. Peering in, down through the glass countertop, the top shelf below displayed various coins sealed in rectangular-shaped, hard plastic holders signifying these particu-lar coins had been graded by an expert. As a numismatist with three hours of experience, I was now aware of such things. He had two gold coins, both in hard plastic holders, side by side.

Trae: You got any more gold coins?

Owner: No, those are the only two I have at the moment. Got them in yesterday.

Both gold coins were dated 1922. I thought, *That's interesting. Nanny and Papa were both born in 1922.*

Trae: How much are the 1922 gold coins?

Owner: Let me look them up. This site will tell me the current trading price for those coins.

Owner: I can sell you either of them for $1,320.

The coins were definitely talking to me, wanting me to take them home, like cute little kittens at a pet store reaching out between the wire cage slats meowing with those precious squinted eyes. In this case though, it was precious metal begging me to take it home. It was five o'clock, and all the storefronts were closing. I'd have to wait until tomorrow to see if any other 1922 gold coins looked better than these two. Just three hours ago, I was not yet a numismatist, nor had a $1,320 gold coin purchase decision even entered into my realm of possibilities.

1922 $20 St. Gaudens Double Eagle

Sitting at the kitchen counter that evening, flipping through my coin book, with my 1873 3-cent nickel and 1887 Morgan Dollar displayed at my right, my wife walked in from her Costco adventure, hugging two cases of strawberries.

My Wife: What are you up to now?

Trae: I am now a numismatist.

My Wife: Whatever. Does this have something to do with ancestry?

Trae: Maybe, well yeah, but it's a pretty cool idea. I'm making a list of my favorite ancestors and then finding a different coin for each one of them. By the time I'm through, I'll have one of each coin ever made, and each one will be a physical connection to a memorable grandmother or grandfather.

With her legendary eye roll, she turned around toward the direction of the laundry room refrigerator to deposit her bounty of favorite fruits.

Focusing back to my seemingly serendipitous ancestors coin collection project, I built a spreadsheet sorted by year, attaching various grandmothers and grandfathers to coins unique to each DNA contributor's respective birth. I imagined the possibility of my ancestors actually once holding in their hands the very coins I would be collecting. Avoiding expensive coins in favor of more reasonably valued options, those 1922 gold coins kept coming back into view.

My grandmother Nanny had recently joined her Savior, and my Papa, in Heaven. As a complete surprise, she had left some money for me, but it wasn't out of character for her, because she had always, always given the best gifts. Having been blessed, I didn't need her money, but I knew she would want for me to buy something special, something outside the realm of possibilities, like the real genuine microscope complete with glass slides she'd bought for me when I was eight years old. Fortunately, I didn't want for anything, except maybe some old coins. That's it! I decided to purchase a 1922 gold coin with some of the money Nanny left me. It wasn't like I was spending the money. I was just converting the digital numbers in my savings account into a liquid asset easily converted back into cash. In the meantime, I could enjoy something tangible to hold.

Pulling up information about the coin online, it was a 1922 $20 St. Gaudens Double Eagle. The front of the coin featured a beautiful woman with flowing hair stepping forward, her bare left leg exposed from beneath the split in her loose-fitting dress. Behind her, rays of sun represented a new day dawning. Her left foot perched elevated upon a stone outcropping. She was stepping up and forward with a lit torch held high in her right hand and an oak branch in her left. With the morning sun at her back, she was heading west toward limitless opportunities. Below and behind her was the United States Capitol building, letting all know she and the gold coin hard currency had the full backing of the U.S. government. The back featured an eagle in flight; extended wings held high signified endless potential energy, pectoral muscles prepared to unleash great strength and determined endurance. Silhouetted by a setting sun, In God We Trust proclaimed she feared not the coming darkness of night and death, believing instead in a new day and eternal life. In perpetuity the eagle flies southbound, toward home.

The next morning, I went to see Calvin's 1922 $20 gold coins. Sharing with Calvin my interest in purchasing the coin, he went to his vault but found no 1922 gold coins. He said he had quantities of any other year. He asked me how much the guy was asking, and I told him $1,320. Calvin suggested I should buy the coin because it was a good price. I then went to the fourth coin shop I hadn't visited yesterday, but like Calvin, they had no gold coins dated 1922. On to the shop where I had purchased the new old book, he, too, could not find a $20 gold St. Gaudens Double Eagle dated 1922 in his inventory. I'd only been a numismatist for twenty-four hours, but how was it that one guy with a brand-new shop had only two gold coins, both 1922, while these other three established shops with hundreds of gold coins combined had not one 1922 gold coin? I called the new shop owner and asked if he still had the 1922 coins. Yes, he did still have them and would hold them until I arrived.

I looked over both coins and picked my favorite. From my pocket, I pulled out the hundred-dollar bills withdrawn from the bank for the purpose. The plastic coin holder felt good in my hand. Inserting my clinched fist deep into the safety of my left pocket, to where I could feel the pant fabric tighten across the top side of my forearm, I deposited the family heirloom. The purchase decision felt right, and I knew Nanny and Papa would be pleased. Once home, I could hardly wait to take photos of the gold coin and text them to my uncles for approval.

A couple weeks later, I traveled to Georgia to help my uncles go through Nanny's final possessions. Uncle James, afflicted with a severe cold, couldn't make the trip, but I called him during my rental car drive.

Trae: Hey, you remember that donkey shirt Nanny made for my dad?

James: Yeah, and my other brother got a tiger.

Trae: What kind of shirt did Nanny make you?

James: A giraffe. I probably threw it away, but I'd wear it every day if I had it now.

Trae: A giraffe? Really?

At that very moment, up ahead about half a mile, I saw a tall billboard sign, and at 75 miles an hour I was closing on it fast. I told James to hold on a minute while I accessed my phone camera feature. Without crashing, I zoomed into the billboard, click, text, send.

Trae: Dude, you aren't gonna believe this. Wait until you open the text photo I just sent you.

James: Holy cow. What are the odds? It's a giraffe!

We both agreed Nanny was with us on this trip.

At my uncle's house, he had all Nanny's boxes filled with her belongings stacked on and around a work bench table in his walk-out basement. He had seen the 1922 gold coin, and I told him the billboard giraffe story. Going through her things, we found a stack of black and white print magazines, all having a World War II-themed photo on the cover. I'd say there were about fifteen of them, and each had about thirty pages. They looked interesting, but they took up a lot of space, and I doubted I would ever get around to reading them. I asked my uncle if he wanted them, and he asked what they were. To find out, I sized up the stack, arbitrarily selected one, and flopped it open to a random page. Immediately I saw a photo of a ship, a familiar ship. The caption read *S.S. Susana*. It was Nanny's brother's ship, the ship that was sunk during the war. The ship where Uncle Griffin was killed. Skimming down the letter associated with the ship photo, the bottom of the letter was signed by my Nanny. She had written a letter to the publisher of this subscription magazine. I just happened to select the edition in which it was featured and opened to the exact page where it was inserted. My uncle was watching and witnessed what happened.

We spent the rest of the evening going through everything, and I mean everything, because there was no telling what might be significant. Starting back at it the next morning, I opened a cardboard box and found a plastic folder stuffed with what appeared to be various pieces of paper trash. I pivoted to my right to toss it behind me into a cull bin, but stopped mid-pitch. I thought to myself, *Don't get lazy now.* I twisted back toward the work bench, set the folder down in front of me, opened it up again, and started visually scanning both sides of every piece of paper stuffed in there. Maybe six or seven pieces of paper into it, a crumpled page torn from a weekly advertisement mailer was next. I pulled at the corners of the page and repositioned it right-side up. What I saw was nothing short of miraculous. It was an advertisement for a gold coin featuring a photo of a gold St. Gaudens Double Eagle, the one I had just bought, with Nanny's money, to commemorate my Nanny and Papa.

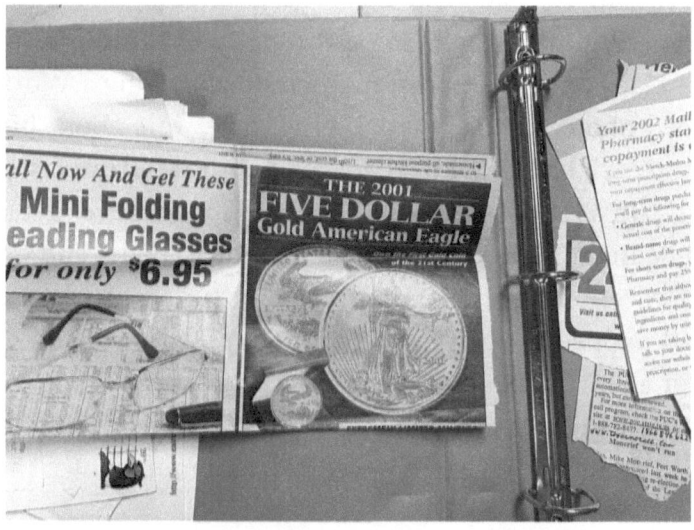

I was already convinced my Nanny was communicating with me through that gold coin, assuring me Heaven was real. Now she was just showing off. While finishing this chapter, I Googled the new coin shop to see if maybe they had a photo of the marketing-wrapped SUV. I recalled the artwork had some stacks of gold coins. There weren't any photos of the SUV, but there was a picture of the storefront with the one and only parking space in front. I clicked that photo thinking maybe I might spy the SUV, but I got something better. At the top of the front of the building was the new company sign. On the left was the word COIN. On the right was the word SHOP. Between the two words, a 3 feet in diameter replica of the $20 gold St. Gaudens Double Eagle. Thanks for the coin, Nanny. And thanks for letting me know you made it home safely.

Chapter 24

SEEKING HISTORICAL CONTEXT

My name is George Carter from Tattnall County, Georgia, and I am most grateful for the opportunity to submit this most unique of contributions for inclusion into the pages of *They Face East*. When I was born 276 years ago in South Carolina, Harvard University had been in existence 106 years, and we the people of the Atlantic coast British colonies were unenlightened subjects of our forefathers' king. I'm sure it must seem rather odd to have a contributor from my time period, but I felt compelled to

Pvt. George Carter, 3rd South Carolina Continental Line, Rev War

share with you my connection to ancestry adventures as it pertains to historical context.

As you can see from my marble headstone, I served in the 3rd South Carolina Regiment during the American Revolutionary War of Independence. Along with my regiment, I saw action against the British and Loyalists at the Siege of Savannah in 1779 and the Siege of Charleston in 1780. What is a Loyalist you say? Well, contrary to the grossly condensed stereotypical modern history texts, not all citizens residing within the colonies desired separation from England, not all enemy combatants wore red coats, and Boston was not the only battleground. Loyalists, also known as Tories, were our neighbors, friends, and family members whose choice it was to maintain allegiance with King George and bear arms against our cause. Those were dark days for our fledgling country, and for me personally, as the entire American army in the South was surrendered to British forces on May 12, 1780. The tide of our quest for freedom was outgoing and would not turn until five months later at the Battle of Kings Mountain.

Monument at Kings Mountain National Battlefield

You may wonder why a Revolutionary War Soldier such as myself from so long ago would insert himself into the pages of this book held within your grasp. As I suffered indescribable conditions offshore Charleston, SC aboard a dank British prison hulk among my fellow 2,571 captive Patriots, I prayed for victory, freedom, and the possibility my sacrifice, and the combined sacrifices of my Compatriots, would one day cast off monarchial dictation, tyranny, and economic surplus siphoning. The eventual outcome of our suffering, courage, and steadfast resolve was never certain, but Divine Providence ultimately favored the ideals set forth in our Declaration of Independence.

Remember us as honorable men, once alive, no different from yourself. Acknowledge our efforts as principled soldiers willing to go all in that you might inherit opportunities unattainable by previous generations. See us in the surroundings and context in which we lived, loved, and died. Comprehend that not all men possess melded attributes necessary for righteous rebellious behavior combined with the fortitude required for victorious perseverance against all odds. And visit our final resting places where few longer trod seeking connection, sharing welcomed words of affection, or placing a warm hand upon our cold marble stones.

—PRIVATE GEORGE CARTER

The physical landscape, generally accepted norms, concerns, and expectations of my 6th Great-grandfather George Carter were very different as compared to my life experience in the 20th and 21st centuries. To begin to imagine him as a breathing human being interacting within his time capsule reality, I must step away from my reality, refrain from judgment, and appreciate how things were 250 to 300 years ago in the 18th and 19th centuries. Different doesn't even begin to describe the dissimilarities, which makes it unreasonable and unfair to frame his decisions within the parameters of 21st century western societal ethics and norms.

The same contextual awareness applies to all of your personal ancestors, and those of human sub-groups specifically distinct from your own, regardless of time period analyzed. They were of different contexts and interacted with their personal environments accordingly. Striving to reach an understanding and appreciation for my discovered ancestors' historical context has been the most unanticipated benefit of my journey to honor my DNA. History was always interesting to me, but placing an actual direct bloodline ancestor into a significant event or turning point truly brings history to a heightened level of caring. This profound sense of caring stoked desire to drill down into fine detail layers never before contemplated or perceived as significantly important.

I found all of my ancestors buried facing east, every single one. Most were buried in church cemeteries. Many of my grandfathers were preachers, pastors, elders, or deacons. Several of my grandfathers donated land or founded churches. All lived their lives in the American South. I wondered, "How was it possible for believers in Jesus Christ, God fearing Christians, to live among slavery?" I found one answer in a book titled, *The Salzburgers and Their Descendants*, by Reverend P. A. Strobel. The book was written in Americus, GA and published in 1855, five years before Abraham Lincoln was elected president and the beginning of the Civil War. Pages 101 through 105 described the dilemma over slavery faced by one group of German speaking immigrants of Protestant Christian faith.

The Salzburgers, with surnames such as Wisenbaker, Zitteraur, Waldhauer, Dasher, and Zipperer, had endured severe religious persecution. Essentially forced to migrate across the Atlantic Ocean to America, more specifically, Georgia, between 1734 and 1750, they left behind their homes, personal property, and even children in Salzburg, Austria. Like so many of the early European immigrants who laid the foundation of the United States of America between 1607 and 1775, the Salzburgers were unwilling to renounce their

Protestant Christian beliefs. Reading and comprehending the red words spoken by Jesus in the New Testament of the Bible, they were unwilling to submit to a church hierarchy, believing instead they could interact directly with God. They prayed directly to God. They asked forgiveness directly from God.

Their laws for their colony at Ebenezer near Savannah forbade the importation of slaves. But with slavery having been established in the British colonies beginning 115 years before the Salzburgers' arrival, the colony of Ebenezer was a landlocked island literally surrounded by the institution of slavery. For many years, the Salzburgers, whose faith in Jesus was unwavering, refused to participate despite relentless peer pressure. A Mr. Whitefield is quoted in the book on pages 103 and 104 as saying he believed with influential writer Alexander Pope that "Whatever Is, is Right; that God had some wise ends to accomplish in reference to African slavery; and that he had no doubt it would terminate in advantage to the Africans." I found this statement made in the 1700s to be extremely profound.

God did have some wise ends to accomplish in reference to African slavery. With the benefit of hindsight spanning four centuries, viewing the world from a macro perspective in both space and time, beyond the boundaries of what's comprehendible within a single lifespan of human experiences, we can glimpse innumerable instances of accomplishments on a human species scale in reference to African slavery. The big picture is simply too big for us as individuals to discern, requiring us to have faith that a higher power was at work with a plan in our best interest as subjects.

My Confederate soldier ancestors had grandfathers in North America dating back to the 1700s, and those grandfathers were Patriots in the American Revolution. To date I have found records indicating forty-three of my 5th, 6th, and 7th great-grandfathers were Patriots. To put forty-three into perspective, I have only been able to identify about 33% of my grandfathers who were of military age during the American Revolution. If I found forty-three Patriot grandfathers in a one-third sampling, then I'm on pace to discover a total of 130 Patriot grandfathers. These were the men who created the United States of America. This fact forms the basis of my question, "Why were my Southern ancestors willing to lay down their lives attempting to create a new nation when their hero grandfathers had just recently fought for freedom from England's rule?"

A stereotypical Civil War history lesson or summary goes something like this:

- The cause of the American Civil War was slavery.
- Northern white people demanded the slaves be freed.
- Southern white people refused to free the slaves.
- Northern white people did not want slavery in the new western territories and states.
- Southern white people wanted slavery to be allowed in the new territories and states.
- President Abraham Lincoln freed all the slaves with his Emancipation Proclamation.
- In response, all the slave states seceded, forming the Confederate States of America.
- Southern white people were traitors for seceding from the United States.
- The South drew first blood when they fired the first shots at Fort Sumter.
- Having exhausted all efforts to end slavery, the North had no choice but to declare war.
- Each person in America had to choose between freedom or continuation of slavery.
- The Union Army was comprised of abolitionist soldiers willing to die to end slavery.

- The Confederate Army was comprised of white supremacists fighting to keep slavery.
- The Civil War was essentially good American brothers vs. bad American brothers.

Sound about right to you? Well, that's the way I had always heard it told. But I thought to myself, *It sure seems strange that all of my ancestors were Confederate soldiers when I expected half of any found to be Union soldiers.*

This book is about honoring my DNA, so I'm taking you deep into the bowels of the Civil War to provide an example of what I did to understand what I discovered about my ancestors when I built my family tree. You can't choose your ancestors. You get what you get, and you can't erase the origins of your DNA. Your ancestors are your people, but it doesn't mean you live within their historical context nor does it mean you should make the same choices as your ancestors. I discovered the Civil War had to happen and men had to die in order for me to have ever been born. I discovered some of my ancestors did in fact own slaves. I discovered a man had to be unfaithful to his wife in order for one of my great-great-grandfathers to have been born. And you, too, will discover facts about the origins of your DNA you could never have imagined until you see it with your own eyes and reconcile it within your own brain.

Every child born on the North American continent between 1619 and 1865, a period of 246 years, was born into the institution of slavery. "Peculiar" was a word used to describe the ownership of human beings of African descent as chattel. While the institution of slavery was an extreme contrast as witnessed by, and lived by, the experiences of blacks compared to whites, the despicable institution itself afflicted all by conditioning those born into it to perceive slavery as a normal order of things. Even Christian church leaders, also born into the institution of slavery, steadfastly justified the existence of slavery to their flock by referencing biblical scriptures. All across America, North and South, the population, black and white, was born into slavery, conditioned to accept the subjugation of black people as fundamentally normal.

I've not heard it said before, but I believe the mass immigration of millions of white people from European countries during the 1840s and 1850s played a major role in igniting the Civil War, because those people were not born into slavery. Those people stepped off the transport ships onto United States soil and sometime soon thereafter were introduced to the concept of slavery for the first time in their lives. The white immigrants didn't land in Southern ports, they arrived in Northern ports where there were very few black people, free or slave. "What the hell is wrong with you people?" is probably what they said to their new Yankee neighbors. It was probably the first time many Northern white people had been confronted with the injustice happening in their midst, the injustice of slavery from which Northerners benefitted both financially and in status.

In addition to bringing their minds not yet polluted by slavery, the millions of white immigrants from Europe also brought with them to the Northern states their spiritual and religious beliefs. Church leaders in their home countries had not ordained from the pulpit that the Bible blessed slavery. To the contrary, slavery had somewhat isolated the Southern white population within their churches. They shared in common a unique homogeneous Protestant faith where pastors and elders found and preached biblical support justifying the enslavement-of-black-people-world in which they, and eight generations before them, had been born and lived. In hindsight, it does make sense that whites in the South prior to the Civil War would have sought spiritual justification for the world around them where upwards of 58% of humans were enslaved blacks (South Carolina). With God as the anchor at the center of their universe, by what other means could slavery have been sustained if not found in the Bible? From a practical standpoint, from a church leader's perspective, how many parishioners benefitting from slave holding would you have in your congregation if your message was that of slavery being unjust?

More than 25% of Union soldiers during the Civil War were foreign born compared to an estimated 9% dressed in grey. Don H. Doyle, professor of history at the University of South Carolina, in his article "The Civil War was Won by Immigrant Soldiers," estimated 43% of Union soldiers were either foreign born or sons of foreign-born parents. This significant fact explained for me the numerous Irish symbols I had observed carved into countless monuments erected along the Union battle lines at Gettysburg. There were so many immigrant Union soldiers from Germany that Southerners sometimes referred to a Yankee as a Hessian, which dates back to the Revolutionary War when Britain hired Hessian mercenaries.

I don't have documentation to support it, because census records didn't track church affiliations, but based on circumstantial correlations, I theorize a large percentage of white Northern men born in the United States and sharing in common with white Southern men a religious faith grounded in presbyterian Protestant worship beliefs, chose to sit out the Civil War. Look at the number of Union soldiers, subtract the number who were foreign born, subtract those of African descent, and then compare the balance to the number of white Northern men who did not serve as Union soldiers. I could certainly be wrong, but if someone digs deep enough into the issue of religion and the Civil War, I am confident they will find a significant divide, a contrast, between North and South along religious lines.

The hero of Little Round Top, Joshua Chamberlain, who achieved the rank of Major General in the Union Army, had this to say in his memoir *The Passing of the Armies.* "We had occasion to observe their religious character. More free thought and wider range of code no doubt prevailed in our Northern army; but what we are accustomed to call simple, personal piety was more manifest in the Confederate ranks than in ours. Not presuming to estimate the influence of particular cases of higher officers, like Stonewall Jackson or General Howard, making prominent their religious principles and proclivities, but fully recognizing the general religious character of most of the officers and men from our Northern homes, it must be admitted that the expression of religious sentiment and habit was more common and more earnest in the Confederate camp than in ours."

Another segment of the American population did not bear arms against the South, and that group was the vast majority of black people (96%), both free and enslaved. Why didn't black people in the South rise up in a slave rebellion behind enemy lines as Lincoln had intended with his Emancipation Proclamation made only after two full years of military losses in the field? Because they loved the same God and worshipped in the same Protestant denominations as the whites who enslaved them. Despite the many ugly manmade issues fabricated to physically and emotionally segregate races in America, from a spiritual standpoint a more powerful force binds blacks and whites as brothers and sisters in Christ. Google it.

If your early ancestors lived in Georgia, and you trace your lineage back to the period 1775 to 1783, you will discover your grandfather of that time period was most likely a Revolutionary War Patriot. The reason is because Georgia was taken from the Indians after the Battle of Horseshoe Bend 27 Mar 1814. Once the Indians were removed from Georgia, the lands of Georgia were divided up and granted to Revolutionary War Patriots or their widows in 1820, 1827, and 1832. Therefore, many of the early settlers of Georgia were Patriots, Protestant Patriots, enticed by tracts of free farmland.

Not all men within the Colonies during the Revolution were Patriots. Approximately 20% remained loyal to the king of England and were known as Loyalists, or Tories. Our liberal schoolbooks tell the story of Minutemen battling Redcoats in and around Boston, when in fact, during the southern campaigns, such as the turning point of the American Revolution at the Battle of Kings Mountain, it was actually a civil war of neighbor against neighbor, or Patriots vs. Loyalists. Truth is, the American Civil War was *not* the first civil war in North America. And many of the Loyalists were members of the Church of England whose head was none other than the king himself.

A seven-volume set could not explain away the issue of slavery, but contrary to popular belief, slavery was an Atlantic Slave Trade sin instituted by European and African Heads of State in the early 1500s. According to the National Museum of African American History and Culture in Washington, D.C., 97% of humans exported out of Africa during the Atlantic Slave Trade as commodity laborers were *not* transported to the North American continent! Slavery became a North American continent sin as early as 1619 when a Dutch ship brought twenty African slaves to the British colony of Jamestown, VA. Slavery became a United States of America sin 157 years later when it was fabricated and instituted within the Constitution itself. Read the Constitution, and slavery is still there today, only altered by the 13th Amendment, which failed to pass during a vote in the House in 1864, while Southern States were not even represented in Congress. As a matter of fact, on June 15, 1864, with the Civil War still raging and just three days after 60,000 Southern men defeated 117,000 Union soldiers at the Battle of Cold Harbor, the United States House of Representatives FAILED to pass the 13th Amendment to end slavery in the United States of America with a vote of 93 in favor vs. 65 against (41% against).

Watch the movie *Lincoln* to see how the 13th Amendment ending slavery barely passed on January 31, 1865, more than four years after the Civil War began, with a pitiful vote of 119 in favor and fifty-six against (32% against). This uncomfortable fact of American history flies in the face of those who shout propaganda the Civil War was fought over slavery. Had the North been truly fighting to free the enslaved people of African descent, the vote tallies in the Senate and the House to pass the 13th Amendment would have been *unanimous* the first time, leaving no need for a second embarrassing vote.

War clouds had been on the horizon well before the presidential election of 1860, eventually leading to the State of South Carolina seceding from the United States of America on December 20, 1860. Mississippi followed, then Florida, then Alabama, then Georgia, then Louisiana, then Texas. The original seven Southern states immediately took back local state-controlled occupation of Federal installations, including coastal forts. Following four long months of failed negotiations to remove Federal forces from South Carolina soil, President Abraham Lincoln decided to call the fledgling Confederate States of America's bluff by ordering United States ships to sail toward Fort Sumter with supplies and reinforcements. Southern leadership knew the vital deep-water port of Charleston would be closed to shipping traffic for many months with just a single resupply.

On April 12, 1861, Confederate authorities gave the order to fire upon Fort Sumter to end the resupply effort. Astonishingly, there were no casualties during the bombardment. Just three days later on April 15, 1861, newly elected President Abraham Lincoln called for 75,000 men to invade the South and quell the rebellion. At this point, the Southern states of Virginia, Arkansas, Tennessee, and North Carolina faced a dilemma.

You may not know American history very well (which you should), but you probably know every detail about the *Star Wars* movies. Do you remember when Luke Skywalker defeated Darth Vader? Do you remember when the Emperor began to jolt Luke with powerful lightning bolts with the intent to kill Luke Skywalker? Do you remember Luke's father, Darth Vader, watching his son being murdered by Darth Vader's master, the evil Emperor? At that point, Darth Vader faced a dilemma. He had to choose sides. Do you see the analogous similarities—the Emperor and Lincoln, Luke and the Deep South states, Luke's father Darth Vader and the states of VA, AR, TN, and NC?

In response to Abraham Lincoln's intent to invade the South, Virginia, Arkansas, Tennessee, and North Carolina chose to stand with their Southern neighbors against Lincoln's central government aggression. This is why Southerners refer to the Civil War as the War of Northern Aggression. Maryland, Delaware, and Kentucky would most likely have followed suit and joined the Confederacy had Abraham Lincoln not exceeded his presidential powers by suspending the writ of habeas corpus (look it up). Lincoln imprisoned any people he felt were empathetic to Southern independence, specifically leaders of border states possessing power to call for secession.

I hope we can all agree slavery was and is wrong. As a product of the Civil War, I have spent a great deal of time thinking about slavery, empathizing over those who were enslaved, and contemplating how I might play a small role in bringing people of diverse backgrounds, sub-groups, and races together as one human people with a common purpose of kindness, tolerance, forgiveness, and patience. In order to get to the Promised Land,

- we each need to discover our ancestral past,
- know from where we came,
- comprehend historical context,
- ask for God to come into our hearts,
- challenge what we assume to be true,
- forgive those who we perceive as having trespassed against us,
- believe in goodness of the human spirit, and
- and put an end to the ugliness of divisiveness.

Until you build your family tree, submit a DNA test, review your DNA matches, and identify your direct lineage ancestors, you have no idea and can't be certain of your heritage. You might find out that hate in your heart toward one group or another is staring back at you in the mirror in direct conflict with the group in which you identify. For example, you may be someone who dislikes a certain race, or makes insensitive comments toward said race, only to find out 3.125% of you was derived from the race you hate. Sally Hemmings' descendants also descend from none other than Thomas Jefferson. I find it interesting, funny almost, to think about how people prejudice toward one group could quite possibly themselves descend from that same group. If you descend from a group, you are that group!

I compiled the following chronological historical context during my efforts to place myself within the shoes of my ancestors and to see the world through their eyes. Many, if not most, of my ancestors, and probably your ancestors, were illiterate. They couldn't read. They couldn't write. They attended church services each and every Sunday learning the word of God from a Bible read aloud by their pastor. They were farmers and dwelled in homes they built with their own hands. They got by without the bountiful comforts, foods, healthcare, and conveniences we mindlessly take for granted today. They lived, loved, raised children, and died within just a few miles of their birthplace. Within this historical context, never yearned for prior to my ancestry adventure, I found an understanding of the past and the present never realized during thirteen years of school, four years in the Navy, four years of college, two years of grad school, and a total of forty-eight years stumbling around the crust of planet Earth trying to better my lot in life.

Sure, many of the stand-alone facts had been read, heard, or memorized along the way, but never with my own flesh and blood intertwined within the fabric of long-ago events. Awareness of my ancestors' presence within stories of the past elevated levels of importance, transforming the once insignificant into personally prized recollections of the human experience. History was no longer George Washington, Chief Osceola, Robert E. Lee, Susan B. Anthony, and Audie Murphy. History for me was now George Carter, Reason Dansby, Leonard Anderson, Isabel Lovett, Mary Surginer, and Ray Mathis. My heroes and heroines were no longer limited to famously recognized figures etched into our history texts, as if those limited few were the only ones involved.

Obviously, this historical timeline of events is extremely concise for a time period spanning 2,000 years, but these are the points I found most impactful for me as I sought to honor my DNA beyond simply a name and couple of dates jotted on a family tree diagram. As a Southerner, I discovered my story is, oddly enough, somewhat similar to other conquered peoples such as the Incas, the Mayans, the enslaved Africans, the Samurai, the Creeks, the Lakota Sioux, the Cheyenne, the Nez Perce, the Spanish, the Japanese, the Germans, and the Mexicans. Throughout human history, there have been countless conflicts resulting in slain and survivors, winners and losers. World maps are ever changing as decided territorial boundaries expand, contract, appear, or disappear. This process continues today as the ever-present yearning for power, influence, and wealth drives certain persons to stoke hatred and patriotism toward their ultimate objective, dividing us from fellow man to fallen fodder.

The victors write the history books and, unfortunately, few have the desire, capacity, and mindshare to seek the truth outside of their own prejudices. When I was a boy, it was common to play Cowboys and Indians, or various games of battle. Guess how many boys wanted to be the Indians? How many boys wanted to be the Japanese soldiers, or the German soldiers? The Confederate battle flag has been transformed into a racist symbol of the Ku Klux Klan and white supremacy. Confederate monuments erected by descendants of Confederate soldiers are being torn down by angry mobs or dismantled by those now in power, or those seeking power, based on perceived popular demand and fearful political correctness. Tell a group of school children they'll be roll playing Civil War soldiers and ask by a show of hands, "Who would like to play a Union soldier?" Not a single hand will rise into the air when asking for Confederate soldier volunteers.

Slavery is not okay, and neither is discrimination, racism, prejudice, sexism, hatred, meanness, jealousy, oppression, prejudging, vilifying the conquered, ignoring the less fortunate, stereotyping, ignoring a person's context, or pitting one group against another for personal gain. And that goes for each and every human being, regardless of one's race, sex, income bracket, or any other manmade category that divides us as members of the same species. This is the chronological order of significant events I compiled during my best effort to honor my DNA by way of attempting to understand why my ancestors lived the lives they lived, why they believed in the God they worshipped, why they migrated to the lands they cultivated, why they fought in various conflicts, and what happened to result in my grandmothers and grandfathers crossing paths. As you read through my summarized observations of dates and facts, consider the following:

- Which of the following events are relevant to your ancestors?
- Which of the following events are new to you, challenging your perceptions and beliefs?
- Which of the following events will you Google and research to learn more?
- Which historical events will help you conceptualize the context in which your ancestors lived?
- Do you feel you can honor your DNA while still empathizing with the plight of others?
- How will you reconcile having ancestors on both sides of an historical event?

Chapter 25

AN HISTORICAL PERSPECTIVE ZERO–1860

- 1 BC|AD 1: Jesus Christ is immaculately conceived and born a Jew. Even the United Nations recognizes the birth of Jesus as the beginning point when counting calendar years. BC stands for Before Christ and AD stands for Anno Domini. AD does not stand for After Death, because Jesus lived approximately thirty-three years. Otherwise, there would be thirty-three missing years between BC and AD. That He lived is indisputable. Based on His well-documented life and deeds, each person must independently choose whether or not he or she believes Jesus was the Messiah. Jesus addressed doubters and skeptics when He said to Nicodemus in John 3:12, "If I have told you earthly things and you do not believe, how will you believe if I tell you heavenly things?" That's a pretty good point. Nicodemus was a ruler of the Jews.
- Read The Gospel According to Matthew, the opening book of the New Testament in the Bible, and you will realize Jesus was a Jew, born in Bethlehem, fled to Egypt, then lived in

the land of Israel preaching and performing miracles for the benefit of His fellow Jews.

- Matthew 15:21–28 described a non-Jew Gentile woman asking Jesus to heal her daughter, who was severely demon-possessed. Jesus said, "I was not sent except to the lost sheep of the house of Israel." Following a verbal exchange where Jesus said to the Gentile woman, "It is not good to take the children's bread and throw *it* to the little dogs." The woman was not deterred from her faith that Jesus was the Son of God. Jesus recognized her steadfast belief and he said to her, "O woman, great *is* your faith! Let it be to you as you desire." And her daughter was healed from that very hour. This is when non-Jews (Gentiles) were accepted and welcomed by Christ as children of God in addition to the lost sheep of the house of Israel whom He was sent to save.
- When Jesus was performing miracles, such as healing the sick, feeding thousands, and raising the dead, those first multitudes who believed in Him and followed Him were fellow Jews. Some Jews believed, some did not, no different from some Gentiles believed, and some did not. Each human, Jew and Gentile alike, reached their own conclusion before they died. The Bible did not provide for free passes to Heaven.
- AD 33: Jesus Christ was crucified.
- The book of Acts in the New Testament of the Bible told the story of the growth of the Christian church following the crucifixion of Jesus and specifically shared the welcoming of Gentiles as believers in Christ, as described in multiple verses such as Acts 10:44.
- 380: Christianity became the official religion of the Roman Empire.

- 476: Roman Empire fell after reigning for 1,000 years. Approximately 15% of the population were slaves.
- The Romans demonstrated how to conquer a neighbor militarily, round up the now defenseless population, and sell the captives into slavery. I think we can all agree slavery, for any human, regardless of race, religion, nationality, or any other categorization, is not acceptable and cannot be justified. However, slavery has been a part of human history, probably back to near the beginning of humans on planet Earth and must be acknowledged for context. Slavery down through the ages has been inflicted upon all races at one time or another, even today.
- Do your own research on the history of slavery to learn who, how, why, and when.
- 1095: The First Crusade began to recapture the Holy Land.
- 1147: The Second Crusade began.
- 1189: The Third Crusade began.
- 12 Oct 1492: Columbus discovered the Americas. He arrived somewhere in the Bahamas.
- Inside the National Museum of the American Indian (NMAI), an information card authored by Paul Chaat Smith described European-designed wooden sailing ships as "…the most advanced technologies Europeans possessed. They were the spaceships of their time."
- Early 1500s: read about the Atlantic Slave Trade to learn who, how, why, and when humans began trading humans between the continent of Africa and the Americas. The slave trade triangle was profitable on all three shipping routes. Africa exported humans to the Americas. The Americas exported commodities to Europe. Europe exported manufactured goods to Africa. This was repeated continuously for the next 350 years.

- 1513: Spanish explorer Juan Ponce de Leon discovered Florida.
- 31 Oct 1517: Martin Luther delivered his *Ninety-Five Theses* challenging practices of the Catholic Church, resulting in the formation of Protestant Christianity.
- 1521: Juan Ponce de Leon attempted to establish the first European colony in Southwest Florida but failed when he was mortally wounded by Calusa Indians.
- 1539: Spanish explorer Hernando De Soto landed on the west coast of Florida. In search of gold, he traveled north through present day Georgia, South Carolina, and North Carolina, then west through Tennessee, Alabama, Mississippi, and Arkansas.
- 21 May 1542: Hernando De Soto died somewhere on the west side of the Mississippi River in either present day Arkansas or Louisiana.
- 1560: The first edition of the Geneva Bible was completed. In disagreement with the established churches, certain Protestants fled to Geneva, Switzerland and translated the Greek New Testament and Hebrew Scriptures into English. The Geneva Bible pre-dated, and was the foundation of, the English language King James Version of the Bible. Learn more by visiting Museum of the Bible in Washington, D.C.
- 1565: The city of St. Augustine, FL was established by Spain, making it the oldest city established by Europeans within the Continental United States.
- 1606: The London Council for Virginia gave the following advice to the soon-to-be-established English colony in the New World: "Lastly and chiefly the way to prosper and achieve good success is to make yourselves all of one mind for the good of your country and your own, and to serve and fear God the giver of all goodness, for every plantation

which our Heavenly Father hath not planted shall be rooted out."

- 13 May 1607: The first English settlement in the New World at Jamestown, VA on the North American continent was established by 104 English men and boys.

- 25 May 1607: More than 200 Virginia Indians drew first blood against the English when they attacked the English men and boys at Jamestown, killing two and wounding ten.

- 1611: The King James Version of the Bible was completed. This translation of the Bible was authorized by England's King James for his Church of England in an attempt to address the conflicting beliefs of episcopal and presbyterian forms of church governance as it pertained to Puritan worship.

- 1616: Inside the NMAI, an information card quoted Thomas Morton, New England Canaan: "The Indians died in heapes, as they lay in their houses…. And the bones and skulls upon the severall places of their habitations made such a spectacle…that, as I travailed in the Forrest nere the Massachusetts, it seemed to me a new found Golgotha." (In the Bible, Golgotha means "place of the skull.")

- 1619: According to History.com, the first African slaves exported from Africa and imported to present-day United States by European traders was "…in 1619, when a Dutch ship brought twenty African slaves ashore in the British colony of Jamestown, Virginia."

- 1619: **The Union Flag of Great Britain became the first flag of slavery on the North American continent**. This flag was created by merging the flags of England and Scotland when Great Britain was formed. The Union Jack flag added the flag of Ireland when the United Kingdom was formed.

- African slaves, with no rights or hopes of ever achieving freedom and equality, declined in status to that of perceived inferiors within effectively an inexplicit caste system.
- 1620: *Mayflower* reached the New World carrying Pilgrims from Plymouth, England. The Pilgrims worshiped Jesus Christ as Protestant Christians.
- 1622: Spanish galleon *Atocha* loaded with silver, gold, and emeralds pillaged from South America and Central America sank in a storm near the Florida Keys.
- 1632: William Spencer, my 11th great-grandfather, arrived at Newe Towne (renamed Cambridge in 1638), Massachusetts Bay Colony.
- 15 Aug 1635: Samuel Haines, my 9th great-grandfather, arrived in Maine and began his life in New Hampshire.
- 1636: Harvard College, the oldest and most prestigious university in the United States, was founded, and my 10th great-grandmother was born, in Cambridge, MA.
- Rules and Precepts of Harvard:

  - 2. Let Every Student be plainly instructed, and earnestly pressed to consider well, the maine end of his life and studies is, to know God and Jesus Christ which is eternal life (John 17:3) and therefore to lay Christ in the bottome, as the only foundation of all sound knowledge and Learning. And seeing the Lord only giveth wisedome, Let every one seriously set himself by prayer in secret to seeke it of him (Prov. 2:3).

- Indentured Servitude was a common form of temporary slavery for white immigrants from Europe to America, whereby a poor person would effectively sell themselves into slavery for a period of three to seven years in return for ship passage to America. Internet search results suggest 50–67% of white immigrants to Colonial America, including my Samuel Haines, were indentured servants, or white slaves.

- Mar 1638: The Ancient and Honorable Artillery Company of Massachusetts was formed, and my William Spencer was a charter member.
- 1685: Code Noir, or Black Code, was a set of rules for slavery in the French Colonial Empire, including North America, authorized by the king of France.
- 1692: Salem Witch Trials.
- 1705: Virginia Slave Code enacted.
- 1717: France imported slaves into Louisiana. **The French "Flag of New France" became the second flag of slavery on the North American continent.**
- 1734: The first group of Salzburgers originating from Salzburg, Austria traveled by ship from England to Savannah, GA, eventually establishing the town of New Ebenezer. Like so many of the Europeans who immigrated to America prior to the Revolutionary War, the Salzburgers were Protestant Christians who were persecuted into exile by the Catholic Church.
- Control of the slave shipping industry in North America was based in Rhode Island.
- 1760: Industrial Revolution began in Great Britain, leading to mechanized manufacturing, rise of factories, population growth, migration from agricultural rural farms to urban cities, cotton textiles, and increased demand for cotton fibers.
- 1762: **The Spanish Flag became the third flag of slavery on the North American continent** when France ceded their

lands west of the Mississippi River to Spain following the
French and Indian War.

- 19 Apr 1775: American Revolution battles of Lexington and
  Concord.
- 4 Jul 1776: Declaration of Independence.

  - Slavery had been an American institution for
    157 years, a period of time spanning six human
    generations.
  - The majority of delegates who signed the Declara-
    tion of Independence owned slaves of African
    descent.
  - Each of the thirteen colonies/states sent a delegate
    who owned slaves of African descent to sign the
    Declaration of Independence including **_NINE_**
    future Yankee Civil War states: Massachusetts,
    New York, New Jersey, Pennsylvania, Con-
    necticut, Rhode Island, Delaware, Maryland, New
    Hampshire.
  - The second sentence reads, "We hold these truths
    to be self-evident, that all men are created equal,
    that they are endowed by their Creator with certain
    unalienable Rights, that among these are Life,
    Liberty, and the pursuit of Happiness."
  - He (King George) has excited domestic insurrec-
    tions amongst us (Loyalists), and has endeavoured
    to bring on the inhabitants of our frontiers, the
    merciless Indian Savages (Native Americans)
    whose known rule of warfare, is an undistinguished
    destruction of all ages, sexes, and conditions.

- The term "men" in the second sentence of the Declaration of Independence clearly refers to white males of European descent based on these facts:
    - all signers of the document were white males of European descent,
    - the majority of males of African descent within the thirteen colonies were slaves,
    - the majority of delegates were slave owners,
    - at least one delegate from each colony/state was a slave owner, and
    - Native Americans were referred to as "Indian Savages"

- Some Native Americans allied themselves with the British against the Patriots.
- 14 Jun 1777: **Continental Congress approved the flag act establishing the fourth flag representing slavery on the North American continent** and **first flag of slavery in the United States**, "Resolved, that the flag of the United States be thirteen stripes, alternate red and white; that the union be thirteen stars, white in a blue field, representing a new constellation." The red, white, and blue United States flag was flown over legal slavery for eighty-eight and a half years, from 14 Jun 1777 until 6 Dec 1865, <u>including all four years of the Civil War</u>, until the 13th Amendment to the United States Constitution was adopted.
- 15 Nov 1777: The original thirteen states agreed to the Articles of Confederation.
- 25 Feb 1779: George Rogers Clark captured British Fort Sackville to secure the Illinois Country for the United States. It was an area almost as large as the thirteen colonies.

- 12 May 1780: entire United States Army of the South surrendered to British forces at Charleston, SC. Among those Patriots surrendered were George Carter and Samuel Cross of the 3rd South Carolina Regiment, both among my 6th great-grandfathers.
- The first civil war in the United States was fought during the Revolutionary War between the Patriots fighting for freedom from England and the Loyalists allied with the British.
- 7 Oct 1780: the Overmountain Men raced on horseback to catch up with British Major Patrick Ferguson and his Loyalists militia before Ferguson could reach the safety of General Cornwallis' army. The Patriots caught up with Ferguson at Kings Mountain, South Carolina in what would prove to be the turning point of the Revolutionary War.
- 19 Oct 1781: Cornwallis surrenders to Washington at the Battle of Yorktown in Virginia.
- 3 Sep 1783: the American Revolutionary War ended.
- 17 Sep 1787: the United States Constitution was signed by delegates.

  - Article I, Section 2, Clause 3: Representatives and direct Taxes shall be apportioned among the several States which may be included within this Union, according to their respective Numbers, which shall be determined by adding to the whole Number of free Persons, including those bound to Service for a Term of Years (indentured servants), and excluding Indians not taxed (Native Americans), three fifths of all other Persons (slaves of African descent). To maintain power within the House of Representatives, the South had an incentive to add to their number of representatives by increasing the number of slaves and reaping the benefit of counting three fifths their number.

- ◆ Article I, Section 9, Clause 1: The Migration or Importation (slave trade) of such Persons as any of the States now existing shall think proper to admit, shall not be prohibited by the Congress prior to the Year one thousand eight hundred and eight (1808), but a Tax or duty may be imposed on such Importation (persons of African descent), not exceeding ten dollars for each Person.

- ◆ Article IV, Section 2, Clause 3: No Person held to Service or Labour (slave of African descent or indentured servant) in one State, under the Laws thereof, escaping into another, shall, in Consequence of any Law or Regulation therein, be discharged from such Service or Labour, but shall be delivered up on Claim of the Party to whom such Service or Labour may be due.

- 1793: Eli Whitney invented the cotton gin, enabling efficient separation of useful cotton fibers from picked cotton bolls. With this mechanical expansion of capacity to process cotton bolls, more cotton could be planted for harvest, thereby increasing demand for slave labor in the cotton belt Southern States, because there were no tractors.
- 1796: Edward Jenner developed Smallpox vaccine.
- 1803: The Louisiana Purchase: United States purchased from France a vast expanse of land from the Gulf of Mexico to Canada, essentially the center of today's United States.
- 1804–1806: Lewis and Clark Expedition sent to discover a northwest passage.

- 1806–1810: Fort Hawkins was built as a military outpost at the border of the southern frontier near present-day Macon, GA, only 300 yards from Ocmulgee National Monument representing 17,000 years of human habitation by ancient Native American peoples.
- 1808: Importation of slaves into the United States ended as per Article I, Section 9, Clause 1 of the United States Constitution. While the importation of slaves was abolished, the selling of slaves within the United States remained legal. (See 1838 slave sale below for example.) The growth of cotton production in the South created a huge demand for labor, specifically slave labor, so the value of a slave in the South was greater as compared to the North. The practice of "Selling Slaves South" began. As northern states passed laws to abolish slavery, typically with a set date in the future when slavery would end, a slave owner in the North could 1) allow the freedom date to arrive, 2) voluntarily free their slaves prior to the law change, or 3) cash in on the value of their human property by selling their slaves to buyers in the South, aka Selling Slaves South, aka Sold Down the River.
- 1812–1815: War of 1812

    ◆ Britain supplied Native Americans with weapons and supplies.
    ◆ 30 Aug 1813: At the Fort Mims Massacre, approximately 1,000 Red Stick Creek Indians killed more than 500 Americans near Mobile, AL. Fort Mims was the fortified property of Samuel Mims, possibly related to my Mims ancestors.
    ◆ 27 Mar 1814: At the Battle of Horseshoe Bend near the present-day city of Daviston, AL, Major General and future president Andrew Jackson led 3,300

men against 1,000 Red Stick Creek Indian warriors, killing more than 800 and claiming 23 million acres of land.

- 24 Aug 1814: British forces burned the capital of the United States, Washington, D.C., including the White House and Capitol Building. Oh, yes they did.
- According to pbs.org, approximately 4,000 refugee slaves of African descent joined British forces against the United States as members of the Colonial Marines. These are probably the "slave" mentioned in the third verse of Francis Scott Key's *Star-Spangled Banner.*
- 14 Sep 1814: Francis Scott Key penned *Star Spangled Banner* while watching the Battle of Fort McHenry located at Baltimore, MD.

- 1816: According to a headstone, my 5th great-grandfather, Thomas Lindsey, a Revolutionary War Patriot, was killed by Indians in Montgomery County, GA.
- 27 Jul 1816: Battle of Negro Fort located on the Apalachicola River in Florida.
- 1820: Georgia land grants for Revolutionary War veterans.
- 1821: Florida became a United States Territory.
- 1822: Isaac Varn, born 1780 in South Carolina and one of the 128 men who were my 6th great-grandfathers, migrated into Florida north of Jacksonville as a Florida Pioneer, qualifying me as a 9th generation Floridian and my children 10th generation Floridians.
- 1827: Georgia land grants for Revolutionary War veterans.
- 1827: Slavery ended in the State of New York.

- 28 May 1830: President Andrew Jackson signed the Indian Removal Act of 1830 leading to the Trail of Tears and Seminole Indian Wars in Florida. Native Americans were forcibly relocated to large reservations in Oklahoma Territory, aka Indian Territory.
- Aug 1831: Nat Turner's Rebellion. Nat Turner, a slave, led a slave uprising killing more than fifty white people before his effort to break out of bondage was ended by militias. More than 100 black people were executed. When found, Nat Turner was hung, drawn, and quartered. Read about Nat Turner's Rebellion and ask yourself if you would have risen up as a slave. Think it through, and you'll understand why slaves didn't, couldn't, revolt in mass. God's intervention was the only way to dismantle the institution of slavery.
- 1832: Georgia land grants for Revolutionary War veterans.
- 28 Dec 1835: Dade Massacre occurred in Sumter County, FL where 108 of 110 U.S. soldiers were killed by Seminole Indians in an ambush, setting off second Seminole War.
- 24 Feb 1836: Commander of Texian forces within the Alamo, William Barret Travis, penned his famous patriotic letter while surrounded by Santa Ana's Mexican Army.
- 6 Mar 1836: Final assault on The Alamo where approximately 250 Texians fought to the death against more than 1,800 Mexican soldiers. Famous Texans killed at the Alamo included William Travis, James Bowie, and Davy Crockett.
- 21 Apr 1836: Texans defeated Santa Anna's Mexican Army at Battle of San Jacinto.
- 1838: Maryland Jesuits sold 272 slaves to pay off debts of what is now Georgetown University. This is just one example of Northern slave owners Selling Slaves South.
- 1845–1849: Irish Potato Famine accelerated migration of low wage earners out of Ireland.

- 3 Mar 1845: Florida became the 27th state in the United States.
- 1846: United States secured the Oregon Territory through negotiations with Britain. This area included all of present-day Oregon, Washington, and Idaho as well as portions of Montana and Wyoming.
- 1846–1848: Mexican–American War. The United States defeated Mexico and secured all or part of the current states of Texas, New Mexico, Colorado, Utah, Wyoming, Nevada, Arizona, and California.
- Contiguous geographic area of the United States established for the first time.
- 24 Jan 1848: Gold was discovered at Sutter's Mill, starting the California Gold Rush.
- 1850: First United States Census to have included names of each household member.
- 6 May 1851: Florida Dr. John Gorrie was issued the first patent for an ice-making machine.
- 10 Mar 1852: *Uncle Tom's Cabin*, by Harriet Beecher Stowe, was published. A novel depicting the lives of slaves in the American South, it was the second best-selling 19th century book, second only to the Bible. The book stoked abolitionism and kindled the Civil War.
- 22 May 1856: Representative Preston Brooks, a Democrat from South Carolina, used a cane to savagely attack about the head, neck, and shoulders Senator Charles Sumner, a Republican and abolitionist from Massachusetts, on the floor of the United States Senate in retaliation for Sumner having mocked the speech impediment of Brooks' uncle, SC Senator Andrew Butler.
- 1858: Third Seminole War ended in Florida.

- 1854–1859: Ulysses S. Grant, future commander of all Union forces, and future President of the United States, was a slave master and slave owner at his in-laws' plantation near St. Louis, MO.
- 16–18 Oct 1859: John Brown's Raid on Harper's Ferry, VA was abolitionist John Brown's quest to capture the United States arsenal, arm the slaves, and initiate a slave uprising. United States President James Buchanan sent U.S. Army Colonel Robert E. Lee to defeat the raiders and retake the federal arsenal. Compare outcome to Nat Turner's Rebellion.

1860 U.S. Population (pop.) Observations:

- Slave pop. as percentage of total pop. 1860 census
  - ◆ SC, MS — 57%, 55%
  - ◆ LA, AL, FL, GA — 47%, 45%, 44%, 44%
  - ◆ NC, VA, TX — 33%, 31%, 30%
  - ◆ AR, TN, KY — 26%, 25%, 20%
  - ◆ MD, MO — 13%, 10%
  - ◆ DE, NJ — 2%, <1%

- Total slave pop. in the United States — 3,900,000
  - ◆ Slave pop. in Union States — 800,000
  - ◆ Slave pop. in Confederate States —3,100,000

- Total free black pop. in the United States — 488,000
  - ◆ Free black pop. in non-slavery states —205,000
  - ◆ Free black pop. in slavery states — 283,000

- Total white pop. in the United States — 27,000,000
  - ◆ White pop. in Confederate States — 5,500,000
  - ◆ White pop. in Union States — 21,500,000

- Total white foreign-born pop. in the U.S. — 4,100,000
  - White foreign-born pop. in Confederate States — 400,000
  - White foreign-born pop. in Union States — 3,700,000

- White pop. growth in the United States 1850 to 1860 — 7,400,000
  - White pop. growth in Confederate States — 1,070,000
  - White pop. growth in Union States — 6,300,000

- White European immigrants landing in Northern ports — 90%
- White European immigrants landing in Southern ports — 10%
- Foreign-born population New York City — 47%
- Foreign-born population New York State — 26%
- Foreign-born population Massachusetts — 21%
- Foreign-born population South Carolina — 2%
- Foreign-born population Georgia — 1%
- 6 Nov 1860: God interceded in the United States Presidential Election, splitting the vote four ways and resulting in Abraham Lincoln being elected President with only 39.8% of the popular vote. No one could have predicted how events would play out over the next five-year period, as each stakeholder in America's future played the hand they were dealt.

Chapter 26

AN HISTORICAL PERSPECTIVE 1860–1981

- 20 Dec 1860: South Carolina, with a white population of only 43%, was the first Southern state to secede from the United States. South Carolina was followed by Mississippi, Florida, Alabama, Georgia, Louisiana, and Texas.
- 9 Jan 1861: President James Buchanan sends the merchant ship *Star of the West* to resupply Fort Sumter. Cadets from The Citadel manning batteries guarding the port of Charleston Harbor, SC open fire on *Star of the West*, turning it away, back to sea.
- 4 Mar 1861: Abraham Lincoln is inaugurated the 16th President of the United States.
- 4 Mar 1861: The Confederate States of America adopted its first national flag, a design almost identical to the current state flag of Georgia, with three stripes—red, white, red—and a blue canton with seven stars representing the original seven states of the Deep South. **This flag became the fifth flag of slavery on the North American continent** and **second flag of slavery in the United States.** The Confederate States of

America adopted several national flag designs, but none were the flag design most believe today was the Confederate flag. The flag design assumed/believed by most today as having been the Confederate States of America flag was actually one of several battle flag designs flown by various units of Southern warrior patriots. The rectangular-shaped flag was The Second Confederate Navy Jack, and another version of the rectangular-shaped flag was the battle flag of the Army of Tennessee. The square version of the battle flag was the battle flag of Robert E. Lee's Army of Northern Virginia. Contrary to these two major armies bearing the names of two states, both armies were comprised of regiments hailing from every Southern state. For example, soldiers from Florida fought with both of these Southern armies.

- Mar 1861: President Abraham Lincoln devised an ingenious plan to start a hot war without appearing to be the aggressor, thereby establishing the moral high ground. Knowing the South would fire on a resupply ship, he would coerce the South into drawing first blood by ordering a naval armada to sail toward Fort Sumter.

- 4 Apr 1861: State of Virginia voted against joining the Confederacy. **Read this again.**

- 6 Apr 1861: President Abraham Lincoln informed Southern authorities and Major Robert Anderson in command of Fort Sumter that an attempt to resupply the fort was imminent.

- 11 Apr 1861: Southern negotiators met with Major Robert Anderson in Fort Sumter to demand he surrender the fort. Anderson respectfully refused to surrender his command.

- 11 Apr 1861: The naval armada sent by President Lincoln to resupply Fort Sumter arrived.

- 12 Apr 1861: Southern cannons fired on Fort Sumter to prevent Abraham Lincoln's resupply ships from reaching

United States armed forces, running out of food and other essentials inside the fort. *No soldier inside the fort was injured during the bombardment.*

- 15 Apr 1861: President Abraham Lincoln called for 75,000 volunteers to invade the South.

  - For perspective, 75,000 troops was nearly five times the size of the United States Army!
  - The Civil War came to be referred to in the South as the War of Northern Aggression.
  - Raising and ordering an army of 75,000 men to invade, attack, kill, and maim your neighbors was not a commensurate response to cannons being fired at a fort, resulting in no casualties. The South had clearly communicated to the North during the entire previous four-month negotiation period that a resupply initiative was a non-negotiable.
  - The vast majority of the white population in the South supported their elected officials' decision to cut ties with the United States, because they were more loyal to their state as compared to the central government of the United States.
  - There were no calls from white citizens in the South to Lincoln asking to be rescued.
  - Secession was the will of the Southern people believing they voluntarily participated as a sovereign independent state in the concept of United States.
  - Lincoln's position was, and the Civil War established as precedence, once a state joined the United States, said state is bound forever and leaving is not an option.

- 17 Apr 1861: In response to Lincoln's call for 75,000 troops to invade the South, the State of Virginia voted to secede and join the newly formed Confederate States of America.

  - Virginia was followed by Arkansas, North Carolina, and Tennessee.

- 22 Apr 1861: President Lincoln suspended habeas corpus to imprison his opposition.
- 21 Jul 1861: United States Union Army of 51,000 men invaded the South and was defeated by 33,000 Southerners at 1st Battle of Manassas, aka Battle of Bull Run. Southern officer Thomas Jonathan Jackson earned his nickname: "Stonewall Jackson."

  - Once this first major battle was initiated by Lincoln, total war could not be avoided.

- Rebel Yell: an eerie battle screech war cry shouted by Confederate soldiers used to stoke courage during attacks and strike fear in Union soldiers as a form of psychological warfare. No recordings of an actual Rebel Yell during battle exists, but it is said to have sounded something like a yipping squall scream derived from Celtic heritage, Southern accents, Native American war cries, and whooping as if communicating with trailing dogs during a fox or coon hunt. In *The Civil War* by Ken Burns, historian Shelby Foote references a description of the Rebel Yell from a Union soldier as being "a peculiar corkscrew sensation that went up your spine when you heard it." The first Rebel Yell may have been unleashed at the 1st Battle of Manassas when Stonewall

Jackson is quoted to have ordered his men to, "give them the bayonet, and when you charge, yell like Furies!"

- The Indian Territory, aka Oklahoma, allied themselves with the Confederacy.
- 9 May 1862: Union Major General David Hunter issued General Orders No. 11 freeing all slaves within his area of authority including Georgia, Florida, and South Carolina. **President Abraham Lincoln cancelled these orders**.
- 20 May 1862: The Homestead Act was approved, opening the West to settlers by offering 160 acres of free land to anyone who could "prove it up" by living on it, farming it, and building a structure for housing.
- 20 May 1862: My 4th great-grandfather, Jr. 2nd Lt. John Matthew Allen, Company A, 50th Georgia Infantry Regiment, died of brain fever contracted at infantry training camp.
- 12 Sep 1862: Pvt. John T. McElhany, Company A, 50th Georgia Infantry Regiment, first husband of my 3rd great grandmother, Mary Ann Allen, was killed in action at Fox Gap, MD during the Battle of South Mountain. My birth was dependent upon the Civil War.
- 1 Jan 1863: President Lincoln issued his Emancipation Proclamation, offering freedom for slaves of African descent located within states currently under rebellion. Approximately 800,000 slaves located within Union/ Northern states and areas controlled by Union military forces were excluded from emancipation/freedom and therefore remained in bondage. A person could read the Emancipation Proclamation delivered twenty-one months after Fort Sumter, learn that Union slaves were not set free, and wonder if Lincoln was simply trying to incite a slave rebellion behind enemy lines while the majority of fighting-age Southern men were far from home.

- 1 Jan 1863: The first Homestead Act claim was in Beatrice, NE by Daniel Freeman.
- 3 Mar 1863: Pvt. James I. Mims, 1st Battalion Georgia Sharp Shooters, my 3rd great-grandfather, was wounded at Fort McAllister, GA during Union ironclads bombardment.
- 1 Jul 1863: Pvt. Reuben Rountree, Company A, 26th Georgia Infantry Regiment, my 5th great-uncle, was killed in action at the Battle of Gettysburg.
- 17 Feb 1864: Confederate States submarine *H. L. Hunley* sunk the *USS Housatonic* off Charleston, SC. Detonation of Hunley's bow harpoon torpedo also sunk the submarine, killing all eight Confederate sailors. These brave Southern men climbed inside this experimental vessel knowing the first two shakedowns had ended with the sub sinking, resulting in the loss of all hands. *H. L. Hunley* was raised to the surface on 8 Aug 2000.
- 6 May 1864: Pvt. Coleman Groover, Company B, 5th Florida Infantry Regiment, survivor of Pickett's Charge at Gettysburg, first husband of my 3rd great-grandmother Lydia Ann Douglass, was killed in action at the Battle of the Wilderness.
- 12 May 1864: During the Battle of Spotsylvania Court House, a salient in the Confederate line would become known as The Bloody Angle, where soldiers on both sides fought desperately, at point blank range, hand-to-hand, for twenty-two consecutive hours, creating 17,000 casualties, bodies piled three, four, and five deep, many literally shot into heaps of chum.
- May 1864: United States Secretary of War Edwin Stanton ordered retaliatory measures to be purposefully inflicted upon Confederate Prisoners of War being held in Union prison camps. Fruits and vegetables were withheld from

daily food rations cut to starvation levels. The intended results achieved was death by diarrhea, starvation, disease, or exposure.

- 11 Jun 1864: 16,000 men on horseback fought the largest all cavalry battle of the Civil War, known as the Battle of Trevilian Station, VA.

- 15 Jun 1864: With no Southern states represented, United States House of Representatives failed to pass the 13th Amendment to abolish slavery with a vote of 93 to 65, which was thirteen votes short of the required two-thirds majority. Wouldn't you think this vote should have been unanimous, especially in the Union/North? This failure to pass the 13th Amendment in 1864 to end slavery in the United States of America cannot be explained away.

- 30 Jul 1864: White Union soldiers killed Black Union soldiers in the Battle of the Crater. Source: Petersburg National Park Visitor Center movie.

- Aug 1864: A delegation of Union soldier Prisoners of War (POW) was sent by commandant Captain Henry Wirz to Washington D.C. from the Confederate prison camp at Andersonville, GA to meet with President Abraham Lincoln to request medical supplies and reinstatement of prisoner exchanges to alleviate suffering and death among Union POWs. Lincoln refused to meet with the delegation.

- 18 Aug 1864: General Ulysses S. Grant refused to exchange POWs with the Confederacy. The delegation of Union POWs returned to imprisonment at Andersonville.

- 25 Aug 1864: Pvt. Ezekiel P. Buford, Company C, 2nd Georgia Sharp Shooters, my 5th great-uncle, a prisoner of war in Union hands, died at Rock Island POW Camp, IL.

- 26 Sep 1864: Union General Philip Sheridan under orders from General Ulysses S. Grant began a two-week period of total war in the Shenandoah Valley of Virginia known as The Burning. Sheridan stated, "...reduction to poverty brings prayers for peace..."

- 23 Oct 1864: The Immortal Six Hundred arrived at Fort Pulaski. These Confederate officer POWs refused to take the Union oath of allegiance even under duress of starvation rations, dark dank cells, and insufficient protection from the elements imposed upon them, which led to the deaths of at least forty-six. A monument was erected at Fort Pulaski National Monument listing the names of the first thirteen who died. The thirteenth name is John H. Talbot. He was the captain and commanding officer of my Coleman Groover's Company B, 5th Florida Infantry Regiment, captured at the Battle of the Wilderness 6 May 1864.

- 29 Oct 1864: Pvt. Samuel S. Moody, Company G, 7th Georgia Cavalry Regiment, my 5th great-uncle, a prisoner of war in Union hands, died at Point Lookout POW Camp, MD.

- 15 Nov 1864: General William Tecumseh Sherman began his infamous scorched earth total war march to the sea, destroying everything from Atlanta to Savannah, GA.

- 24 Nov 1864: Pvt. Hiram L. Bland, Company I, 1st Georgia Infantry Regiment, my 1st Cousin 6x Removed, a prisoner of war, died at Camp Chase, a Union death camp near Columbus, OH. His body was removed from a freshly dug grave by Northern body snatchers and sold to a medical college in Cleveland, OH for dissection.

- 9 Dec 1864: Pvt. James Anderson Self, Company B, 55th Georgia Infantry Regiment, my 4th great-uncle, a prisoner of war in Union hands, died at Camp Douglas, Chicago, IL.

- 31 Jan 1865: United States Congress passes the 13th Amendment, ending slavery with a Senate vote of 38 to 6 and a House vote of 119 to 56. As portrayed in the movie,

Lincoln, the majority in the House was achieved via votes from fourteen lame duck Democrats.

- 11 Feb 1865: Cpl. Edmond W. Mathis, Company K, 29th Georgia Infantry Regiment, my 5th great-uncle, a prisoner of war in Union hands, died at Camp Chase POW Camp, OH.
- 9 Apr 1865: Confederate General Robert E. Lee surrendered the remnants of his Army of Northern Virginia at Appomattox Court House, VA.
- 14 Apr 1865: John Wilkes Booth assassinated President Abraham Lincoln at Ford's Theater in Washington, D.C.
- 26 Apr 1865: Confederate General Joseph E. Johnston surrendered his army to Union General William Tecumseh Sherman at Bennett Place, NC.
- 26 Apr 1865 – 9 Dec 1865: **The United States flag became the sixth flag of slavery on the North American continent** and **third flag of slavery in the United States.**
- According to Wikipedia, approximately 30,000 Union soldier POWs died in Confederate prison camps while nearly 26,000 Confederate soldier POWs died in Union prison camps.
- 10 Nov 1865: Confederate Captain Henry Wirz, commandant of Andersonville POW camp, was executed by hanging following conviction for war crimes.
- 1865 to 1877: Southern Reconstruction

    - 13th Amendment ended slavery
    - 14th Amendment distributed significant percentage of national federal surplus wealth to Union soldier veterans by way of bounties and pensions. It also appears to have been a ploy by the victorious North to quash the windfall allocation of additional members of the House of Representatives for Southern

states when freed slaves would become counted as a whole number instead of three/fifths of a person. It excludes "Indians not taxed" as persons to be counted.

- 15th Amendment established that the right to vote cannot be denied based on race, color, or previous condition of servitude.
- Lincoln's Republican Party, solidly in political control of the United States, established state governments controlled by the Republican Party candidates within the formerly rebellious Southern states, which had historically been firmly in the hands of Democratic Party politicians.
- Former slaves, now allowed to vote, overwhelmingly voted for Republican candidates, including candidates of African descent.
- The Southern population was ruled by Northern leaders in Washington D.C. in the forms of Republican puppet governments, deployed Union troops, and local police forces comprised of officers of African descent.
- The Southern population responded to Reconstruction by creating organizations such as the Ku Klux Klan to suppress voting by former slaves and anyone supporting Republican Party candidates.

- 1866: Replacement treaties were signed between victorious Union/North United States and the Indian tribes of Oklahoma effectively claiming Indian Territory of Oklahoma for homesteading as punishment for Indians siding with the Confederacy during the Civil War. Each Indian was assigned 160 acres of land, the same amount given to any homestead settler.

- 1866: The United States federal government exhumed 187 Union soldiers from the Confederate Section of the Old City Cemetery in Lynchburg, VA. These 187 Union soldiers were moved to a National Cemetery near Norfolk, VA. However, the federal government chose to leave one Union soldier behind. His name was Talbot, USCT.
- 30 Mar 1867: United States purchased Alaska from Russia.
- 1866–1870: My ancestors in Georgia and Mississippi began to migrate southward into Florida. Georgia was devastated during the Civil War while Florida remained relatively untouched, wild, and open for homesteading.

Flags of Slavery on North American Continent

1619-1783

FRANCE 1717-1763

SPAIN 1763-1800

1777-1865

1861-1865

UNTIL 6 DEC 1865

Once aware that the American flag flew over slavery for eighty-eight years, including seven and a half months after the South was conquered, one can appreciate why some of African descent grapple with visiting places like Gettysburg, standing for the national anthem, or reciting the Pledge of Allegiance.

Segregated Cemetery in Gettysburg, PA

- According to historical markers placed at segregated Lincoln Cemetery in Gettysburg, PA by three different organizations—including Pennsylvania Historical and Museum Commission, Civil War Trails, and The Sons of Goodwill—black men who volunteered as United States Colored Troops and served as Union soldiers during the Civil War were denied burial in Gettysburg National Cemetery, where President Abraham Lincoln gave his famous Gettysburg Address.

- 10 May 1869: Transcontinental railroad was completed at Promontory Summit, UT commemorated by the driving of a golden spike. At the time, this event in history was comparable to landing a man on the moon.
- 25 Jun 1876: Battle of Little Bighorn, aka Custer's Last Stand. To put things in perspective, the population of Indians at the area of the battle was approximately 11,000 while the population of the United States was approximately 45,000,000.
- 14 Oct 1878: Thomas Edison invented the electric light bulb.
- 1892: First version of the United States Pledge of Allegiance was written.
- 1892: First gasoline powered tractor was invented.
- 18 May 1896: Plessy vs Ferguson, United States Supreme Court ruled racially segregated schools were constitutional, promoting separate but equal schools for both white and black students. This was thirty-five years after the Civil War ended.
- 1898: Spanish American War resulted in Cuban independence and the United States taking over Puerto Rico, Guam, and the Philippines.
- 1 Jul 1898: Battle of San Juan Hill in Cuba included future President of the United States, Theodore Roosevelt and former Confederate Cavalry General Joseph Wheeler.
- 1898: United States annexed Hawaii.
- 1902: Willis Carrier invented the air conditioner.
- 17 Dec 1903: Wilbur and Orville Wright flew the first airplane at Kitty Hawk, NC.
- 1908: Ford Model T automobile was manufactured on an assembly line, bringing affordable transportation to the masses.
- 15 Apr 1912: Luxury liner *Titanic* hit an iceberg and sank in the North Atlantic.

- 1914: World War I began.
- 1916: Great Migration of 6 million African Americans from South to North began.
- 6 Apr 1917: United States declared war on Germany to enter World War I.
- 1918–1919: 1918 Flu Pandemic, aka Spanish Flu, killed more than 50 million worldwide.
- 11 Nov 1918: Armistice Day ended World War I.
- 18 Aug 1920: 19th Amendment to the Constitution adopted, giving women the right to vote.
- 1921: The 1890 census burned in a Washington, D.C. fire.
- 1924: The term Bible Belt was first used to describe an area of the United States essentially identical to the geographic area of the Confederate States of America.
- 1925: Florida land boom bubble burst.
- 1928: Alexander Fleming discovered Penicillin, the first antibiotic.
- 1929: The Great Depression began.
- 1939: The Great Depression subsided.
- 7 Dec 1941: Japan attacked Pearl Harbor, HI. My grandfather, Baker 1st Charles Robert Zipperer, was en route to Pearl Harbor from Long Beach, CA aboard USS Sepulga.
- 18 Apr 1942: Doolittle Raid—sixteen modified B25B bombers were launched from the deck of the USS Hornet on a one-way mission to China, dropping their 2,000 lb. payloads of bombs on the Japanese city of Tokyo along their route in retaliation for Pearl Harbor.
- 4 Jun 1942: Battle of Midway. American aircraft carriers USS Enterprise and USS Hornet were all that stood between four Japanese aircraft carriers and the west coast of the United States. Carrier USS Yorktown, severely damaged at the Battle of Coral Sea had limped back to Pearl Harbor en route

to Bremerton, WA for several months of repairs. Admiral Chester Nimitz, knowing he was outnumbered, and the west coast naked, commanded all hands at Pearl Harbor they had seventy-two hours to prepare *USS Yorktown* for battle. An impossible task, seventy-two hours later, *USS Yorktown* sailed into naval lore on a one-way mission to Midway Island to save the United States of America.

- 7 Jun 1942: Having saved the United States from invasion, and with her battle flags flying, *USS Yorktown* rolled upside down and sank to the bottom of the Pacific Ocean.
- 13 Oct 1942: S1 Griffin Monroe Haynes, USNR, my great-uncle, was killed in action by German U-boat *U-221* during the Battle of the Atlantic when *SS Susana* was torpedoed.
- 5 Nov 1942: My thirty-five-year-old great-grandfather, Walter Ray Mathis, a civilian pilot, enlisted in the United States Army, became an enlisted Flying Sergeant, and Flew the Hump over the Himalayan Mountains transporting fuel to the Chinese, keeping that front open and a million Japanese servicemen away from the fighting against Americans. The Hump was also known as The Aluminum Trail, because the pilots could see sunlight reflecting off the aluminum wreckage of planes that didn't make it.
- 6 Jun 1944: D-Day. Within six days, my grandfather, nineteen-year-old Pvt. Esly Paul Surgnier, 79th Infantry Division, would land on the beaches of Normandy at Utah Beach.
- 17 Jul 1944: Port Chicago Naval Magazine explosion disaster near San Francisco, CA.
- 7 May 1945: Germany surrendered for Allied victory in Europe "V-E Day."
- 6 Aug 1945: United States destroys Hiroshima, Japan with atomic bomb Little Boy.

- 9 Aug 1945: United States destroys Nagasaki, Japan with atomic bomb Fat Man.
- 2 Sep 1945: Japan surrendered for Allied victory in the Pacific "V-J Day."
- 1946: Baby Boom began.
- 14 May 1948: State of Israel declared.
- 1950–1953: Korean War, The Forgotten War, 37,000 U.S. Servicemen died defending South Korea from combined North Korean, **Chinese**, and Soviet Union forces.
- 1954–1968: Civil Rights Movement

  - 17 May 1954: Brown v. Board of Education, To-peka, KS, Supreme Court ruled segregated schools were unconstitutional based on 14th Amendment to the United States Constitution.
  - Sep 1957: Little Rock Nine was a group of nine black students who faced fierce resistance when they tried to attend the historically segregated Little Rock Central High School in Little Rock, AR.
  - 16 Apr 1963: Martin Luther King, Jr. wrote his Letter from Birmingham Jail.
  - 28 Aug 1963: Martin Luther King, Jr. gave his *I Have a Dream* speech at the Mall in Washington, D.C.
  - 4 Apr 1968: James Earl Ray assassinated Martin Luther King, Jr. in Memphis, TN.

- 1954–1975: Vietnam War, 60,000 U.S. Servicemen killed or missing in action.
- 1962: Engel v. Vitale Supreme Court case ended composed prayers in public schools.

- 1963: Abington School District v. Schempp Supreme Court case ended school-initiated Bible reading in public schools.
- 20 Jul 1969: United States Astronaut Neil Armstrong stepped onto the moon's surface.
- 1974–1988: Boston, MA implemented the 1965 Racial Imbalance Act in an effort to desegregate schools by bussing students, resulting in angry protests and violent rioting.
- 4 Apr 1981: Chicago, IL Board of Education announced a plan to desegregate schools.

Chapter 27

INTERPRETING THE PAST

In less than two years, through my curiosity, initiative, and efforts to become inquisitive about what was going on during various time periods, I learned a great deal about the contexts in which my ancestors interacted during their limited lifespans. Taken out of their contexts, they were no different from myself, no different from you. Regardless of skin color, they were designed in the likeness of their Creator; they were constructed perfectly at conception as per the Potter's blueprints (DNA), life was breathed into them by their Creator, they were sinners, they faced temptations, they did their best under circumstances not entirely of their choosing, and they prayed. They prayed with vigor, believing, leaning on God, relying on God, putting their fate in God's hands, because God was the center of their lives. They understood they had nothing else, and no one else to turn to when their wife was giving birth, when their child was sick, when their crops needed rain, when a wound became infected, and when the enemy was at their gate.

Humans have been competing for limited resources, happiness, freedom, and power since the beginning. Our ancestors faced and met challenges unlike anything we may feel is difficult today. Lying in bed on my Tempurpedic® space-age foam mattress, I wasn't quite comfortable and realized I had earlier in the day adjusted my air conditioning thermostat up one degree to 75. Begrudgingly, I pushed the covers back, got out of bed, walked to the living room, adjusted the thermostat down one degree to 74, and went back to bed. Looking through my eyelids I thought to myself, *How spoiled we've become.*

Various ancestors' experiences flashed in front of me. They didn't leave Europe because things were going so well for them. There was no guarantee they would survive the ocean voyage. They landed and set foot in a New World with barely a beachhead to cling to as the ships sailed away back toward the east. Their view toward the west was of dense virgin forests and the unknown beyond. And there was no air conditioning to adjust that one degree to achieve optimal comfort conditions.

The questions I ask you to answer for yourself are the same questions I asked myself.

- Have you made an honest attempt to look at history with an open mind?
- Are you capable of acknowledging that your ancestors lived in a time period when the context in which they lived was vastly different from your own?
- Now that you are more aware of historical events and your ancestors' roles, how does your new awareness of the past help you reconcile what you observe in society today?
- What will you do to improve the way your generation is perceived 100 years from now?
- Which of your ancestors stand out as your favorites, and why?

- Are the headstones of your ancestors facing east? If so, why was that important to them?

Jesus said in Matthew 24:27, "For as the lightning comes from the east and flashes to the west, so also will the coming of the Son of Man be."

The process of placing my ancestors within perspective of their historical context by enthusiastically researching events and details of years past has been a most enlightening experience. I read about their time periods, their military service, and their migration patterns. I visited the places where they lived, where they worshipped, where they fought, where they were laid to rest. I listened to my grandparents describe their grandparents, tell their life stories, and identify long-since-grown-old-and-died youthful, smiling faces captured in aged, yellowed photos of black and white. Not in control of the date and place of their conception, nor the macroeconomic and political landscapes of their times, they lived, breathed, loved, and prayed upward toward the heavens no differently than me. As I look back, imagine, envision, and focus on how they interacted with their surroundings, I turn, look toward the future, and see my descendants 100 years from now wondering who I was, the time period in which I lived, and why I did or did not make choices congruent with futuristic mainstream beliefs. How will history judge me? How will history judge you?

As mentioned previously, the chronological historical events, information, and data provided here are those points of reference chosen by me that I found helpful toward understanding the contexts in which my ancestors lived and from which I came. Use my historical outline as an example for creating your own timeline relevant to your ancestors and your interests. The broad brush used to label people as White, Black, Indian, Hispanic, Asian, Middle Eastern, and other archaic "buckets" is truly unfortunate. I find it interesting that English, French, and Germans speak different languages and have been killing each other for thousands of years, but all are poured into the convenient White bucket. Oddly enough, I descend from all three!

Trying to comprehend humans categorizing their fellow man by race determined solely based on similarities limited to physical characteristics of appearance, I recalled meeting a man by the name of Yellow Bear at the Grand Teton National Park Visitor Center. For more than a week, we had been exploring Montana and Wyoming, where much was noted about people native to America, specifically the genocide imposed upon the original caretakers of the continent by the United States government. The gift shop was bustling with tourists, but not one person acknowledged Yellow Bear's presence despite him standing there in his art exhibit looking into the crowd, waiting for someone to enter his space. Being a friendly, outgoing Southerner, and recognizing the disrespectfulness of the situation, I approached him and introduced myself. Like most people who meet me for the first time, I caught him off guard, but he sensed my genuineness and introduced himself. Continuing with my charm, I asked him, "Are you from around here?"

Talking with Yellow Bear, he helped me become aware of his perspective, whereby humans native to the Americas do not identify whatsoever with the label Indian placed upon them by Europeans. For one thing, they aren't from India. He didn't even identify with the label Native American, preferring instead to consider his heritage to align with First Nations. There were, and are, hundreds of distinct clans of proud people differentiated from other unique groups by numerous factors, including language. He emphasized the absurdity of the label "Indian" by comparing the practice to deciding one day to begin referring to all birds of prey as being falcons. A golden eagle is not a burrowing owl nor is a red-tailed hawk an osprey. The same goes for human groups on the African continent and of African descent.

My initial main objective was to reach the Civil War period of 1861–1865, but you can't help but find a few well-documented lineages during your search, which will take your tree out another couple hundred years or more. Turns out most of my original ancestors who migrated across the Atlantic Ocean to North America did so between the early 1600s and mid-1700s, giving me 275–400 years along what is now the east coast of the United States to research. It has been common for me to reach back eight generations to my 6th great-grandparents, finding them already here on American soil. Many of the people I speak with today about their family know of a grandparent who came to America during the 1900s. Their historical timeline to understand the context of their ancestors, and from where they came, will focus on their ancestors' countries of origin instead of simply the United States of America.

In my case, one such line took me back to the year 1632 when two of my 8,192 11th great-grandparents, William Spencer and Agnes Tucker Spencer, arrived at Newe Towne, Massachusetts Bay Colony, later renamed Cambridge, MA. To put this event into perspective, William and Agnes had been living in Cambridge for four years when their daughter Sarah Spencer, my 10th great-grandmother, was born in 1636, the same year Harvard College was founded. I, too, would arrive at Cambridge, MA, 359 years later, to attend Harvard Business School. Walking across the Anderson Memorial Bridge spanning the Charles River, I stood in Harvard Square where unbeknownst to me, my ancestors had arrived there as pioneers of a newly established British colony in the New World.

Yes, you, too, have 4,096 11th great-grandfathers and 4,096 11th great-grandmothers for a total of 8,192 11th great-grandparents! Good luck finding all of them to add to your tree, but it's possible. Each lived. Each had a name. And each had a story.

Chapter 28

THE WORLD NEEDS A BAPTISM—A FRESH START

Honoring my DNA by taking the time and making the effort to truly get to know my ancestors made me a better person. Uncertainty during the process of discovery enabled an acceptance of all human subgroups without prejudice. Knowing the next card I would turn over was mine, regardless of what it looked like or from what country it originated, took me to a place of unconditional love. That next grandma identified could have been white, black, yellow, red, fat, skinny, beautiful, unattractive, nice, or mean. It didn't matter. And because it no longer mattered, the same applied to the diverse new faces I came into contact with daily. For all I knew, the black man and Asian woman next to me in the grocery line may have had centimorgans of DNA in common with me.

Aren't we all just making our way in life? Isn't a worldly death awaiting each of us in the very near future? Haven't we all been done wrong in some way? Don't we all have ancestors who were persecuted and exploited in some way by some other group? Doesn't the Bible state each of us was made in God's image?

Rewinding my life record to that sidewalk leading from the hotel room to the battlefield at Gettysburg, I was oblivious an adventure of such magnitude awaited. All had been forgotten in three generations. My wildest of creative brainstorming could never have foreseen what I accomplished in fifteen months while honoring my DNA:

- Traveled more than 12,000 road trip miles.
- Visited all seventy-two known cemeteries where my ancestors were buried.
- Cleaned all 143 headstones at my ancestors' known gravesites.
- Placed flowers at the graves of all my grandmothers.
- Placed flags at the graves of my military veteran grandfathers.
- Added more than 1,450 ancestors to my family tree.
- Using a thin metal rod, located an ancestor's gravesite.
- Visited and interviewed all my oldest known living relatives.
- Collected DNA samples from my grandparents or their siblings.
- Using atDNA, discovered 3rd great-grandmother from 145 years ago.
- Using atDNA, discovered 3rd great-grandfather from 150 years ago.
- Using Y-DNA, solved a 145-year-old paternity question.
- Gathered more than 1,500 photos of my ancestors.
- Stood where my ancestors fought at twenty-five Civil War battlefields.
- Met distant cousins during cemetery visitation road trips.
- Learned historical facts I had never heard about my country.
- Identified with 125 surnames as significant as my last name.
- Came to the realization all my ancestors were facing east.

I trust in Him and have faith I am doing what God has guided me to do. Why He chose to encourage a guy like me, with hundreds of Confederate soldier ancestors, to put it all out there as an advocate for veteran headstone cleaning, DNA testing, building family trees, and visiting graves of ancestors, I don't know for sure. I have no doubt things happen for a reason, orchestrated by a higher being. I do not give credit to randomness any more than I give credit to evolution resulting in a pancreas capable of producing sufficient quantities of insulin and distributing it in just the right amounts at just the right times twenty-four hours a day every single day.

If I had to guess why God sent me on this mission, I'd say it's about reconciliation, second chances, and salvation. Personal demons like alcohol, drugs, and pornography are too powerful to rely solely on ineffective earthly remedies. Macro demons like slavery, genocide, racism, and modern versions of what happens after death can be cast out.

As a whole, the world needs a baptism. Each of us needs a second chance to recognize our commonalities, reconcile our differences, discontinue our ugly behavior, forgive, and be forgiven. What we need as a human species is a mass baptism where we all get a fresh new start, a rebirth, a do over, where all of our trespasses against one another effectively never happened. What each of us chooses to do from that day forward, good or bad, right or wrong, is of our own doing for which we will be held accountable on our judgement day. All it takes is a willingness to make the world a better place, an emersion under water, and emergence from the water symbolizing rebirth. A baby in the mother's womb is encapsulated, immersed, in water, not yet blemished. Maybe a global baptism is how we move beyond trespasses, beyond wars, beyond persecution, beyond slavery, beyond race, beyond genocide, just beyond.

While honoring my DNA, I experienced the greatest of adventures I had never contemplated. Forgotten in three generations, they remained, readily accessible to be remembered, to be heard, steadfast in their belief, facing east. My ancestors each left behind a message, a perpetual lasting form of communication, their testimonies, easily decipherable, in the form of burial sites, their graves. A pilgrimage to my ancestors' final resting places was the trip of my lifetime, enabling me to disconnect from my worldly minutia, and be still.

THE END

www.ingramcontent.com/pod-product-compliance
Lightning Source LLC
Chambersburg PA
CBHW021000150626
46549CB00012BA/80